Japan's Economy

Also of Interest

Japan and the United States: Economic and Political Adversaries, edited by Leon Hollerman

† *Japan: Profile of a Postindustrial Power*, Ardath W. Burks

† *The Hidden Sun: Women of Modern Japan*, Dorothy Robins-Mowry

The Sogo Shosha: *Japan's Multinational Trading Companies*, Alexander Young

Business in Japan: A Guide to Japanese Business Practice and Procedure, Fully Revised Edition, edited by Paul Norbury and Geoffrey Bownas

How Japan Innovates: A Comparison with the U.S. in the Case of Oxygen Steelmaking, Leonard H. Lynn

OPEC, the Gulf, and the World Petroleum Market, Fereidun Fesharaki and David Isaak

Critical Energy Issues in Asia and the Pacific: The Next Twenty Years, Fereidun Fesharaki, Harrison Brown, Corazon M. Siddayao, Toufiq A. Siddiqi, Kirk R. Smith, and Kim Woodard

OPEC and Natural Gas Trade: Prospects and Problems, Bijan Mossavar-Rahmani and Sharmin B. Mossavar-Rahmani

U.S. Foreign Policy and Asian-Pacific Security: A Transregional Approach, edited by William T. Tow and William R. Feeney

† *The Theory and Structures of International Political Economy*, edited by Todd Sandler

Trading Blocs, U.S. Exports, and World Trade, Penelope Hartland-Thunberg

World Economic Development: 1979 and Beyond, Herman Kahn

---

†Available in hardcover and paperback.

Contents

Figures and Tables

Tables

Acknowledgments

Publication of this book would not have been possible without help and support from several institutions and individuals. The editor began the process of organizing this book under a National Fellowship from the Hoover Institution, Stanford University. A grant from the Japan–United States Friendship Commission gave him the leeway to continue working on it from 1980 to 1982. Special thanks go to the Northeast Asia–United States Forum, Stanford University, for research and editorial assistance, typing, and a variety of other services; Gerry Bowman, Anne Blenman Hare, Helen Morales, Nancy Okimoto, Meg Young, Barbara Johnson, Susan Morita, and Marilyn Webber were especially helpful and generous with their time and effort. The editor also wishes to thank Ted Eimon for graphic work and Jeff Seward for editorial assistance, and members of the Westview Press staff, particularly Susan McRory and Deborah Lynes.

Daniel I. Okimoto

Introduction

Daniel I. Okimoto

The early postwar period was an era of unprecedented prosperity and growth worldwide. Japan, one of the "big losers" in World War II, became one of the major beneficiaries of the relatively stable and open economic order created and sustained by the United States. Its economy grew at an average annual rate of 8.8 percent, fastest of all the major industrial states. Not only did Japan surge to the forefront of the world's most productive market economies, but, in the process of doing so, it also managed to find the security that had eluded it in the prewar period, when it had used brute military power to realize national interests.

The establishment of a liberal postwar order permitted Japan to turn its foreign policy completely around. In lieu of military conquest and colonial expansionism, postwar Japan's foreign policy came to be characterized by military meekness, political subordination, and concentration on the pursuit of economic interests. Its international orientation — which could be considered an extension of its domestic course of rapid growth — seemed to hinge on three basic strategies:

1. extending and maintaining economic, political, and military ties with the United States and making this alliance the central axis of foreign policy;
2. separating economic issues from political and military entanglements and pursuing economic interests, wherever possible, with all nations of the world — except in those instances where this course clearly threatens to damage relations with the United States; and
3. procuring resources overseas and securing access to foreign technology and markets as part of an overall strategy of achieving high growth.

1

These three strategies could be counted on to steer Japan through the maze of bewildering questions and multiple policy options that regularly confront nation-states. Adhering to these guidelines gave Japan's international orientation the predictability that had been so sorely lacking before the war.

This postwar course, centered around alliance with the United States, yielded rich dividends. Not only did Japan's economy flourish, but its political system also became stabilized. Japan's transformation from military to merchant state, as Daniel I. Okimoto points out in Chapter 7, permitted it to attain the status of economic superstate without destabilizing the structure of the postwar order, because gains in economic productivity were not converted into advances in military power. This course seemed safe and rewarding.

Problems and upheavals in the international system, however, have rendered it increasingly difficult and costly to continue along this path. In Chapter 1, Hideo Kanemitsu describes the dramatic developments that undermined the Bretton Woods system and led to the restructuring of the international economic order—among them the Organization of Petroleum Exporting Countries (OPEC) oil cartel, rising costs of energy, balance-of-payments disequilibria, worldwide recession and unemployment, trade friction, erosion of international rules governing trade, and protectionist pressures. Such upheavals in the external environment have deeply affected all areas of Japan's economy and its international orientation.

The oil crisis hit Japan where it was allegedly most vulnerable: namely, its extraordinary level of dependence on imported oil supplies. Herbert I. Goodman recounts in Chapter 2 how Japan came to be so dependent on oil from the Persian Gulf. Although its initial reaction to the first oil crisis, in 1973–1974, was one of panic, Japan has coped far more effectively with subsequent oil crises and their ripple effects than most Japanese had believed possible. Energy conservation, conversion to alternative sources, and effective macro-economic management have reduced the cost of the oil shocks. But in the process of coping, Japan has had to make a series of adjustments, shifting gears from "rapid" to "steady" growth. The process of adjustment is still going on and is likely to continue, as Japan attempts to reorient institutions and practices heretofore geared to full-throttled growth in response to the changing realities and needs of a less stable world environment.

It would be a mistake to assume that, because Japan has demonstrated a remarkable capacity for adaptation, energy-related problems are no longer worrisome. As Goodman points out, Japan still has a long and hard road to haul before reaching its goal of lowering its dependence on oil imports to halve its total energy consumption. The possibility of further supply interrruptions and steep price increases cannot be ruled out, and depending on their severity and duration, such developments could throw Japan's economy and the world into even greater turmoil. Enormous power has come to be concentrated in OPEC's hands — not simply over oil supplies and prices but also over linkage areas, such as transportation, distribution, financing, investments, and so on. Such power, and the many uncertainties surrounding politics in the Persian Gulf, might subject the Western alliance, and the United States–Japan partnership in particular, to tremendous stress. What can Japan, acting either alone or in concert with the United States, do about the energy threat? Goodman assesses the steps Japan has already taken and suggests others.

Sudden price hikes, as seen in the 1970s, can also disrupt patterns of world trade. Japan's trade relationships, particularly with the United States, have gone through the pangs of a major adjustment process. In Chapters 4, 5, and 6, Gary R. Saxonhouse, Hugh T. Patrick, and Ryutaro Komiya analyze Japan's economic relationship with the United States from differing perspectives. Saxonhouse examines the macroeconomic policies of the two countries and evaluates their bilateral implications. He asks whether some form of policy coordination, aimed, for example, at smoothing out dissynchronous business cycles, might have been either feasible or beneficial. Patrick places bilateral economic transactions within the context of what might be called the political economy of the two allies. In what ways, he asks, do the political processes affect the handling of trade conflicts? How might these conflicts be better managed? From the Japanese economist's perspective, Komiya holds a variety of stereotypes commonly held in the West up to logical and empirical scrutiny: Is Japanese protectionism responsible for the huge trade and current-accounts imbalance? Are nontariff barriers more serious in Japan than elsewhere? How might the U.S.-Japan trade and current-account imbalance be rectified?

Saxonhouse, Patrick, Komiya, and Kanemitsu each deal with facets of the underlying causes of Japan's trade problems: the sudden oil price hike, fluctuations in the yen exchange rate, sharp deterioration in the terms of trade, the comparatively high ratio of savings to dissavings. What do these developments portend for Japan's economic future? Is its huge current-accounts surplus with the

United States likely to continue? Will the bilaterial imbalance be deemed intolerable by the United States, which is already saddled with severe problems of unemployment? These economists take a look at these and other central questions through slightly different but complementary lenses: the systemic, bilateral, and national levels of analysis.

In addition to the impact on Japan's trade patterns, changes in the international environment have unleashed forces that are working to reshape other aspects of Japan's economy and world posture. In Chapter 3, Eric W. Hayden focuses on the forces of change in Japan's financial system. This system, which played a critical role in capital formation and allocation during Japan's era of rapid growth, has received its share of foreign criticism for its tight controls over capital flows, foreign investments, and guidance of credit allocation. Because of the unusual power vested in the Ministry of Finance and the Bank of Japan (to set interest rates, for example), the financial system has been perceived as one of the prime mechanisms by which the government has maintained a measure of control over the economy. In what ways is this financial system changing? Is "internationalization" inevitable? What are the implications of internationalization, in terms of domestic institutions and processes as well as foreign economic policies? If Japan becomes a net exporter of capital, will this relieve some of the political pressures arising from the imbalance of merchandise trade? Will the yen play a bigger role as an international reserve currency?

Closely related to questions concerning Japan's changing economic position and role are criticisms of its reluctance to assume greater political and military responsibilities. There is a fairly widespread perception in the United States that Japan cares only about its own narrow economic interests and is unwilling to shoulder more of the costs of collective security. Many people in the United States believe the burdens of maintaining peace, stability, and an open and prosperous economic order are falling disproportionately on their shoulders, even though Japan benefits as much as any other nation and is capable of "paying" more of a "fair" share. Indeed, commonly heard charges of "unfair" trade practices can be seen as part of the same "free rider" syndrome that lies at the heart of criticisms about Japan's politico-military irresponsibility. There are even causal links forged in the minds of some Americans between Japan's low defense burden and its commercial competitiveness and capacity to penetrate the U.S. market.

In Chapter 7, Daniel Okimoto explores the interrelationship of economics and military security. He traces the origins of Japan's "one percent of GNP" formula for military expenditures and assesses the systemic, bilateral, and domestic consequences of a low military posture. Questions discussed in his chapter include: How would higher defense spending—say, around 2 percent of GNP—affect Japan's economy? What are the primary constraints on, and what would be the consequences of, a significantly expanded military capability? The United States's loss of clear military supremacy—like the decline of its economic dominance—has altered the world balance in ways that raise questions within the U.S.-Japan alliance about the possibility and desirability of Japan's carrying more of its own military weight. Clearly, the minimalist military stance, one of the three foreign policy guidelines cited earlier, can no longer be automatically assumed in the face of major changes in the outside world.

All the contributors to this book address the question of how Japan's political economy is coping with the complex and far-reaching changes that have already taken place and that continue to transform the international environment. The golden era of 1952–1972 has ended and, with it, the highly favorable environment that had given Japan the opportunity to combine policies of high-speed growth at home and the optimization of economic interests and politico-military inoffensiveness abroad. Where Japan goes, and how it responds to its external environment, are bound to have a profound effect, in turn, on the shape of the world to come. Readers are invited to explore and reflect upon Japan's passage through this difficult period of transition as it searches for a new definition of its proper role in a world of growing uncertainty and potential turmoil.

1
Changes in the International Economic Environment

Hideo Kanemitsu

Changes in the international political and economic environment in the 1970s were so far-reaching that the fundamental framework of the post–World War II order was shaken. Japan's rise to the status of an economic superpower was accompanied by the relative economic decline of the United States and the emergence of OPEC as a major politico-economic power. The free-world economy has made an unmistakable transition to a multiple-power system. In this new order Japan has already played a key role in determining the shape of the international economic system, even though Japan neither sought nor willingly accepted this responsibility. Japan's growing economic power makes it vitally important to recognize that country's responsibility in the 1980s for managing the world economic system in concert with the United States, Western Europe, and the OPEC countries.

My concern here is to trace the ways in which the events of the 1970s affect developments in the 1980s. In the first section, I will review the most salient features of the last decade compared with the world situation in the 1950s and 1960s. In particular, this means an examination of the gradual crumbling of some of the principal organizational rules of the postwar order that was dominated by the International Monetary Fund (IMF) and General Agreement on Tariffs and Trade (GATT), the reemergence of conservative nationalism and protectionism, and the shift from strategies of economic confrontation to collaboration within the framework of the economic summit conference. During the 1970s the industrial economics of the capitalist bloc suffered such problems as rampant inflation, an enormously high rate of unemployment, and large-scale trade deficits—all partly triggered and clearly aggravated by the oil crises of 1973–1974 and 1979–1980. The success, and even the existence, of the Economic Summit Conference distinguishes the difficult transition period of the 1970s and 1980s from the strikingly similar period of the 1930s and another historic transition period of a century ago, 1870–1890. It is sobering to remember that the failure of the major powers to resolve the economic and political issues raised by those earlier transitions set the stage for two catastrophic world wars.

In the second section, I will attempt to clarify the principal issues of the 1980s that have been created by the turbulent transition in the 1970s, particularly in connection with international trade and finance among the developed countries. Some policy suggestions will be outlined to address the chief difficulties of the coming decades. As I see it, what is at stake is the choice between free trade and protectionism; at the policy level, critical choices have to be made between the various rules and codes of conduct based on international agreements and discretionary foreign economic policies of individual nations.

Finally, in the third section, I will attempt to assess the crucial problems Japan will face during this continuing process of world transformation, problems that affect not only Japan's own short-term economic interests, but also the interests of the world economy. In my judgment, Japan's active participation in the shaping of the world economy is bound to grow, and the character of that participation will be an important determinant in how well this transition is handled and how effectively the international economic system functions over the next several decades.

The Basic Characteristics of International Political and Economic Systems in the 1970s

Crudely speaking, the transition period of the 1970s can be characterized as a time of political instability and continuing unrest on a worldwide scale and the breakdown of international economic systems. We witnessed many structural, *systemic* changes. The economic hegemony of the United States and the old IMF regime of fixed exchange rates and gold convertibility collapsed; the free-trade system was in danger of breaking down; the nonaligned bloc of Third World nations appeared to be disintegrating; and OPEC's oil cartel challenged the status quo of world politics and economic management. Although there were encouraging developments in such areas as Western relations with the Soviet Union and China and diplomatic normalization between Egypt and Israel, there is no denying that the international political and economic environment during the 1970s suffered from the destabilizing impact of systemic disturbances.

Responses to the shocks of the 1970s were largely ad hoc, but three adjustment mechanisms emerged as particularly noteworthy. After the collapse of the fixed (but adjustable) exchange-rate system in 1971, one obvious mechanism was to invoke free-market forces and let exchange rates be determined, not by par value, but primarily by forces in the international exchange market. The Eurocurrency market has played an indispensable role in recycling the huge surpluses accumulated by OPEC. This adjustment is an example of how market forces helped solve one of the difficult international currency problems of the 1960s.

A second type of adjustment is exemplified by government discretionary policy, often on a trial-and-error basis. Efforts to achieve internal and external economic equilibrium simultaneously often took the form of nationalistic confrontations, especially on the part of the major advanced countries. Protectionist trade policies like discriminatory import restrictions, which became rampant during the 1970s, are a classic example of this sort of "beggar-thy-neighbor" policy. Obviously, OPEC's forceful oil cartel is another example of this approach.

The third type of adjustment is typified by the creation of the economic summit, which started in 1975 through the brilliant initiative of the French president, Giscard d'Estaing. Other cooperative efforts have been made continuously through various international agencies, notably the IMF, GATT, and Organisation for Economic Co-operation and Development (OECD) meetings.

The adjustment mechanisms, however, failed to cure what ailed the international economic system. Throughout the 1970s the world suffered from slow growth, high unemployment, global inflation, a fundamental disequilibrium of both domestic and external balances, pollution and considerable destruction of the natural environment, and heated and highly politicized trade disputes.

To distinguish the transition period of the 1970s from the preceding decades, I have singled out six characteristics as the *differentia specifica* of the 1970s (without pretending that these provide a comprehensive description of this whole period):

1. The decline of the economic hegemony of the United States and the consequent decentralized structure of the world economy.
2. The sudden emergence of the OPEC oil cartel as a major world power.

3. The rapid erosion of international legal rules and the turn to both international market forces and discretionary policy-making by the advanced countries.
4. The development of market adjustments and government policy responses and the deficiencies of these adjustments and responses.
5. The predominance of a confrontational political approach toward international economic problems.
6. The use of the economic summit.

1. *The decline of the economic hegemony of the United States and the consequent decentralized structure of the world economy.* During the two prosperous decades of the 1950s and 1960s, most countries of the world, developed and developing alike, made unprecedented economic progress. U.S. leadership created and maintained the Bretton Woods system, consisting of the IMF, the World Bank, and GATT. The axial principle of the system was nondiscriminatory free trade to promote stable and multilateral trade, foreign investment, and financial transactions. The very success of other economies, particularly in Western Europe and Japan, however, inevitably undermined the hegemonic position of the United States.

In 1971 the U.S. trade balance recorded a $2.2 billion deficit, the first such deficit in this century, and the overall balance registered a deficit of more than $30 billion. This accelerated the drain on U.S. foreign reserves that had occurred through the 1960s as the trade surplus declined, foreign investment expanded, and military expenditures abroad steadily climbed during the Vietnam War. As a result, in 1971 the foreign reserves of the United States were reduced to $12.2 billion (of which gold accounted for $10.2 billion), while the overseas official liquid assets, i.e., U.S. liabilities, amounted to more than $50 billion. Confidence in the value of the U.S. dollar (the only currency that was officially guaranteed convertibility in the IMF charter in 1944) was seriously undermined. When that confidence finally collapsed and the dollar came under attack from large-scale speculation, the Nixon administration abandoned the IMF exchange-rate rule rather than devalue the dollar, suspended the dollar's convertibility, and requested a change in the rules of the international currency system.[1]

Through the 1960s the United States's expansionist policies and large balance-of-payments deficits had given the country the role of world banker. The demands of international liquidity were satisfied by the continuing supply of U.S. dollars. The value of the U.S. dollar was kept artificially high as a consequence of the IMF exchange-rate system. This overvaluation, in effect, eroded the international competitiveness of the U.S. economy vis-à-vis European countries and Japan. The asymmetric system for managing the world economy has now been replaced by a more or less decentralized managing system that includes the United States, the European Economic Community (EEC), Japan, some of the other OECD countries, and OPEC.

In the wake of OPEC's new-found clout, many developing countries in Asia, Africa, and South America have challenged the existing international economic order and demanded a New International Economic Order under the auspices of the United Nations Conference on Trade and Development (UNCTAD). All of this clearly indicates that the free world has made an unmistakable transition from a stable, well-organized system under the hegemony of the United States to an unpredictable, decentralized system with multiple centers.

2. *The sudden emergence of the OPEC oil cartel as a major world power.* From October 1973 to January 1974, during the fourth Middle East war, OPEC succeeded in quadrupling the price of oil and announced its intention of reducing world oil production by as much as 25 percent. OPEC also agreed to make selective use of oil embargoes against unfriendly countries, including the United States. In 1979 OPEC once again stunned the world by doubling the price of exported oil.

OPEC's price hike during the first oil crisis immediately created problems. First, the world external payments system, and the economic situation in advanced countries in particular, experienced a drastic change. Except for the United States and West Germany, oil-importing countries suffered current-accounts deficits; recycling OPEC's enormous short-term liquid assets to pay for this mounting oil bill became an acutely pressing problem for international financial markets. Non-oil-producing developing countries also suffered severe problems and required some recycling of "petrodollars."

Second, the quadrupling of oil prices aggravated inflationary trends in the world economy, which were already firmly entrenched in 1973. Third, the combination of external deficits and external inflation forced both developed and developing nations to apply sharply deflationary policies. Worldwide recession and high levels of unemployment were the result. Fourth, the excess savings of the Arab members of OPEC in particular, which had indirectly caused the recession, meant that a systemic adjustment was urgently needed. OPEC's cartel policy had become a crucial part of world economic management. Fifth, OPEC's moves to decrease oil pro-

duction threatened to restrict the economic growth rate of the world
by regulating the available supply of energy.

3. *The rapid erosion of international legal rules and the turn to
both international market forces and discretionary policymaking by
the advanced countries.* The Bretton Woods system, which fell
apart in the 1970s, was the first international economic system constructed and managed under the authority of supranational legal
rules and agreements among the major industrialized countries.
When the "dollar shock" of 1971 took place, it was clear that international currency problems were deeply rooted in the deficiencies of
the adjustable-peg system, which prevented prompt and necessary
adjustments. The resulting disequilibria in world financial payments had been well understood during the traumatic period of the
late 1960s. After the Smithsonian Agreement in December 1971 and
the 10 percent devaluation of the dollar in February 1973, a floating
system of exchange rates was established.

Under the new IMF agreement those mechanisms that will determine the fundamental framework of the international monetary
system are left essentially to the policy direction of individual nations. Accordingly, the new international system emphasizes the
autonomous functions of the international market in such aspects
as the free-floating exchange-rate system, but at the same time it
stresses policy interference and control by governments coping with
both external and internal economic difficulties. Therefore, the
floating exchange-rate system is subject to management by the
monetary authority of each country.

Throughout the 1970s many GATT countries pursued trade
policies that were in obvious conflict with GATT rules, including
import surcharges and various import restrictions going under the
name of "orderly marketing arrangements" or "voluntary export
restraints." These clearly violate the fundamental principle of
GATT, namely, the most-favored-nation principle of Article I. The
purpose of the advanced industrialized countries in imposing these
import surcharges and restrictions was to shield domestic industries
from foreign competition, but the safeguard clause (Article XIX), the
principal escape clause under GATT rules, has rarely been invoked
to justify such protection.

Trade conflicts over agricultural commodities also became increasingly serious, particularly between the EEC and the United
States and between Japan and the United States. U.S. frustration
with both the EEC's Common Agricultural Policy and Japan's
similar effort to maintain a protectionist agricultural policy shows

the difficulty of reconciling domestic goals with GATT rules designed to harmonize international trade policies.

4. *The development of market adjustments and government policy responses and the deficiencies of these adjustments and responses.* Despite the repeated traumas of the 1970s, the world economic order did not collapse as it had in the 1930s. On the contrary, after the breakdown of the Bretton Woods system, market mechanisms succeeded to a considerable extent in making appropriate adjustments. The freely fluctuating exchange-rate system has played a valuable, indeed indispensable, role in providing a certain degree of workable stability. For example, this system mitigated the enormous balance-of-payments disequilibrium after the first oil crisis.

The Eurocurrency market, operating purely on the basis of private market forces, also played a remarkable role by facilitating urgently needed capital transfers. A sizable quantity of petrodollars was recycled from the Eurocurrency market to deficit countries, especially into the non-oil-producing less developed countries. Indeed, without the smooth functioning of the Eurocurrency money market, an international financial panic would have been a distinct possibility. However, official intervention in the foreign exchange market and the rampant use of exchange controls by the monetary authorities of each country have very much distorted the efficient adjustment of the free-market mechanism. Japan's exchange-rate policy during the early 1970s was an example of such a distortion.

Of course, the market mechanism itself has shown deficiencies in coping with the structural difficulties inherent in this transition period of world economics. For example, in the case of many important decisions taken by large corporations and organized labor, long-range considerations or expectations of future economic events reduce the impact of immediate market pressures. In fact, in the transition period of the 1970s the concept of "economic equilibrium" may have lost its operational meaning. No wonder various market signals ("price parameters"), such as commodity prices, wage rate, interest rate, and exchange rate, have fluctuated repeatedly in a wide band around an "insignificant level of equilibrium," i.e., an unstable equilibrium level.

Moreover, the policies of the advanced countries, particularly in the early 1970s, were inappropriate, poorly timed, and confusing. Policies designed to correct the imperfections of the market instead helped to undermine the smooth functioning of the IMF system in its external adjustments. The attempted cures were probably worse than the disease. Clearly the adjustment capability of the free market was hampered significantly by governmental mishandling of inflation policy, incomes policy, and related regulatory measures.

5. *The predominance of a confrontational political approach toward international economic problems.* The turbulent 1970s began with the breakdown of the U.S.-Japan textile negotiations, ominously ushering in a period of political confrontation between major countries over attempts to deal with international economic problems. In contrast to economic behavior conducted according to the rules and procedures of international agreements such as GATT, political negotiations emphasize the strategic use of confrontation. Bilateral rather than multilateral negotiations tend to give high priority to ad hoc political settlements of difficult economic problems, as occurred in the textile settlement between Japan and the United States in 1972. This politicized approach to economic negotiations also means that specific economic issues are inevitably linked to broad questions of political strategy. For example, a concrete economic problem can be used as a principal negotiating weapon, a bargaining chip, when two allied countries sit down to discuss the sharing of defense burdens.

Why this trend toward the politicization of economic issues? In the first place, protectionist advocates have gained considerable political power in several countries. Industry, the agricultural population, and labor unions are all powerful pressure groups lobbying for strong protectionist trade policies. Second, to prevent its economic hegemony from completely unraveling, the United States felt little hesitation in asserting its political power in the world. Third, as dramatic, systemic changes took place in the world economy, no stable set of rules and codes of conduct emerged as the basis for a new consensus. In such an environment, noncooperative strategies were bound to dominate among countries jockeying for position in a new order. Every specific economic negotiation became simultaneously a negotiation over the political rules of the game.

It may be possible for a hegemonic power (and perhaps for a firmly established international cartel) to carry out a political settlement of economic issues through confrontation. But such political settlements achieved through confrontation and unilateral demands will probably not last long. The validity and stability of such arrangements are very dubious unless the negotiating countries are willing to cooperate with one another on the basis of their own interests and generally accepted economic principles.

6. *The use of the economic summit.* Despite the first oil crisis in

1973–1974, we have avoided a chaotic, nightmarish replay of the 1930s. The disintegration of the world economy has been averted, and economic and political warfare have not broken out. One key factor in this success is the continuing economic summit among the major industrialized countries of France, West Germany, Italy, Japan, the United Kingdom, the United States, and later Canada.

The heads of the participating governments quickly recognized the importance of summit meetings as a way of coping not only with international monetary problems but also with a variety of fundamental problems in international economic relations. Coverage at the summit meetings has been expanded to encompass problems of trade, foreign aid, energy, and even the limited coordination of the various countries' domestic economic policies.

The economic summit has thus strengthened the ability of leaders in the advanced countries to take concerted action. This was demonstrated in particular at the Bonn Summit (1978) and at the Tokyo Summit (1979), where the participating countries together with the EEC authorities set out to design a coordinated set of economic policies in the interests of the world economy—from both short-run and long-run points of view. From a historical perspective, such concerted leadership and coordinated actions have successfully replaced the political and economic hegemony of the United States, which prevailed until the end of the 1960s.

Vital Issues in the Free-World Economy in the 1980s

In this section, I will try to clarify the key issues of the 1980s, focusing primarily on the following aspects of international trade and investment policy:

1. free trade versus protectionism
2. international rules versus discretionary national policy
3. the economic principle of comparative advantage versus the political principle of the "merit industry" protection.

1. The fundamental choice between free-trade policy and protectionism. Whenever political forces of nationalism prevail, free-trade policy is quickly replaced by protectionism in the international economic environment. Indeed, protectionist trade policies are probably the most powerful and subversive tools of political nationalism.

Protectionism has been advocated under various names and slogans, such as "fair" trade, "stable" trade, "orderly marketing" trade, and "managed" liberal trade. The various slogans all indicate the grave concern of governments about international private transactions, which are not always compatible with national policy targets, such as national security. The essence of protectionism is always the same: Governmental decision making is suggested as a replacement for the free market in order to protect a particular industry from foreign competition.

In fact, the economic case for protectionist trade policy is almost identical with the case for a planned economy. The fundamental premise is that the government should correct "market failures" due to either the imperfections of competition or serious externalities (such as environmental issues). The arguments for the fair distribution of income (for beleaguered farmers, for example) are often used to support policies favoring government interference in general and protectionist trade policy in particular.

Clearly contemporary free-enterprise economies do need the intervention of government to meet the demand for public goods such as defense and law enforcement, to redistribute national incomes via appropriate tax systems, and to promote macroeconomic stability in the form of high employment and stable prices. The real issue, then, is not a pure choice between absolute free trade or protectionism but rather to what extent government interference should be allowed to restrict free-market forces in order to accomplish the national goals of each country. In this sense, the difference between free trade and protectionism rests upon a careful assessment of what protective measures are taken, to what degree, and for how long. The complexities of these choices will make tension between free trade and protectionism a vital issue of the 1980s.

2. *The conflict between international rules and discretionary national policymaking.* Historical experience demonstrates that a free-trade system requires leadership from a single dominant nation (like Great Britain in the nineteenth century and the United States in the post-1945 period) whose national interests coincide with the stable working of an open world economy. A supranational legal system to support such a free-trade order is bound to be weakened when no one superpower can effectively exercise political and economic leadership in the world.

Both the IMF rules (such as gold convertibility and the adjustable-peg exchange rate system) and the GATT rules (such as the most-favored-nation principle, general eliminations of quantitative restrictions, and the nondiscriminatory safeguard rule) were covertly and overtly violated during the 1970s. For example, it was most unfortunate that the safeguard mechanism (Article XIX of

GATT) has by and large been ignored and rarely invoked in an appropriate manner when needed. Instead, most of the advanced countries, notably the United States, favored prompt application of a discriminatory safeguard, particularly against developing countries and Japan. The United States strongly urged the Japanese government to accept "orderly marketing agreements" (OMA) and "voluntary export restraints" for textiles, steel, and color televisions during the 1970s, measures that amounted to import quotas.

Such discriminatory application of safeguard measures has been strongly supported by particular interest groups, such as the steel industry, while the economic interests of the country as a whole have been often overlooked. The sectoral benefit to the U.S. steel industry that resulted from the OMA in 1976 has contributed significantly to accelerating inflation in the ensuing period and has also weakened the international competitiveness of U.S. industries. Protected industries, not to mention the economy as a whole, are bound to be left behind by newly developing technology and will be unable to use scarce economic resources efficiently in the long run.

Another conflict between international rules and discretionary governmental policies is import relief for senescent industries under the cover of "adjustment assistance." It is very tempting for governments to abuse adjustment assistance to prop up import-competing industries that have lost comparative advantage, thereby jeopardizing the efficient allocation of resources in these countries. Although such assistance is sometimes politically unavoidable, each government should carefully weigh sectoral benefits in terms of the costs incurred, not only for the national economy but also for the world economy.

What is needed is a kind of international surveillance mechanism (probably under the auspices of GATT) to restrain the abuse of discretionary protective policies. Within such an international framework, temporary import restrictions and import relief could be properly assessed according to internationally agreed upon rules of conduct.

3. *The fundamental conflict between the economic principle of comparative advantage and the political principle of "merit industry" protection.*[2] The threat of control of imports for political or even security reasons has led almost all the major countries of the world to justify a certain level of production in "strategic" or "essential" industries. Not only defense industries, but also agricultural and steel industries (or at least some portions of them) have been well protected even when there has been a clear conflict with the principle of international comparative advantage.

Article XX of GATT mentions general exceptions to free trade that are similar in spirit to the idea of "essential" or "merit" products. It refers to measures designed, for example, "to protect public morals," "to protect human, animal or plant life or health," and to conserve "national treasures" or "exhaustible resources." However, from the standpoint of the efficient utilization of economic resources, political considerations concerning merit industries are in obvious conflict with the full application of the principle of comparative advantage. The more each country gives priority to the merit industry argument, the more the economic resources of the world at large will be wasted.

The same analysis is appropriate with respect to so-called positive industrial policies, under which each country tries to foster a promising sector of the economy as an "infant industry." Arguments for government aid for the research and development efforts of high-technology industries, for example, should be carefully scrutinized from the standpoint of global economic efficiency.

Japan's Role in the Changing World Economy of the 1980s

The watershed decade of the 1970s clearly marks a historic transition for the world economy, but it is much easier to see where we have been than where we are going. Moreover, not everyone seems willing to face the realities of the transition. The Japanese people in particular are still clinging to a traditional psychology that emphasizes the insularity of Japan, a state of "seclusion" with respect to the rest of the world. In fact, however, the 1980s and 1990s will require Japan to exercise new forms of leadership in shaping the character of the new global order. What should be the basic principles of such a new Japanese foreign policy? In what follows, I will discuss three aspects of Japanese foreign policy, namely, the political, the economic, and the social.

First, the utmost political priority for Japan should be to continue to seek stable world peace. This implies vigorous efforts in many areas to reduce international tensions, but Japan should not move to develop its military power. The renunciation of armaments is stated clearly in the Japanese Constitution in a clause virtually dictated by the United States at the close of World War II, but recently the United States has been urging Japan to increase its defense forces substantially for a number of reasons.

The first reason is economic. The United States wants Japan to share the defense burden of the free world, particularly in the Far East. However, an increased military presence for Japan in the Far

East might well increase rather than reduce military tension. Moreover, it is naive to assume that Japan would automatically use its increased military power in ways that are necessarily compatible with the political interests of the United States. Finally, a concerted effort to build up Japan's military forces would inevitably raise the issue of nuclear armaments. That in turn would create tremendous domestic political turmoil and in the long run could also pose a new threat to world peace and stability. Japan's postwar economic success is partly attributable to the fact that Japan has not burdened itself with massive military expenditures. But it is not only in Japan's interest, but also in the interest of the world as a whole, for Japan to avoid turning itself into a major military power.

In my judgment, Japan can make the most appropriate contribution to a system of international stability and security, first, by dramatically increasing its nonmilitary foreign aid. Obviously, this kind of nonmilitary aid must come from taxes and voluntary contributions by all the Japanese people. In this sense, *foreign* economic policy is indeed *domestic* economic policy, but idealistic humanitarianism in international politics is quite consistent with Japan's nationalistic interests.

Second, Japan's foreign economic policy should be to strengthen the fundamental principle of free trade and oppose de facto protectionism all over the world. As part of this effort, Japan must take practical policy measures to avoid disrupting the domestic markets of other countries. Temporary adjustment assistance of various kinds will be needed to ease the social costs of phasing out senescent or inefficient industries in importing countries, while appropriate self-restraint will be required over a reasonable period of time in the case of efficient and hence growing firms or industries in exporting countries. In this regard, appropriate safeguard measures should be promptly invoked based on GATT rules.

Third, Japan's foreign policy should emphasize as its overriding task the establishment of the social identity of the Japanese people in the international community. Historically, Japan has made a great effort to adapt itself to the existing rules and orders of the international environment, especially since the end of World War II. However, Japan has almost never attempted to assume a responsible and influential role as one of the "rule-makers" of the international community.

It is increasingly clear that Japan can no longer be allowed to maintain the position of a small country in the contemporary international community. Given the tremendous impact of Japan's actions and policies on the world economy, Japan's failure to assume a responsible role appropriate to its position reveals a lack of serious concern about maintaining the stability of a precarious international system.

Japan's foreign policy should also be based on the unique vision that developed out of the long history of Japanese culture and traditions. The rich and creative economic activities of the Japanese people should continue to inspire people in parts of the world where social and material progress are both urgently desired. The Japanese have sometimes been described as "economic animals." The constructive performance of such economic animals is needed in the international economic environment and would certainly contribute more to the improvement of the world than the performance of most "political animals."

During the hundred years that followed the Meiji Restoration of 1867, and especially during the thirty-five years following Japan's defeat in World War II, the Japanese people have succeeded in producing rapid economic growth and remarkable social progress while maintaining political stability and preserving some of Japan's traditional cultural solidarity. If the achievements of the Japanese people are to have a significant place in world history, it will be because the creativity and the nonmilitary stance of the Japanese people can make a substantial contribution to the prosperity and stability of the world economy. And it should not be forgotten that this contribution, and indeed Japan's economic development since the beginning, has been based essentially on a market-oriented, free-enterprise economy.

Notes

1. The Japanese, stunned by this set of moves, referred to this incident as the "dollar shock."

2. "Merit goods" are theoretically to be distinguished from "public goods" such as defense expenditures, which are by their intrinsic nature consumed collectively and to which the "exclusive principle" is not applicable. Merit goods, such as compulsory education or public health expenditures, on the other hand, involve the imposition of governmental preference on consumer sovereignty with respect to goods that could be provided and consumed privately by individuals.

2
Japan and the World Energy Problem

Herbert I. Goodman

Introduction: The International Background

It sounds dramatic, but perhaps it is not an exaggeration to say that the world is entering a new economic era — an era that will be shaped and constrained by shrinking energy resources available only at rapidly escalating prices; an era in which available incremental energy supplies are disproportionately in the hands of a few less developed countries. It will also be, we must hope, an era in which communication, understanding, and awareness of interdependence and of shared ultimate interests will result in the coordination of the objectives and economic progress of those countries with vast energy resources and those with few.

The present period, one of transition to that uncertain future stage, is characterized by an enormous and intricate worldwide mosaic of interlocking debates, controversies, and conflicts about energy. Questions being debated include the cost and availability of various types of energy, trade-offs between economic growth and protection of the environment, the safety and utility of nuclear power, and the potential role of renewable energy sources. Also widely discussed are the political and strategic implications of the industrial world's dependence on a few petroleum-producing countries; the possible limits to world economic growth implicit in finite hydrocarbon availability and in the cost of alternate energy sources; the dilemma of the world's poor countries, unblessed with indigenous energy resources, but striving to satisfy their people's rising expectations. The list could go on.

Increasingly, these questions can be solved only within an international context, as the problems inherent in the debate transcend both national and regional boundaries. Limited agreements have been reached by some countries for specific types of energy cooperation. The seventeen member countries of the International Energy Agency (IEA) have discussed specific issues; the European Economic Community and the Organization of Petroleum Exporting Countries have talked about meeting to discuss some of these problems. For the most part, however, individual countries have sought national solutions to their energy problems, with only the most limited acknowledgment of their ultimate dependence on and shared interest with other nations. Few nations, whether oil-rich or oil-poor, have acknowledged the need for coordinated and cooperative programs to deal with this truly international dilemma.

It is the thesis of this chapter that, in order successfully to navigate the economic difficulties that inevitably will arise in this new energy era, Japan in particular would be well advised to play a *leadership* role in developing cooperative international solutions. Before we turn to an outline of some of the basic elements of such a solution and some suggestions as to the role Japan might play, it is perhaps useful to look briefly at Japan's stake in the energy problem, to analyze the current and prospective world energy picture, and to place the Japanese energy economy within that perspective.

Japan's Stake in the Problem

The international energy dilemma may be more poignant and more meaningful for Japan than for any other industrialized nation. In 1978, Japan's consumption of energy (all sources) was equivalent to 7.0 million barrels of oil per day, representing 5.2 percent of total world energy use. This may not seem an enormous amount when compared with consumption of other major consumers: U.S. consumption in the same year was 36.2 million barrels per day of oil equivalent (27.6 percent of world consumption); the Soviet Union consumed 22.1 million barrels per day (16.8 percent); and the EEC, 18.9 million barrels per day (14.4 percent).[1] Japan, however, imported 85.4 percent of its total energy requirements, contrasted with 21.6 percent for the United States and 54.0 percent for Western Europe; the Soviet Union remained a net exporter.[2] The percentage of energy imported by Japan has risen precipitously since the 1950s. In 1955, total Japanese energy consumption was equivalent to only 1 million barrels of oil per day. Fifty percent of this was provided by coal; petroleum supplied 20 percent.[3] Today, in startling contrast, petroleum accounts for more than 70 percent of the more than 7 million barrels of energy consumed per day, and coal has dropped to only 15 percent. From about 24 percent in 1955, imports of total energy requirements had risen by 1978 to more than 85 percent.[4]

This percentage can be expected to rise even higher during the next several years before starting to decline.

Thus, Japan accounts for approximately 8 percent of the world's oil consumption and imports virtually all of it.[5] Japanese and international oil companies have made huge efforts and large investments to develop indigenous oil resources, yet total proven Japanese crude reserves are only about 55 million barrels,[6] less than 1/125 of 1 percent of the 686 billion barrels of proven world reserves.[7]

This degree of reliance on imported energy provides a fair measure of Japan's stake in solving the international energy problem. The overwhelming dependence on imports for the energy needs of a populous and crowded archipelago underlies the policies of the government, whether economic or political, foreign or domestic. On the one hand, it is essential for Japan in the near term to assure foreign supplies of needed energy and to earn through exports the foreign exchange required to pay for them. On the other hand, it is almost as important for Japan to attempt to lessen its dependence on these easily interrupted supplies through diversification of sources and types of imported fuels, as well as through the development of indigenous substitutes. Japan has made major efforts since the early 1960s to liberate itself from its dependence on Middle East oil, but a quick survey of these efforts shows that the results have been slim.

First, with organizational and financial backing from the government, Japanese companies have for twenty years searched for oil in various parts of the world. As early as 1961, one of these companies started producing foreign crude oil for shipment to Japan. In the late 1960s and early 1970s, importation of liquefied petroleum gas (LPG) and liquefied natural gas (LNG) began, along with the commercial introduction of nuclear power. In 1980, these sources provided an amount equal to Japan's entire 1955 energy requirements, but this fulfilled only about 15 percent of the country's requirements.

Second, to provide some cushion against abrupt interruptions of petroleum supply, the Ministry of International Trade and Industry (MITI) programmed stockpiles of crude oil and refined products in 1972. In early 1979, Japan had stockpiles equal to 90 days' consumption, which were drawn down to about 81 days during the first six months of the Iranian revolution.[8] By early 1980, these stocks had been rebuilt to about 105 days' requirement, including 7 days' supply in laid-up tankers.[9]

Third, efforts have been made to improve the security of crude oil supplies by diversifying the geographical sources. Despite efforts initiated in the late 1950s, in 1967 Japan was still dependent on the

Middle East for more than 90 percent of its crude supply.[10] Twelve years later, after concerted efforts and investments totaling more than $4 billion, this reliance had decreased markedly—but it was still more than 80 percent.[11]

Fourth, events in the 1970s—the interruption of world oil supplies during the 1973 war in the Middle East, accelerated nationalization of oil companies by producing governments, the enormous strengthening of OPEC, and the quintupling of oil prices in the early 1970s—panicked Japan into intensifying diversification efforts. Funds were allocated for the development of less conventional energy sources such as solar, geothermal, coal gasification and liquefaction, and hydrogen. In spite of these efforts, some realistic estimates suggest that by the year 2000 Japan may still depend on oil imports for nearly three-quarters of its total energy needs.[12] According to this calculation, nuclear energy would contribute only one-seventh of total energy requirements, and the remainder (less than one-seventh) would be supplied by coal, hydroelectric, and nonconventional energy sources.[13] Even under the assumptions of a more optimistic estimate, almost two-thirds of Japan's energy requirements in 1990 will still have to be supplied by imported oil.[14] In addition, all uranium for the nuclear option and most coal must also be imported, although these come principally from Australia, Canada, the United States, and other Pacific Basin countries with which Japan is closely allied.

Finding secure supplies of petroleum will continue to be a problem. Prior to the Iranian revolution, 67 percent of Japan's crude supply was furnished by the major international oil companies, 20 percent was purchased directly from producing governments, and 9 percent came from overseas sources developed by Japanese companies.[15] The abrupt ending of Iranian oil exports temporarily cost Japan about 18 percent of its crude supply. About half of this was replaced by increased deliveries from other countries, and the remainder was replaced by drawing down the strategic stockpiles so that there was minimal volumetric effect on domestic industry.[16] Japanese oil and trading companies have now made direct deals with Iran for future supply, but the volumes are only about one-half of previous supply. All the international major oil companies have phased out their crude oil sales to Japanese independents. Japan can now expect about 40 percent of crude imports to be supplied by those companies that have equity ownership in Japanese affiliates; the remaining 60 percent of their requirements must be purchased directly from the producing governments.[17]

Current World Energy Picture and
Prospects for the Future

The Organization of Petroleum Exporting Countries

During the last few years a rather loosely knit organization of thirteen oil-producing countries has assumed an unprecedented influence on the world's economy.[18] The Organization of Petroleum Exporting Countries was formed in 1960 by five major producing nations—Venezuela, Saudi Arabia, Kuwait, Iran, and Iraq—in order to wrest control of crude oil prices from the international oil companies, which as concessionaires had discovered and developed the oil reserves of these countries and were marketing the crude oil worldwide.[19] The OPEC members felt that the oil companies were underpricing their oil and managing their resources so as to optimize the interests of the consumers rather than those of the producers.

In 1960, the founding members of OPEC controlled 67 percent of the world's petroleum reserves, 38 percent of world oil production, and 90 percent of oil in international trade.[20] In 1980 the thirteen members of OPEC controlled 70 percent of the world's petroleum reserves,[21] 49 percent of production,[22] and 80 percent of oil in international trade.[23] The organization has grown not only in size, but, almost immeasurably, in power.

The Supply and Demand of World Energy

Before relating the dimensions of this growth in power and importance and of OPEC's impact upon the oil consumers of the world, it is useful to provide a brief overview of the world's present and forecast supply and demand parameters for primary energy. The demand for OPEC oil is a residual; that is, it constitutes the difference between total world demand for energy and the supply of energy from all non-OPEC sources.[24] Thus, OPEC oil is the critical balancing factor for fueling the world's machinery; it influences the market price for all energy.

Figure 2.1 shows the world demand for energy for 1978 and how this demand was supplied from various energy sources. Oil was the single largest source, supplying 46 percent of the world's total demand. (The OPEC countries contributed about 48 percent of world petroleum production, thus supplying 22 percent of the world's total energy requirements.) Coal was second in importance, supplying more than 27 percent of energy demand, followed by gas, hydroelec-

FIGURE 2.1
1978 Total World Energy[1] Consumption by Energy Type [millions of barrels
per day (MMB/D) of oil equivalent]

Nuclear	2.3%	3.2 MMB/D
Water Power	6.0%	8.2 MMB/D
Natural Gas	18.6%	25.5 MMB/D
Coal	27.1%	37.2 MMB/D
Oil	46.0%	63.1 MMB/D
	100.0%	137.2 MMB/D

[1]Excludes other energy sources such as solar, radiation, wind,
wave, ocean gradient, geothermal, etc.

Source: British Petroleum Statistical Review: 1978 (London:
Britannic House, 1979), pp. 8-9.

tric power, and finally, nuclear power, which contributed a mere 2.3
percent.

Figure 2.2 divides the world energy demand by class of user. We
see that the largest amount is used to operate industrial plants,
which draw upon a wide spectrum of energy sources, including
petroleum, coal, natural gas, hydroelectric, and nuclear. Interfuel
substitution takes place most easily in industry. In contrast, the

FIGURE 2.2
1978 Total World Energy[1] Consumption by End Use [millions of barrels per day (MMB/D) of oil equivalent]

Energy Sector Own Use	9.8%	13.4 MMB/D
Transport	17.7%	24.3 MMB/D
Domestic Public and Commercial	33.6%	46.1 MMB/D
Industry	38.9%	53.4 MMB/D
	100.0%	137.2 MMB/D

---

[1]Excludes other energy sources such as solar, radiation, wind, wave, ocean gradient, geothermal, etc.

Sources: Percentages calculated from "World Energy Resources 1980-2020," London, World Energy Conference, 1979 (mimeo), p. 186. Figures calculated from British Petroleum Statistical Review: 1978 (London: Britannic House, 1979), pp. 8-9.

transportation sector currently relies almost totally upon petroleum.

Table 2.1 shows how major energy sources developed during the 1970s. Nuclear power grew steadily, although not at the accelerated rates once anticipated. The rate of growth in oil consumption

TABLE 2.1
Historical Analysis of Total World Energy Consumption by Energy Type (Millions of Barrels Per Day –
MMB/D – of Oil Equivalent)

	1970		1972		1974		1976		1978	
	MMB/D	%	MMB/D	%	MMB/D	%	MMB/D	%	MMB/D	%
Natural Gas	19.61	18.5	21.51	18.8	22.87	18.9	23.81	18.6	25.46	18.6
Oil	46.49	43.8	52.59	46.0	56.05	46.2	59.14	46.2	63.12	46.0
Coal & Other* Solid Fuels	33.30	31.4	32.74	28.6	33.78	27.9	35.23	27.6	37.17	27.1
Water Power	6.28	5.9	6.70	5.9	7.17	5.9	7.51	5.9	8.29	6.0
Nuclear	0.41	0.4	0.79	0.7	1.29	1.1	2.18	1.7	3.13	2.3
TOTALS	106.09	100.0	114.33	100.0	121.16	100.0	127.87	100.0	137.17	100.0

*Includes lignite, peat, wood, and shale.

Source: British Petroleum Statistical Review: 1978 (London: Britannic House, 1979), pp. 6–8.

decreased from 6–7 percent (pre-1973) to 2–3 percent (1974–1978), due largely to OPEC's fivefold price increase in 1973–1974. Although coal reserves represent a very substantial share of the world's energy reserves—especially in North America, Australia, and Asia—coal consumption has grown only slightly and its share of the total has decreased, largely because of labor requirements, environmental problems, and the relative attractiveness of other fuels. Petroleum is still the most attractive and versatile fuel. It is easily transported, readily refined, comparatively low in cost, and produces a variety of energy products for industrial, residential, commercial, and transportation uses.

Table 2.2 breaks down world petroleum production and consumption in 1978 according to what we may call geopolitical groups. The single largest consumer of petroleum is the United States, which, with 5.3 percent of the world population, consumed 29.1 percent of world oil production. The thirteen OPEC nations produced 47.9 percent of world oil production, while consuming only 3.5 percent. As previously noted, Japan produces an insignificant amount of oil and is almost entirely dependent on oil imports to meet its energy needs. Apart from the OPEC countries, the free world (all countries except the People's Republic of China [PRC] and the Soviet bloc countries) was a net consumer of petroleum. The Soviet Union and the PRC between them exported approximately 2 million barrels per day of crude oil and petroleum products to the noncommunist world. The PRC exported 225,000 barrels per day, or about 12 percent of their 2 million barrels per day of production.[25] Sixty-seven percent of these exports went to Japan, which is expected to remain the major recipient of Chinese exports during the next several years.[26]

Many industry observers and the Central Intelligence Agency (CIA) consider that Soviet-bloc exports will cease in the early 1980s, at which time these countries will become net importers, with East European imports from the noncommunist world offsetting Soviet exports. The CIA in mid-1979 predicted that by 1982 Soviet-bloc countries would be net importers of 700,000 barrels per day.[27]

In order to isolate oil and energy supply available to satisfy demand in critical markets, we must differentiate between total production and the amount moving in international trade. Table 2.3 shows the international trade in crude oil from 1975 to 1979. Although the OPEC countries contributed only 46 percent of world petroleum production in 1978, they provided 82 percent of the crude oil moving in international trade. This amounted to more than half of total free-world oil consumption. Although there has been a

TABLE 2.2
1978 Total World Oil Data (Thousands of Barrels Per Day - MB/D)

Geo-Political Group	Production		Consumption[1]	
	MB/D	%	MB/D	%
Soviet Bloc	12,135	19.3%	10,455	16.6%
People's Rep. of China	1,930	3.0	1,705	2.7
Japan	10	-	5,420	8.6
USA	10,265	16.3	18,345	29.1
Western Europe	1,820	2.9	14,600	23.1
Latin America & Mexico	2,525	4.0	4,190	6.6
Other Free World				
- OPEC nations	30,155	47.9	2,200	3.5
- Others	4,125	6.6	6,205	9.8
Subtotal	34,280	54.4	8,405	13.3
World[2]	62,965	100.0%	63,120	100.0%

[1]Some values for the consumption data contain both crude oil and refined product quantities (e.g., estimated product imports to Japan are 600,000 b/d for 1978).

[2]Differences between world oil production and consumption figures are attributed to stock changes and unknown military liftings.

Source: British Petroleum Statistical Review: 1978 (London: Britannic House, 1979), pp. 6-8.

steady increase since 1973 in oil supplies from non-OPEC areas—notably from Mexico, the North Sea, and the North Slope of Alaska—the rate of growth of non-OPEC production has slowed down and will be even smaller in future years. Into the foreseeable future, the world's consumers, while fully utilizing all other available energy sources, will continue to need OPEC supplies to fulfill a large portion of their critical requirements. Table 2.4 shows that even under very conservative assumptions of demand growth, OPEC countries will still be supplying 43 percent of total world production and more than 57 percent of free-world production in 1990.[28]

Table 2.5 shows how critically important the OPEC suppliers have become for Japan, whose dependence on OPEC-supplied crude oil increased from 80.5 percent of total crude imports in 1976 to 87.9 percent in 1978. Petroleum contributed almost 73 percent of

TABLE 2.3
Free World Internationally Traded Crude Oil (Millions of Barrels Per Day - MMB/D)

Source of Exports by Geo-Political Area	1975		1976		1977		1978		1979 (Estimate)	
	MMB/D	%	MMB/D	%	MMB/D	%	MMB/D	%	MMB/D	%
OPEC	25.9	86	28.9	86	29.5	85	27.7	82	28.3	82
OECD	1.1	4	1.1	3	1.2	4	1.5	4	1.9	5
Non-OPEC Developing	1.3	4	1.5	5	1.8	5	2.2	7	2.4	7
Communist	1.8	6	2.1	6	2.2	6	2.3	7	1.9	6
TOTALS	30.1	100	33.6	100	34.7	100	33.7	100	34.5	100

Source: Derived from Petroleum Economist, 1979.
OPEC Statistical Yearbooks (1976-1978).

TABLE 2.4
Worldwide Production of Crude Oil: 1970-1990 (Thousands of Barrels Per
Day — MB/D)

Producers	1970		1980		1990	
	Vol.	%	Vol.	%	Vol.	%
Free World						
OPEC	23,500	51	29,000	47	31,000	43
Non—OPEC	14,860	32	18,700	30	23,200	32
Total Free World	38,360	83	47,700	77	54,200	75
Communist Countries						
(USSR, E. Europe, China)	7,835	17	14,300	23	17,800	25
TOTAL WORLD	46,195	100	62,000	100	72,000	100

Sources: 1970 data from Oil and Gas Journal, December 28, 1970.
Future projections are calculated from various issues of the Oil
and Gas Journal, Petroleum Intelligence Weekly, Arab Press
Service, and Platt's Oilgram News.

Japan's total 1978 energy requirements; OPEC crude oil supplied 64
percent of Japan's total energy in that year. IF LPG and LNG imports
from OPEC members are included, Japan's total dependence on
OPEC becomes even greater.

The Evolution of OPEC's Power

For years to come, the OPEC nations collectively will be the
world's "swing" supplier of needed energy. The power this gives to
OPEC is enormous, frightening, and unprecedented. How did this
situation come about?

Prior to the creation of OPEC, petroleum production, pricing, and
movement into world markets were managed by the numerous
companies making up the world's oil industry and were governed essentially by market requirements. Economic considerations were
paramount, and these, by and large, reflected the needs of the
world's consumers. The U.S. market was the largest, and U.S. com-

TABLE 2.5
Total Crude Oil Imports into Japan (Thousands of Barrels Per Day - MB/D)

Geo-Political Area	1976		1977		1978	
	MB/D	%	MB/D	%	MB/D	%
From:						
OPEC Nations	3,824.6	80.5	3,740.8	78.3	4,091.5	87.9
U.S.S.R.	1.6	-	1.4	-	1.1	-
China	125.3	2.6	138.4	2.9	146.6	3.1
Other	801.8	16.9	901.1	18.8	416.8	9.0
TOTAL	4,753.3	100.0	4,781.7	100.0	4,656.0	100.0

Note: (1) Estimated petroleum product imports to Japan are 600,000 barrels/
day for 1978.
(2) Petroleum product imports are not included in the above data.

Source: 1976/1977 - Japan Petroleum and Energy Yearbook, 1978, pp. G52-G57.
1978- Japanese Oil Statistics Today, November 1979, pp. 6-7.

panies, joined by a handful of European competitors, were in the forefront of technical and commercial development. Beginning in the 1920s, the largest of these companies went abroad to explore and develop the world's hidden petroleum resources, which were almost always located in forbidding and undeveloped wastelands. The objective of these companies, for the most part, was to develop crude oil to be moved into the large and growing U.S. market.

During the 1950s, after their overseas efforts had been crowned with spectacular success, the pioneering companies were joined by a large number of smaller U.S. oil companies. The smaller companies anticipated adverse effects on their U.S. market positions from the large amounts of low-cost foreign oil that would soon be entering the United States. They particularly saw the need to acquire access to Middle East and North African oil, whose reservoirs were understood to be very large and whose production costs were very low. By the end of the 1950s, just as large amounts of newly developed foreign crude oil were beginning to enter the U.S. market, the U.S. government imposed an import-control program that effectively closed the U.S. market to almost all foreign oil.[29] The producing companies were required by their concession agreements to make substantial royalty payments to the host governments and faced the loss of their concessions and their investments unless they met those obligations. The companies therefore looked for Eastern

Hemisphere markets to replace the lost U.S. demand for which the investments had been intended. With so much new oil competing for limited European and Far Eastern markets, which were already being satisfactorily supplied, the inevitable result was lower and lower international crude oil prices.

As the competing oil companies brought crude prices ever lower, revenues to the producing government from royalties and taxes declined apace. The governments strenuously contested the companies' control of the pricing mechanism and in 1960 formed OPEC to wrest control of pricing from the companies. The OPEC governments henceforth assumed control of price-setting for the crude oil produced in their countries.[30] The ambitions of the oil-producing governments evolved during the 1960s to include total nationalization of their oil industries, a process largely completed by the time of the Arab-Israeli war in October 1973. The war gave the producing countries an opportunity to test the reality of the power that had fallen almost unnoticed into their hands during the previous decade. The Arab members of OPEC announced an oil embargo of the Netherlands and the United States and quadrupled the price of their oil. The price rise was successful, but the embargo was thwarted by the international oil companies. The worldwide logistics infrastructure of terminals, tanker fleets, and know-how allowed the companies to trade with each other and between the consuming countries so that nonembargoed crude could be delivered to the embargoed countries and embargoed crude to destinations permitted by the Arab governments.

The experience of 1973–1974 taught the OPEC countries two lessons: First, it confirmed for them the reality of their control of crude oil pricing and demonstrated that as long as they maintained some semblance of coordination of production volumes, they could price their oil however they agreed; second, it brought home to them the need to extend their control beyond pricing to areas that were still in the hands of the oil companies, such as production scheduling, types of oil produced, and the markets for which shipments were destined. By 1979, most oil-producing governments had extended their total control into these areas as well.

Since the end of 1973, crude oil prices have risen steadily. In 1979 dollars, the average of the official prices of crude in the Persian Gulf increased from $3.25 per barrel in 1973 to $13.75 in 1975 and $26.60 in January 1980.[31] Higher prices have brought increasing revenues and increasing foreign exchange surpluses. The aggregate of the current-account surpluses of the OPEC members after the 1979 price increases was estimated to total $44 billion per annum.[32] The events of these years gave the oil-producing countries new insight into the extent and nature of the power they collectively wield, as well as some sense of the problems arising from that power—problems for the oil consumers, but also for themselves.

The reality is that the oil-producing countries now collectively have the power to decide how much revenue they want and how much oil they are willing to produce and then to decide what the unit price of that oil should be in order to generate the desired revenue. If consumers decide to reduce their oil consumption through conservation efforts, the producers, if they stick together, can reduce their production to meet the new lower demand level and raise their unit prices enough to return their total revenues to the previous level. The phenomenon is the result of a combination of the short-run inelasticity of demand for petroleum and the control of the necessary marginal supplies by a few producers operating as a cartel.[33] The problem this presents to oil-consuming countries and to the existence of a stable international economic order is obvious.

The Producers' Question: How Much to Produce?

The difficulty facing OPEC members is to use this immense power so as to optimize their own long-term benefits while not crippling the industrialized countries on which they depend for markets, supplies of industrial and consumer goods, and investment opportunities for their savings and foreign exchange surpluses. At present, neither OPEC nor its member governments have a clear idea of how to deal with this problem. Indeed, there are great divisions on this complex of questions among the OPEC members, as well as between conflicting groups within many of the member nations. The economic interests of the OPEC countries vary widely in accordance not only with the differing volumes of their oil reserves and their differing foreign exchange requirements, but also with their political orientations, which range across a spectrum from extreme traditional conservatism on the right to extreme radical commitment on the left.

Endless speculations and theories circulate, both among the OPEC nations and in the industrialized countries, as to how these international economic issues should be resolved. The oil producers themselves are probing to find safe and possible limits to which they can push crude oil prices and other demands on the consuming nations. On one important point, at least, the producers are in approximate agreement: Their aggregate production should be kept very close to the total world demand for their oil.

Figure 2.3 shows the relationship between: (1) historic and pro-

FIGURE 2.3

Noncommunist World Production Capacity and Potential Petroleum Supply, 1976–1982 [millions of barrels per day (MMB/D) of oil equivalent]

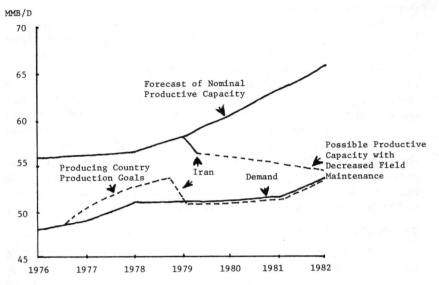

Sources: The Petroleum Outlook (Menlo Park, Calif.: Sherman H. Clark Associates, 1979); Gulf Oil Crude Oil Economics Committee, "World Petroleum Outlook 1978–1995," Houston, Tex., Gulf Oil Exploration and Production Company, November 1978.

jected free-world demand for oil; (2) historic and projected physical capacity to produce oil; and (3) the actual amounts produced from 1976 to 1979 and the amounts producers intend to produce in the future.[34] The first point, which is dramatically apparent, is the significant surplus of production capacity. Productive capacity in the noncommunist world in 1980 was estimated to exceed 60 million barrels per day.[35] Six million barrels per day of potential production, two-thirds of which is in the OPEC countries, is shut-in. The remaining balance is in Canada, the United States, Mexico, the United Kingdom, Norway, and Angola, but in each case the amount is relatively small.

A caveat that should be given here is that neglect of the oil fields will result in a decline in the immediately available productive capacity. Some producing countries do not seem to be continuing development programs to maintain the capacity of their fields. Iran has ceased gas-injection programs and field development, and its available capacity may already have declined from 6 million barrels per day to little more than 3 million. Kuwait's capacity has been 3 million barrels per day, but in 1980 it may have been less than 2.5 million. This trend toward reduced technical maintenance may develop in all the OPEC countries with excess earning power and/or bureaucratic inefficiency. The potential impact of this type of neglect is shown by the dotted line in Figure 2.3.[36]

Figure 2.3 also shows that from late 1976 until late 1978 the aggregate production goals of the individual producing countries exceeded the free world's aggregate demand for crude oil. During this period, oil prices declined, and inventories in the consuming countries were built up as consumers purchased relatively low-cost crude to build strategic reserves. Japan, for example, purchased about 400 million barrels more than it needed for current consumption and increased its stockpiles to 90 days of consumption.[37] By the second quarter of 1978, one-half year before the Iranian revolution, the OPEC governments were discussing how they might reduce their aggregate production to strengthen prices. In June of that year, they agreed on a program for such a reduction, which began to take hold almost immediately.[38] By December the Iranian revolution temporarily terminated Iranian production, taking 6 million barrels per day off the world market. The events of 1978 taught the OPEC members the importance of coordination of their aggregate production levels in order to realize the benefits of their control of prices. In the future, they can be expected to keep aggregate production very close to the level of expected demand, as shown in Figure 2.3.

The Producers Are Testing the Limits

Underlying the natural desire of the OPEC countries to take maximum advantage of their power over both pricing and programming production is their consciousness that their oil is a wasting asset. To place this in a world perspective, Table 2.6 shows the international distribution of total crude oil reserves. The world has currently discovered and proven reserves sufficient to supply 39.4 more years of consumption at the 1979 level. The OPEC member countries control almost 80 percent of total free-world oil reserves and more than 68 percent of total world reserves.[39]

These are obviously valuable resources. But the OPEC governments are aware of great problems for their economically underdeveloped societies. If world consumption were to continue to increase at the rates of the 1970s, it is clear from Table 2.6 that the bulk of supply would have to come from OPEC, whose reserves would then be depleted much more rapidly than indicated. Unless

TABLE 2.6
Total World Crude Oil Reserves as of January 1, 1979 (Millions of Barrels
Per Day - MMB/D - of Oil Equivalent)

	% of Total	MMB/D	Years Remaining Life*
OPEC - Middle East	56.7%	389,570	51.4
OPEC - Other	11.7	80,150	22.2
U.S.A., Canada	5.0	34,500	9.3
Mexico	4.4	30,000	54.8
United Kingdom/Norway	3.2	22,100	31.0
U.S.S.R.	10.3	71,000	16.6
People's Republic of China	2.9	20,000	26.1
Others	5.8	39,500	23.3
TOTAL	100.0%	686,820	(average) 39.4

*Assuming 1979 production rates.

Source: *Oil & Gas Journal*, December 25, 1978.

the OPEC governments plan carefully, they could be left with massively underdeveloped countries, with little to show for the immense resources they once possessed and the immense economic power they once enjoyed. A determination to avoid such an outcome and to use their depleting oil resources to assure future prosperity for their countries largely explains the response of the oil producers to the world's apparently insatiable demand for their oil.

With production levels held approximately equal to demand, the producers have been raising crude oil prices as rapidly as possible. They seem intent on testing the upper limits to which prices can be pushed without crippling the industrial world. At the same time, they are experimenting with payment devices that would protect their mounting foreign exchange reserves from the high rates of inflation in the industrialized countries.

During 1979, while steadily raising official prices, the producers also began to shorten the duration and decrease the volumes of their crude oil sales contracts. This increased their flexibility and gave them the option of either decreasing production volumes or selling the freed-up oil at even higher prices on the spot market. In late 1979, spot-market prices were as high as double the official OPEC prices. At this time, the producing governments were, by various estimates, selling an unprecedented 10–20 percent of their total production in this manner.[40]

In the view of many oil-producing governments, these are volumes that they have no need to sell. Greatly increased crude oil prices have lowered the production levels necessary to generate the foreign exchange needed for their current and development budgets. One can characterize as "discretionary" oil the difference between the production volumes required to provide the producing country's foreign exchange requirement and the volumes required to satisfy the crude oil needs of the consuming countries.

Worldwide demand for OPEC crude oil was around 28.4 million barrels per day in 1980, whereas the OPEC countries had to sell less than 20 million barrels per day to generate their aggregate foreign exchange requirements, as shown in Figure 2.4.[41] This left 8.4 million barrels per day of discretionary oil. The producers' objectives for these discretionary barrels are evolving from receiving the maximum price to creating various other mechanisms to assure themselves of inflation-proof payment in the form of real assets, assistance in developing their economies, and support for various political goals. Demands placed on crude oil customers by various producers include the following:

- signature bonuses (key money)
- exploration activity in producing country
- advance payment for crude oil, giving the producer the use of the money before oil is delivered
- utilization of producer-owned tanker fleets
- purchase of petroleum products from producer-government refineries
- purchase of LPG from producer governments
- technology transfer to producing country
- downstream investments in producing country
- giving producers positions in downstream facilities in consuming countries
- support for producing-government foreign policy goals[42]

This experimentation and testing of limits will continue and will grow until some new modes of relationship are developed to accommodate the needs of both the producers and the consumers of oil.

The Realities and Limits of Alternative Fuels

Until a viable framework is established for both producers and consumers, the world will continue to experience the chaotic and damaging conditions of the recent past. It can be expected that the real price of oil will continue to rise through the 1980s, with increasing economic damage to both industrialized and developing consuming countries. Most analysts believe that a minimum real

FIGURE 2.4
Current Changes in OPEC Government Crude Oil Marketing [millions of barrels per day (MMB/D)]

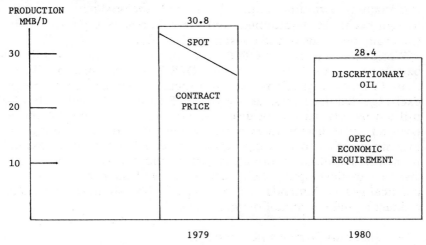

Source: Gulf Oil Corporation Internal Reports, 1979–1980.

economic growth of 3 to 3.5 percent per year is necessary in the industrialized countries in order to provide minimum markets for the exports of the developing countries.[43] In recent years, a 3 percent growth rate in the industrialized nations of the free world has required a 1.5 percent increase in energy use.

Bringing these realities together with the concerns and aspirations of the oil-producing countries, many estimates project an increase in the real price of oil of about 2 percent per year over the 1980s and at a somewhat higher rate after that; or a nominal rate of increase of 10–12 percent per year until 1990.[44] Thus, nonconventional alternative energy sources (shale, fuel synthesis from coal, solar, geothermal, etc.) will become economic during this period, as the price of oil reaches the cost of producing each of these sources.[45] At the same time, higher prices will slowly result in decreased energy consumption.[46]

Table 2.7 shows a possible scenario for world energy consumption through 1990, based on the assumptions of limited production, rising cost, conservation in the industrial countries, and substitutions of nuclear and other alternative fuels.[47] Conventional crude oil production from 1980 to 1990 for the world is forecast to increase at

TABLE 2.7
Total World Energy Consumption[1] by Energy Type (Millions of Barrels Per
Day - MMB/D - of Oil Equivalent)

ENERGY TYPE	1978 (Actual)		1985		1990	
	MMB/D	%	MMB/D	%	MMB/D	%
Natural Gas	25.5	18.6	32.0	20.0	39.0	21.0
Oil	63.1	46.0	72.0	44.0	77.0	41.0
Coal and Solid Fuels[2]	37.2	27.1	44.0	27.0	52.0	28.0
Water Power	8.2	6.0	9.0	6.0	10.0	5.0
Nuclear and Other[3]	3.2	2.3	5.0	3.0	9.0	5.0
TOTALS	137.2	100.0	162.0	100.0	187.0	100.0

[1]Combined values for domestic and imported supply/demand
[2]Includes lignite, peat, wood, and shale
[3]Includes geothermal energy

Source: Gulf Oil Corporation Internal Document, "Environmental Forecast,"
December 1978.

about 1.5 percent per year.[48] OPEC production is shown holding
fairly constant during the period, with the increase coming from
non-OPEC areas like Mexico. The production of some low-reserve
OPEC countries, like Iran, Venezuela, and Indonesia, will decline as
reserves are depleted, while that of others, like Saudi Arabia, will increase moderately. If this projection were continued for a few more
years, we would see that world conventional petroleum production
is expected to peak at about 75–80 million barrels per day around
1990 and then start to decline.[49]

Conservation has already been seriously undertaken in the consuming countries and will accelerate under the pressure of rising
prices and political imperatives. The growth rate of energy use in
the free world during the period 1974–1978 was 1.4 percent per
annum, or only one-quarter of the 5.2 percent per annum experienced from 1965–1973. This figure of 1.4 percent per annum is sufficient to maintain the 3 percent GNP growth rate considered to be a
minimum for world economic health.[50]

Similarly, energy substitution is taking effect almost everywhere,
and this process also should accelerate. The easiest and most obvious substitutes are natural gas, coal, and nuclear energy, despite
the environmental problems associated with coal and nuclear en-

ergy and the large infrastructure needs associated with coal. Many possibilities are being considered for large-scale production of non-conventional fuels, but the problems are enormous.

A major problem associated with energy substitutes is finding the necessary capital. At the present level of technology, it could cost as much as $700 billion to replace the 1979 oil imports of the United States (roughly equal to twice Japan's present oil imports) with synthetic oils from oil shale or coal. Exxon's chairman, C. C. Garvin, has estimated that successful implementation of a synthetic oil program could take as long as thirty years.[51] The very long lead times required to make these investments are a serious constraint; on the other hand, they dilute and help to ease the problems caused by diverting such large amounts of capital funds from the rest of the economy. One of the questions being debated is how this large investment should be shared between the private and public sectors. U.S. energy companies fear that the capital requirements are too great a burden for private enterprise to bear alone, and they have been soliciting governmental participation. Until synthetic fuel projects become economically viable vis-à-vis alternative energy sources, they probably will not contribute significantly to the alleviation of the world energy problem. Commercial quantities of these fuels will probably not be produced before 1990.

Solar power for electric-power generation, where solar energy is expected to have the most significant impact, is thought to be forty years away by some experts in the U.S. electric utility industry.[52] Ths U.S. government's long-range plans for utilization of solar energy—with an ultimate goal of 20 percent of all energy requirements' being supplied by solar technologies by the year 2020—is considered unrealistic by many scientists.[53] The science of photovoltaics, the direct conversion of solar energy to electric power, is in its infancy. Indirect utilization of solar energy through solar heat-collecting panels, although now practical, has efficiency limitations and large capital requirements.

Thus, as shown in Table 2.7, more than 40 percent of the world's energy in 1990 will still be provided by oil, and the world will still be dependent on OPEC, even if every effort is made to conserve energy and to develop coal, nuclear, and other energy sources. Moreover, the OPEC countries will have to be persuaded that it is in their economic and political interest to produce the volumes of oil required to meet these goals. In the best case that can be foreseen (Table 2.4), the OPEC countries will produce 31 million barrels per day of oil in 1990, almost exactly the level of their 1979 production.[54]

Japan and Energy: Dependency and Survival

The ending of World War II served as a new beginning for Japan. During the early postwar years the nation's objectives were, first, to survive, and second, to grope its way back to its prewar level of economic health. By 1955 the economy had reached prewar levels of GNP and energy consumption and had begun a long and extraordinary ascent. Japan now faces the challenge of adjusting to the dramatic changes in available international oil supplies if it is to continue that growth process or, at a minimum, to preserve its hard-won prosperity.

The Scarcity of Domestic Resources

Table 2.8 and Figure 2.5 show the evolution of the energy-supply patterns that fueled this economic development.[55] Despite strenuous efforts, ingenuity, and capital expenditures, the total energy supplied by domestic sources has declined since 1950. As a percentage of total energy use, domestic supply fell from 93 percent in 1950 to 12 percent in 1979.

Changing Energy Patterns

The statistics in Table 2.8 illustrate the degree to which Japan's economic growth has been fueled by imported energy. They also illustrate Japanese frugality, pragmatism, and organization in the thoroughness and efficiency with which the nation's limited energy resources have been exploited. The importance of wood and charcoal in the early postwar years is remarkable in a modern industrial society. About 8.9 percent of the total energy used in Japan in 1950 was provided by wood products. As late as the early 1950s, firewood remained the primary household fuel; it was used in several industrial applications and, in combination with charcoal, propelled 40 percent of the nation's automotive vehicles. A total of 199 trillion BTUS was supplied from this source annually.[56]

By the mid-1950s, energy derived from charcoal and firewood had virtually disappeared from national statistics. The remaining traditional indigenous sources of energy are hydropower and coal. Lignite was introduced in 1940 in response to wartime fuel shortages. By 1950, lignite contributed 1.4 million tons per year, out of estimated recoverable reserves of 800 million tons. Indigenous coal's percentage slowly declined as this resource was depleted and was replaced by imports, mainly from Australia, the United States, and recently China.[57] From 22 million metric tons per year in 1945, coal production reached a high of 57 million tons per year in 1960

TABLE 2.8
Japanese Primary Energy Supply (Thousands of Barrels Per Day - MB/D - of Oil Equivalent)

	1950	%	1960	%	1970	%	1975	%	1977	%	1978	%	Estimated 1979	%
Crude Oil	66.6	4.7	543	33.6	3,333	62.3	4,268	67.6	4,506	67.5	4,438.9	66.5	4,605.6	66.4
Imported Oil Products	21.2	1.5	67	4.1	394	7.4	242	3.8	323	4.8	133.5	2.0	256.6	3.7
Imported LPG	--	--	--	--	60	1.1	122	1.9	153	2.3	300.4	4.5	152.6	2.2
Natural Gas	1.4	0.1	16	1.0	46	0.9	46	0.7	51	0.8	46.7	0.7	41.6	0.6
Imported LNG	--	--	--	--	22	0.4	116	1.8	192	2.9	273.6	4.1	319.0	4.6
Coal	725.5	51.2	671	41.5	1,107	20.7	1,037	16.4	988	14.8	914.5	13.7	971.0	14.0
Nuclear Power	--	--	--	--	19	0.4	106	1.7	134	2.0	240.3	3.6	263.6	3.8
Hydropower	463.4	32.7	247	15.3	338	6.3	363	5.8	322	4.8	320.4	4.8	319.1	4.6
Firewood	87.8	6.2	44	2.8	25	0.5	16	0.3	4	0.1	6.7	0.1	6.9	0.1
Charcoal	38.3	2.7	18	1.1	2	--	1	--	--	--	--	--	--	--
Imported Coke	--	--	--	--	1	--	1	--	--	--	--	--	--	--
Lignite	12.8	0.9	10	0.6	1	--	--	--	--	--	--	--	--	--
TOTAL	1,417	100	1,616	100	5,350	100	6,315	100	6,673	100	6,675	100	6,936	100

Sources: Data for   1950 - Ministry of International Trade and Industry (MITI)
1960, 1970 and 1975 - MITI, quoted in Japan Petroleum & Energy Yearbook - 1978
1977 - MITI, quoted in Japan Petroleum and Energy Weekly, March 15, 1979
1978 and 1979 - MITI

FIGURE 2.5

Japan's Primary Energy Supply [millions of barrels per day (MMB/D) of oil equivalent]

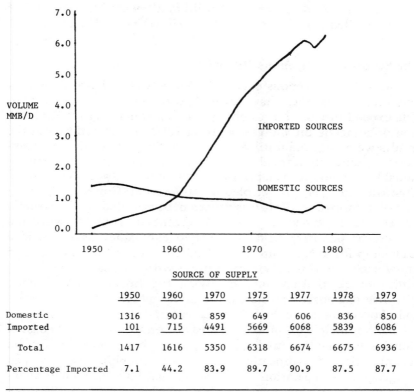

SOURCE OF SUPPLY

	1950	1960	1970	1975	1977	1978	1979
Domestic	1316	901	859	649	606	836	850
Imported	101	715	4491	5669	6068	5839	6086
Total	1417	1616	5350	6318	6674	6675	6936
Percentage Imported	7.1	44.2	83.9	89.7	90.9	87.5	87.7

Sources: Data for 1950 – Ministry of International Trade and Industry (MITI); for 1960, 1970, and 1975 – MITI, quoted in Kiyotaka Kurokawa, ed., Japan Petroleum and Energy Yearbook: 1978 (Tokyo: Japan Petroleum Consultants, 1978); and for 1977 – MITI, quoted in Japan Petroleum and Energy Weekly, March 15, 1979. 1978 and 1979 – MITI.

and has since declined to 18.6 million tons in 1978.[58] Imports multiplied forty-five times, from 1.3 million tons in 1945 to more than 58 million tons in 1978.[59]

The contribution to energy needs of hydropower in this mountainous, high-rainfall country has grown slowly and steadily from 6.8 million kilowatts in 1952 to 27 million kilowatts in 1979 (about 4 percent of total energy needs).[60] Coal-fired thermal plants were first constructed in Japan to provide dry-season supplemental capacity but grew rapidly in number as the need for electricity outstripped hydroelectric capacity. Economics soon dictated the replacement of coal by oil as boiler fuel. By 1979, oil provided 57 percent of electric-power generation.[61] The number of thermal plants increased from 273 (with installed capacity of 4 million kilowatts) in 1950 to 756 (with installed capacity of 91 million kilowatts) in 1979.[62]

The Search for Indigenous Oil and Gas

With other indigenous energy sources scarce and already largely exploited, the Japanese have focused great effort and very consider-able expenditure on the search for domestic oil and gas.[63] Exploita-tion of domestic oil and gas began in 1890, but the effort and the results were minimal until World War II. Since that time two com-panies specifically formed for this purpose have been the organiza-tional focal point of the Japanese search for oil and gas: Teikoku Oil Company and Japan Petroleum Exploration Company (Japex). Teikoku, formed in 1941, was government-initiated but is privately owned; Japex, formed in 1955, is 65 percent government-owned and 35 percent privately held. These two companies have provided leadership for keeping up with world advances in technology and knowledge, entering into joint ventures with international oil com-panies in exploration, and involving the financial and human resources of a host of Japanese oil-refining and marketing companies and of other industrial and financial enterprises.

Japan's principle oil-producing areas lie on the northwest coast of Honshu, but the fractured volcanic geology has resulted in limited accumulation of hydrocarbons in the stratigraphic reservoirs and the geographic separation of oil and gas pockets with small quan-tities of reserves, low recoverability, and high costs. In 1946, the Japanese petroleum production of 4,200 barrels per day was barely one-third of the very depressed consumption level, and by 1950 pro-duction had only increased to 5,500 barrels per day, or 13.9 percent of that year's consumption. Discoveries of natural gas were simi-larly sparse, and in 1950 only 2.5 billion cubic feet (0.75 million cubic meters) were produced, equivalent to 1,130 barrels of oil per day.[64]

By 1978, 112 exploratory wells had been drilled in Japan at a cu-mulative cost of 68.5 billion yen, or about $350 million.[65] In 1980 oil production was a bare 8,000 barrels per day, with reserves of 55 million barrels, compared to consumption of 5.4 million barrels per day.[66] Beginning in April 1980, Japan's fifth five-year plan for economic development provides for drilling some 15 exploratory wells per year on the continental shelf at water depths of up to 200 meters, with estimated capital expenditures reaching 150 billion yen ($750 million) over the plan period.[67]

Availability of Low-Cost Foreign Oil

With such paucity of domestic resources, yielding slight returns even with massive and determined efforts, it was fortunate for Japan that circumstances in the outside world were exactly appropriate for the purchase and importation at very low prices of massive and increasing quantites of crude oil and petroleum-related hydrocarbons like liquefied petroleum gas and liquefied natural gas. Otherwise the economic miracles of Japan's development would not have occurred.

Between 1950 and 1973, Japan's GNP grew at an average annual rate of 8.9 percent, fueled by petroleum imports that grew from about 82,000 barrels per day in 1950 to some 5.3 million barrels per day in 1973.[68] Expressed in 1970 prices, Japan's GNP rose from 12.6 billion yen in 1951 to 29.9 billion yen in 1961 and 90.5 billion yen in 1973. During that entire period, as shown in Figure 2.6, the average delivered cost of Japan's imported crude oil from all sources was close to $2.00 per barrel.[69]

The availability of virtually unlimited quantities of low-cost energy, which contributed importantly to Japan's ability to price its exports competitively for world markets, was assured by two developments in the late 1950s. One of these, mentioned earlier, was the U.S. government's 1957 decision to limit drastically the importation of foreign oil, which forced into European and Far Eastern markets large amounts of crude oil produced from the major new discoveries made in North Africa and the lower Persian Gulf during the 1950s. The resulting lower crude prices in the Eastern Hemisphere provided Japanese manufacturers with low energy costs, giving them a competitive edge in the U.S. market. The energy costs of U.S. manufacturers remained at higher levels as a result of the import quota program. Between 1957 and 1973, the average wellhead price of U.S. domestic crude was about $3.06 per barrel and by 1973 had reached $3.89, compared to the $2.00 average delivered cost to Japan.[70]

The second development leading to low Eastern Hemisphere crude oil prices was the increasing desire of the governments of Middle East oil-producing countries for higher revenues. These governments, especially in Iran, Kuwait, and Saudi Arabia, pressed the international oil companies to increase their annual crude oil output at the same time that crude oil from the new North African and lower Gulf fields was also being forced into the market.

FIGURE 2.6
Average Delivered Cost of Crude Oil Imported into Japan

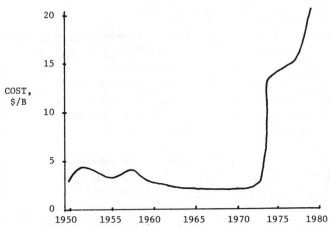

Note: 1979 Average Estimated

Sources: Data for 1950-1960 - Japan Exports and Imports;
for 1960-1977 - Kiyotaka Kurokawa, ed., Japan Petroleum
and Energy Yearbook: 1978 (Tokyo: Japan Petroleum Consultants, 1978); for January 1978-September 1978 - Japanese Oil Statistics Today, October 1979.

A special relationship, which developed between the Japanese
government and the Japanese refining industry during this crucial
period of economic development, enabled Japan to take maximum
advantage of international petroleum developments and to maintain
a constant downward pressure on crude oil prices. Until 1962, MITI
allocated foreign exchange for the purchase of oil, relating each importer's allocation partly to his allotment for the preceding three-
month period and partly to the physical quantity of oil he obtained
with that allotment. As a result, Japanese refiners were highly
motivated to negotiate the lowest possible crude oil prices, with
MITI maintaining pressure by publicizing the price arrangements.
Other refiners could then use this evidence to force their own suppliers to remain competitive. Between 1957 and 1962, the average
f.o.b. prices that Japanese importers paid for Persian Gulf crude oil
decreased by 17-18 percent.[71] The crude oil contracts Japan thus
squeezed out of its international suppliers profoundly affected the
entire international oil market and helped to reinforce the tendency
to low crude oil prices that ultimately led to the rise of OPEC.

The mechanics of this system of assuring low-cost oil supplies changed in 1962, when—as part of the admission fee for joining the OECD—Japan made commitments to the International Monetary Fund to remove foreign exchange restrictions, thereby diminishing MITI's control of the supply arrangements of Japanese refiners. But an alternative control mechanism was quickly developed. Japan's 1962 Petroleum Industry Law required the ministry to produce a five-year oil plan, to be revised annually for the purpose of controlling both the production of refined petroleum products and the import of crude oil and products. Refinery construction and expansion programs henceforth required MITI licensing, which depended in turn upon MITI approval of every detail of each refiner's plans, including those for crude oil supply. In addition, MITI retained the power to establish "standard selling prices" for petroleum products. In spite of foreign exchange liberalization, the Japanese government retained considerable power to "assure the stable and cheap supply of petroleum."[72]

The Role of the International Oil Companies

Since World War II, the Japanese oil industry has had a close association with the international oil industry, benefiting from the transfer of technology and know-how as well as easy access to worldwide crude oil systems. Table 2.9 shows the structure of these relations, whereby a number of international oil companies own up to 50 percent of Japanese refining companies and several others have close ties with Japanese refiners through the provision of loans, technology, and long-term crude oil contracts.[73] In 1965, international oil companies had equity positions in Japanese refining companies that together supplied 68 percent of the market. The foreign companies traditionally supplied all their affiliates' crude oil requirements. The remaining 32 percent of the market was supplied by completely Japanese-owned refiners, who purchased the bulk of their crude supplies on long-term contract from international companies that offered loans and technology but did not participate in the domestic operations of the Japanese refiners. These refiners market their products through their own retail operations.[74]

Seeking markets for their supplies of Middle East crude oil, a number of international oil companies subsidized much of the growing Japanese refining industry's plant expansion during the 1960s through the provision of long-term, low-interest loans tied to the supply of crude oil for the increased refinery capacity.[75] Seventy percent of Japanese crude oil purchases were tied to such loans.[76] As shown in Table 2.10, the dominant position of the international oil companies in the supply of crude oil to Japan continued through the

TABLE 2.9
Who's Who in Japanese Oil

Crude Supplier	Refining		Capacity 1,000 b/d		Marketing		Market Share 1964 (est.)
	Company	Equity	July 1965	Approved Exp.	Company	Equity	
Caltex	Nippon Oil	100% Japanese	15.8		Nippon Oil*	100% Japanese	18.6
	Nippon Petroleum Refining	50% Caltex 50% Nippon Oil	232.0				
	Koa Oil	50% Caltex 50% Japanese	148.3				
Esso **Mobil**	Toa Nenryo	25% Esso 25% Mobil 50% Japanese	230.5		Esso Sekiyu	100% Esso	5.1
					Mobil Sekiyu	100% Mobil	5.8
	Nichomo Sekiyu	70% Toa Nenryo 30% Nihon Gyomo Sengu	27.0		Nihon Gyomo Sengu	100% Japanese	2.8
Esso	General Sekiyu	50% Esso Sekiyu 50% General Bussan	115.0		General Bussan	100% Japanese	5.1
Shell	Showa Oil	50% Shell 50% Japanese	102.0		Showa Oil	50% Shell 50% Japanese	5.0
	Showa Yokkaichi Oil	50% Showa Oil 25% Mitsubishi Group 25% Shell	180.0		Shell Sekiyu	100% Shell	8.1
Tidewater	Mitsubishi Oil	50% Tidewater 50% Japanese	124.4	80 (1966)	Mitsubishi Oil	50% Tidewater 50% Japanese	8.6
Union Oil	Maruzen Oil	32.9% Union Oil 67.1% Japanese	137.5	35 (1966)	Maruzen Oil	32.9% Union Oil 67.1% Japanese	8.8

Foreign Affiliates

Esso, Gulf Sojuzneft	Idemitsu Kosan	100% Japanese	240.0		Idemitsu Kosan	100% Japanese	15.8
French Oil	Daikyo Oil	100% Japanese	115.0		Daikyo Oil	100% Japanese	4.8
Gulf	Nippon Mining	100% Japanese	109.4				
Gulf, Sojuzneft	Toa Oil	100% Japanese	50.0		Kyodo Oil	100% Japanese	11.3
Esso, Mobil, Sojuzneft	Asia Oil	100% Japanese	55.0	40 (1966)			
Mobil	Fuji Kosan	100% Japanese	29.0		Mobil Sekiyu	100% Mobil	
B.P.	Kyushu Oil	100% Japanese	40.0		Nippon Oil	100% Japanese	
Sojuzneft	Taiyo Oil	100% Japanese	38.5		Taiyo Oil	100% Japanese	0.2
Esso, Gulf	Toho Oil	100% Japanese	40.0		Idemitsu Kosan Mitsubishi Shoji	100% Japanese	
Domestic	Teiseki Topping	100% Japanese	3.2		Teiseki Oil	100% Japanese	

National Companies

*Includes 2.0% petrochemical naphtha sales by Koa & N.P.R.C.

Source: Oil and Gas International, August 1965.

TABLE 2.10
Japanese Crude Imports by Supplier (Units: Thousand Barrels Per Day - MB/D)

Supplier	1970	1973	1975	1978	First Half 1979
International Oil Companies					
Caltex	561	777	600	687	640
Exxon	359	582	531	622	495
Mobil	315	393	364	455	384
Gulf	265	395	290	320	272
Shell	425	539	486	558	484
B.P. (including Unoco)	382	361	200	352	185
Total	76	98	55	78	72
Getty	146	141	107	46	23
Total Internationals	2,529	3,286	2,633	3,118	2,555
Other Foreign Suppliers	101	81	55	114	100
Producing Country National Oil Companies	33	288	500	644	798
Japanese Overseas Concessions	346	424	400	445	466
Japanese Trading Companies	691	893	796	333	693
TOTAL	3,700	4,972	4,384	4,654	4,612
Share of International Oil Companies	68.4%	66.1%	60.1%	67.0%	55.4%

Sources: Data for   1970 - Petroleum Industry in Japan - 1975
                       1973, 1975, and 1977 - Petroleum Industry in Japan   1978
                       1978 and 1979 - MITI

1970s, despite Japanese efforts to diversify supply sources and channels and government efforts to bypass the companies.[77]

The combined effect of the links established in the 1950s and 1960s between the Japanese oil industry and MITI on the one hand and industry and the international oil companies on the other brought an increasing supply of low-cost Middle East oil into Japan. Table 2.11 shows the degree and breakdown by supplying country of Japan's dependence on Middle East crude oil, which by the mid-1950s accounted for more than 80 percent of Japan's imports.[78] This dependence rose to more than 90 percent in the late 1960s be-

TABLE 2.11
Origins of Japan's Crude Oil Imports (Thousands of Barrels Per Day – MB/D)

	1960	%	1965	%	1970	%	1975	%	1977	%	1978	%	1979	%
MIDDLE EAST	452	80.1	1,338	89.0	2,859	84.7	3,541	78.2	3,733	78.0	3,645	78.3	3,689	76.3
Saudi Arabia	110		292		490		1,156		1,465		1,336		1,372	
Iran	23		326		1,470		1,122		820		785		479	
UAE	---		8		156		418		538		481		489	
Kuwait	218		356		287		387		376		372		442	
Neutral Zone	29		248		349		232		170		232		313	
Oman	---		---		97		129		169		168		191	
Iraq	70		96		---		94		150		163		259	
Qatar	2		12		4		3		45		108		144	
Others	---		---		7		---		---		---		---	
PACIFIC BASIN	83	14.7	108	7.2	449	13.3	850	18.8	1,024	21.4	994	21.3	1,123	23.2
Indonesia	61		106		445		518		653		598		696	
Malaysia	---		---		---		23		70		93		111	
Brunei	22		2		4		149		163		152		164	
China	---		---		---		159		135		147		150	
Australia	---		---		---		1		3		4		2	
OTHER	29	5.2	57	3.8	68	2.0	137	3.0	31	0.6	18	0.4	22	0.5
Africa	---		---		46		131		24		10		13	
Venezuela	---		7		12		5		7		7		8	
U.S.S.R.	29		50		10		1		---		1		1	
TOTAL	564	100	1,503	100	3,375	100	4,528	100	4,788	100	4,656	100	4,834	100

Sources: Data for 1960 – Petroleum Association of Japan.
1965 – Tokyo Petroleum News, January 26, 1968.
1970, 1975 – Ministry of International Trade and Industry (MITI), quoted in Japan Petroleum and Energy Yearbook: 1978.
1977, 1978, and 1979 – Japan Oil Statistics Today, December 1979.

fore starting to decline.[79] In 1979 it was still more than 76 percent. The large subsidized loans and other advantages Japanese refiners received from their international crude oil suppliers throughout the late 1950s and 1960s translated into additional discounts from the price of crude oil, so that the real prices paid by Japan for its crude imports were even lower than the $2.00 per barrel figure cited earlier. The sharply increased supply of crude oil imported at such low cost fueled Japan's rise as a formidable international economic competitor.

Japan's Efforts to Lessen Its Dependence

By the early 1960s there was a growing concern in Japan that the country's vigorous petroleum-based growth carried with it the seeds of problems arising from a triple dependence—on imported petroleum, on foreign-owned international oil companies, and on the Middle East. Despite the enormous benefits these sources brought to the Japanese economy and would continue to bring for another twenty years, it was felt that dependencies as such must be reduced, and a massive effort was mounted toward this end.

The Petroleum Industry Law of 1962 marked the beginning of a new period for Japan's oil industry. MITI used the law, as we have seen, to keep imported oil prices low and to encourage foreign "impact loans" to finance Japanese refinery expansions. But the ministry also began to use its licensing power to strengthen Japanese-owned companies by increasing their refinery and marketing shares at the expense of the local affiliates of international oil companies. MITI fostered that objective in other ways, including the consolidation of a number of small refiners into a single marketing company, Kyoto Sekiyu, and the purchase by Japanese interests of Maruzen Oil shares owned by the Union Oil Company of California.[80] The share of total refining capacity owned by affiliates of foreign companies declined from 70 percent in the mid-1960s to 40 percent in 1978.[81]

As we have seen, the government had begun as early as 1955 an accelerated program to find oil in Japan by establishing the Japan Petroleum Exploration Company. By the mid-1960s, with the domestic program almost a complete failure, the government developed new plans involving both stepped-up domestic exploration efforts and the direction of sizable Japanese resources into an overseas exploration program. In December 1963, a special government committee recommended (1) diversification of crude supplies, (2) development of overseas crude oil interests, and (3) increasing Japanese control of the refining industry.[82] The Overall Energy Council was established by the Diet in August 1965. A report issued by the council in October 1966 strongly supported the recommendations of the 1963 committee.[83] This three-pronged program was greatly moved along by a timely Japanese entrepreneurial initiative.

In February 1958, eleven important Japanese companies formed the Arabian Oil Company (AOC) to operate an oil concession negotiated the previous year by a predecessor company in the Neutral Zone between Saudi Arabia and Kuwait. With no oil experience, a concession agreement financially less attractive to investors than the industry norm, and a very small investment, the new company struck oil in January 1960 and began to export to Japan sixteen months later.[84] As the Khafji crude oil from this discovery was relatively high in cost and low in quality, Japanese refiners had no economic incentive to purchase it during a period when better-quality crude was readily available in large volumes at more attractive prices. Therefore, in pursuit of diversification and decreased dependence, MITI decided to mandate Japanese purchase of the Khafji crude, allocating a proportional share to each refiner.

Thus was born the concept of "national interest crude" — foreign-source crude oil produced by Japanese interests and given a preferential position in the Japanese market. Following the AOC success, the North Sumatra Oil Development Corporation was established in 1960 to provide technical and material assistance to the Indonesian state oil company, Pertamina; payment was received in crude oil. During the same period, Teikoku and Japex increased their activities in Japan and abroad, and other Japanese oil companies expanded their activities to include exploration. In 1967, the government established the state-owned Japan Petroleum Development Corporation (JPDC) to promote and provide low-cost financing for Japanese domestic and overseas oil-exploration efforts.[85]

By mid-1978, there were sixty-eight companies engaged in petroleum exploration and development either outside Japan or in its offshore waters; forty-one of these companies had received financing from JPDC. By the end of 1977, Japanese companies had invested a total of 803.90 million yen in search of oil outside Japan.[86] Japanese-interest foreign oil has been significant in Japan's supplies since the mid-1960s, growing rapidly to about 10 percent of crude imports and averaging more than 400,000 barrels per day (9 percent of imports) during the 1970s.[87] AOC's Neutral Zone concession and the Indonesian operation provided the bulk of these imports until the middle 1970s, when other ventures in the Middle East and Africa began to prosper.[88]

Japan-China Agreements: Optimistic Expectations

In the search for geographic diversification of supply, the Japanese have directed major efforts to acquire energy supplies from China and the Soviet Union. The Japan-China Trade Agreements of 1977 provide for imports of up to 300,000 barrels per day of Chinese oil and up to about 3 million tons per year of Chinese coal by 1982 in exchange for Japanese plants and industrial equipment.[89] In 1978, the agreement was extended to 1985, at which time China is supposed to supply Japan with 800,000 barrels per day of oil and 9 million tons of coal per year. No targets are specified for 1983 and 1984.[90] Chinese oil is important, but has not yet made a really significant contribution to Japan's total imports. (In 1979, 150,000 barrels per day were imported by Japan.) However, if the volumes targeted in the 1978 amendment are achieved, Chinese oil could represent as much as 12–15 percent of Japanese imports in 1985.

It is most unlikely, however, that China will be able to increase its output enough to achieve these 1985 supply targets. China is very likely to continue to make some of its crude oil production available for export, especially to Japan, in order to generate needed foreign exchange; but the CIA, for example, does not expect China to become a major exporter during the critical 1980s.[91] Although oil production of 2.12 billion barrels per day makes China an important producer, its own development programs are greatly increasing domestic energy requirements, and this demand growth is expected to stay ahead of increased production from probable future oil discoveries.[92] In 1979, China's GNP increased by 8 percent, while its oil production was up by only 1.9 percent.[93] The Chinese volume commitment to Japan is based on a very optimistic estimate of the potential output from the Po Hai Gulf, where China and Japan have agreed to a joint development effort. It also assumes rapid development, with foreign help, of coal production to supply much of the growth in domestic energy requirements, leaving offshore and coastal oil discoveries available for export. However, in January 1980, the Chinese reportedly advised Japan that 1980 exports to Japan would be 140,000 barrels per day rather than 160,000, as called for in the agreement.[94]

In addition to the uncertainty about how much Chinese crude oil will be available to Japan, these crudes have serious quality problems. Japanese refiners have been reluctant to purchase the relatively heavy and waxy Chinese crudes, which are difficult to process and can damage refinery equipment. Costly additional equipment is required to overcome these problems. To promote these otherwise less desirable purchases, the Japanese government has treated Chinese oil as national-interest crude and allocated volumes for purchase by Japanese refiners. Early in 1978, the government announced plans for the construction of cracking facilities with a capacity of 500,000 barrels per day to upgrade the Chinese crudes.[95] However, the facilities, which were to be operational by 1982, have not materialized, probably due to the uncertainty about how much Chinese crude oil Japan can expect to receive.

Japan-USSR: A Delicate Balance

When the Japanese began seriously to orchestrate their energy-diversification program in the middle 1960s, discussions were undertaken with the USSR. Cooperative schemes were considered under which Japan would help develop Soviet energy resources in return for Soviet purchases of Japanese pipe and equipment and the sale to Japan of part of the oil and gas from the projects. Three such projects were discussed for nearly ten years before one joint exploration project off Sakhalin Island finally came to fruition.

On January 30, 1975, Japan and the USSR signed an agreement under which Japan provided $100 million of credit for the purchase of Japanese equipment for the Sakhalin project. Technical assistance was to be provided by the Gulf Oil Corporation, and Japan was to receive one-half of any oil and gas that might be produced.[96] The Japanese also agreed to extend credits of $450 million for the development of coal reserves near Yakutsk and $500 million for forestry development in eastern Siberia.[97] In 1977, the USSR-Japanese group announced that four test wells were producing crude oil at a combined daily flow of 7,000 barrels.[98] In 1978, natural gas was found in a test well that tested at a rate of about 3 million cubic meters a day. In August 1979, Japan and the USSR agreed to continue cooperation in the development of oil and gas off Sakhalin until the end of 1982. Japan agreed at that time to provide an additional $70 million in credits.[99] To commercialize the discovery, the Sakhalin Oil Development Corporation was formed. It is currently 40 percent owned by the Japanese National Oil Company (JNOC) and 60 percent by private companies.[100]

Two other proposed projects with the USSR to which the Japanese have devoted much time and effort involve joint development of oil fields in the Tyumen region of the Urals and large natural gas fields in the Yakutsk area of Siberia. Western Siberia in 1978 provided 41 percent of USSR petroleum production and 30 percent of its natural gas.[101] It is expected to supply 50 percent of Soviet oil output in 1980. The Samotlor field in the Tyumen region, the largest and most productive in the USSR, is leveling off and may already have peaked at 3 million barrels per day.[102] This field's decline is considered to be the principal factor in the slowdown of the growth of Soviet oil production. Natural gas production at Tyumen, however, is increasing and is thought to have reached 125 billion cubic meters in 1979.[103] Assuring the continued growth of gas production and arresting the declining trend in oil production at Tyumen are major objectives of the Soviet Union, which has announced that it will spend $2.2 billion on natural gas development there during the next several years.[104] Great efforts have also been devoted to obtaining foreign financial and technical help for this development. The Soviets are also eager to develop the natural gas reserves in Yakutsk, which are thought to total 1 trillion cubic meters.[105]

Joint development of both the Yakutsk and the Tyumen projects would require huge investments, long payout periods and very advanced technology and would involve a large element of risk. The Tyumen project requires construction of a 2,500-mile (4,000-kilometer) oil pipeline to the port of Nakhodka, and the Yakutsk project, the construction of an approximately 800-mile (1,300-kilometer) gas pipeline to a liquefaction plant at Magaden on the Sea of Okhotsk.[106] Although preliminary agreements were signed by Japan and the USSR concerning Tyumen in February 1972 and Yakutsk in November 1974, both the Soviet and the Japanese sides need the participation of Western companies with the necessary technology and know-how. The Japanese were also reluctant to undertake such a large capital commitment without U.S. participation in view of the political risks thought to be inherent in investing in the Soviet Union.

Following President Nixon's visits to Beijing and Moscow in 1972, the U.S. government began to encourage U.S. companies to seek investment opportunities in the Soviet Union. Consequently, the USSR brought Occidental Petroleum and El Paso Natural Gas Company into the Yakutsk discussions, and the Japanese brought the Gulf Oil Corporation into the Tyumen talks. Both negotiations ultimately faltered over the differing expectations and conditions of the two sides and the passage of U.S. legislation limiting Export-Import Bank credits to the Soviet Union. Contacts between Japan and the USSR were continuing in the early 1980s concerning the Yakutsk project, but the Japanese did not expect an agreement to result.[107]

Japan's Pioneer Initiatives in Producing Countries

The acquisition of crude supplies from China and the development of other national-interest crudes somewhat lessened Japan's dependence on its traditional major oil-company suppliers and, to a very small extent, on its primary Middle East supply sources. However, as nationalization of oil-company properties accelerated in the Middle East, the Japanese opened contacts with the newly organized national oil companies of the producing countries. These companies sought to bypass the dispossessed international oil companies and to deal directly with consuming countries. As shown in Table 2.10, Japanese oil imports from the national oil companies rose from 1.5 percent in 1972 to 20 percent in 1978. In 1979, following the Iranian revolution, this figure increased to approximately 33 percent.[108]

The turning point in this shift of supply from the international oil companies to the national companies of the producing governments was the Yom Kippur War in October 1973. Producing governments had assumed controlling ownership in the production companies prior to 1973. However, the operations of these companies were still largely managed by the old concessionaire companies, which handled the sale of most of the nationalized oil as well as their own remaining equity oil.[109] After 1973, the trickle of oil sold directly by the producing countries rapidly increased to a flood.

In late 1973 Arab oil producers reduced production by 25 percent (followed by further reductions), embargoed oil sales to the Netherlands and the United States, and raised their oil prices. The Japanese looked first to the United States and Europe for guidance and leadership in resolving the crisis.[110] However, much Arab rhetoric was directed at the Japanese, and pressure was applied to persuade Japan to break diplomatic relations with Israel and declare support for the Arab states. The Japanese rather quickly understood that the United States was unwilling and unable to do very much. The shift of control over Middle East oil was irreversible; the Arab governments had finally understood the extent of their power. Circumstances were ideal for those governments to use what they had begun to call the "oil weapon" to pursue their political objectives. Early in 1974, as the Japanese government realized that those events represented a turning point, Japanese oil and trading companies flooded the Middle East, prepared to buy oil from the producing governments under any terms the sellers demanded.[111] Japanese companies were in the forefront of the panicked buyers who, by the end of 1974, had bid up the average price of Middle East oil to about five times the mid-1973 level.[112]

While joining in the scramble to get an appropriate share of reduced oil supplies, the Japanese began to experiment with schemes to assure a continued supply of oil into a future that they recognized would be very different from what they had experienced in the past. Since then, both the Japanese government and private companies

have made an impressive number of loans to oil-producing countries
for a variety of industrial and infrastructure projects, fostered joint
ventures in producing countries between Japanese and local enterprises, and in a variety of other ways cemented economic and political relations with producing countries.

Other industrial countries have followed Japan's example and involved themselves in oil-producing countries and, indeed, in other
Third World areas. Japan has clearly been the leader in such efforts
and has engaged in a wider variety of initiatives than any other industrial country. Industrial projects have been promoted in almost
every country in the Middle East, including Egypt and Jordan, which
export little or no oil; in Southeast Asian oil-producing countries
like Indonesia and Malaysia; in West Africa; and in Latin America.
Unlike the practice of other industrial countries, the Japanese
government has often participated directly in these activities, either
through government companies or by arranging consortia of industrial companies, banks, and trading companies with government
financial backing.[113]

Excluding expenditures for actual oil-exploration and -production
activities, Japan by the end of 1978 had committed more than $17
billion in direct investments, grants, and loans for hundreds of industrial and infrastructure projects in oil-producing countries.[114] A
comprehensive analysis of these activities would be very useful in
demonstrating how a modern industrial nation can use its capabilities to pursue its objectives in the Third World to the mutual advantage of itself and the recipient countries. A few examples will serve
here to illustrate some of the important types of activities Japan has
undertaken.

1. The 1974 Japan-Iraq Agreement for Economic and Technical
Cooperation, supplemented in 1977, provided Iraq with $1.7 billion
in government and private credits to finance a number of industrial
projects. In return, Iraq was to supply Japan with a quantity of crude
oil, petroleum products, and liquefied petroleum gas on a long-term
basis (annual volumes fluctuate according to oil prices and financing provided during each period). In 1979, Japan received 115,000
barrels per day under this arrangement.[115]

2. A major petrochemical complex is under construction in Iran as
a fifty-fifty joint venture between the National Petrochemical Company of Iran and the Iran Chemical Development Company, a consortium of five Japanese companies.[116] This project was estimated
in 1976 to cost $1.9 billion. Construction delays and inflation have
raised this estimate to $3.0–3.5 billion. The financing includes
loans from the Japanese government, the Japanese Export-Import

Bank, Japanese consortium companies, and the Iranian government.[117]

3. A consortium of fifty-four Japanese companies, led by the Mitsubishi group, has staked out an area for construction of an oil refinery and a petrochemical complex in the new Jubail industrial area on the east coast of Saudi Arabia. The new company, the Saudi Petrochemical Development Company, Ltd., is developing engineering plans and negotiating an arrangement with the Saudis for construction of the complex, the cost of which is estimated at $1.3 billion, in return for a Saudi crude oil and natural gas supply for the new plants, plus additional volumes for direct export to Japan.[118] Firm export volumes have not been set, but the figure being quoted is 1,000 barrels per day for every $1 billion of equity investment.[119]

4. In 1979, $500 million was lent to the Mexican government oil company, Pemex, by the Japanese Export-Import Bank (70 percent) and twenty-two Japanese city banks (30 percent) in connection with a long-term crude oil supply contract. This contract involved 100,000 barrels per day through 1981, with the volume to be renegotiated for subsequent years. The money was to be used to help finance development of Pemex's oil-related facilities.[120]

5. In October 1979, Japan made a loan to Indonesia to cover the major costs of building a urea plant in northern Sumatra. Although the project is sponsored by five nations (Indonesia, Thailand, Malaysia, Singapore, and the Philippines), Japan is providing the funding through a low-interest loan of $140 million, which includes a seven-year grace period. The plant, with a proposed capacity of 570,000 metric tons per year, will export to Asia. Another 7 billion yen loan was made in February 1980 to develop two new Indonesian oil fields, with Japan to purchase 40 percent of the field's output.[121]

This type of activity, pursued by Japan to assure a supply of oil resources from producing countries, has not only been copied by other industrial nations but has also been adopted by the oil producers as a model for the kind of arrangements they will require from consuming countries as inducements to sell their increasing volumes of discretionary oil.

Oil and Gas Potentials in East Asia

The development of oil and gas production in Southeast Asia, for which Japan is the natural market, has been important in reducing Japan's dependence on the Middle East. Increasing quantities of crude from Indonesia, Malaysia, and Brunei are being imported to Japan by Japanese companies and the major oil companies operating in these countries. By 1979, Southeast Asian crudes supplied 23.2 percent of Japan's imports; Middle East crudes had dropped from more than 90 percent in 1967 to 76.3 percent, as detailed in Table 2.11. Dependence on the Middle East has also been eased by the importation of Chinese crude, which in 1979 contributed 3 percent of total imports. Although the development of these Pacific Basin imports is significant, Japan's dependence on the Middle East is still enormous and is not likely to decline much further in the foreseeable future.

Pacific Basin Oil Potentials

Much has been made of the petroleum reserve potential of the East Asian continental shelf, and early estimates were almost certainly overly optimistic. In any case, adequate exploration to prove that potential will require the investment of huge sums, which will have to be either allocated against competing requirements by the nations involved or secured from foreign sources. It will also require advanced technology, which can only be provided by Western companies. Securing the necessary foreign commitment is impeded by a maze of disputes as to sovereignty over the shelf among the coastal states — China, Taiwan, Japan, and Korea in the north and China, Vietnam, Cambodia, Thailand, Malaysia, and the Philippines in the south. Major foreign investment is unlikely until these disputes are resolved. (There is a possibility that some form of Japanese-Chinese cooperation could open up exploration in parts of the shelf in the north.) The importance of the potential offshore resources and the nature of these territorial disputes constitute one of the most potentially destabilizing issues in East Asia today. If major oil or gas reserves are found on the continental shelf, the possibilities for conflict will increase.

Japanese dependence on Middle East imports and the problems and uncertainties that surround possible oil and gas discoveries in Asia have broad and crucial policy implications for the three other great powers involved in the East Asian balance, as well as for Japan. The Soviet naval buildup in the Indian Ocean and its increasing presence in the Pacific directly threaten the security of the huge Japanese imports of Middle East oil. Japan will watch carefully the U.S. reaction to this potential threat to its ocean lifeline. Similarly, the political stability of Southeast Asia, through whose waterways those crucial oil supplies must pass, is vital to Japan and to other Asian countries.

The available data on known or potential oil reserves in the Pacific Basin suggest that the likelihood of decreasing Japan's dependence on Middle East oil through regional production is small. Current estimates indicate that the entire western Pacific area contains 39 billion barrels, or 6 percent of the world's 686 billion barrels of proven crude oil reserves, compared to approximately 56 percent for the Middle East. An estimated 2.9 percent is located in China and 1.4 percent in Indonesia, with the remainder split among several countries.[122]

Estimates of undiscovered potential reserves for the area as a whole are much higher but also more speculative. In a recent study, two distinguished petroleum geologists estimated the world's total undiscovered potential reserves at 986 billion barrels. Some 10–12 percent of this amount is assumed to be in the western Pacific area.[123] There are a number of such estimates, all of which are based on analysis and extrapolation of geophysical data from areas that are relatively well studied as well as areas for which little information exists. The estimates are understood to be conditional and directional, but there is general agreement on the order of magnitude.

Another critical factor in calculating the availability of Pacific Basin oil to Japan is the investment capital needed to develop fields, should exploratory drilling prove substantial crude oil reserves. Investment requirements vary over a broad range, depending on the size of the deposit, geographical location (onshore or offshore), depth of pay, and rate at which the reserve can be produced. To illustrate this point, development costs in 1977 dollars for each new daily barrel of production range from a low of about $500 in some Middle East areas to $7,000 for some fields in the North Sea.[124]

If we assume that development costs in the western Pacific will average $4,000 per new daily barrel, total investments required would be about $4 billion to place 1 million barrels per day of new production onstream. If we further assume that these fields will be developed for a 10 percent per annum depletion rate, then the volume of proven recoverable reserves needed to support 1 million barrels per day of new production will be about 3.5 billion barrels. Accordingly, development of 100 billion barrels of recoverable reserves in this region would require investments in excess of $100 billion (1977 dollars). These capital costs do not include the day-to-day expenses required to operate and maintain production. Considering even reasonable escalation of costs, the required investment would be even greater by the time the money is actually spent.

The Offshore Reserve Situation

Of the potential offshore reserve areas, the highly promising seismic readouts from Western studies of the Yellow and East China seas have attracted the most attention. "Undiscovered potential" estimates for the Yellow Sea (3–6 billion barrels), East China Sea (6–13 billion barrels), Taiwan Basin (4.7 billion barrels), and the Ryukyu Basin (2–3 billion barrels) give a total range of 15–29 billion barrels. In China's Po Hai Basin, the estimate is 3–6 billion barrels.[125]

However, since 1968, when the seismic survey series conducted by the United Nation's CCOP (Committee for the Coordination of Joint Prospecting for Mineral Resources in Asian Offshore Areas) released these estimates of undiscovered potential reserves in the Yellow and East China seas area, more than two-hundred tests have been drilled. There have been several shows of oil, but nothing suitable for commercial production has yet been discovered.

In the South China Sea area, seismic studies and the overall thrust of exploration activities have been less comprehensive. In some places water depth has been measured in excess of 2.5 miles (4 kilometers), far beyond the reach of even the most modern deep-sea production technology. Not all the basin areas are so deep, and it appears that promising geophysical strata exist primarily in the Tonkin Basin northwest of the Chinese island of Hainan (4–8 billion barrels), in the Viet Trough (2–3 billion barrels), in the "High Sea" area of the China Basin (2–5 billion barrels), and off the Malaysian states of Sabah (3–5 billion barrels) and Sarawak (4–8 billion barrels) and the sultanate of Brunei (4–7 billion barrels). Offshore production exists in the three latter areas, where total production in 1977 amounted to approximately 80,000 barrels per day, 100,000 barrels per day, and 220,000 barrels per day, respectively. Thus current data, admittedly incomplete, suggest a South China Sea potential of 19–36 billion barrels.[126]

In sum, the Asian continental shelf area (including the Viet Trough and the Malaysian and Brunei coasts) may contain 37–66 billion barrels of undiscovered potential reserves.

The Onshore Reserve Situation

In comparison, overall prospects remain dim for the discovery of additional onshore recoverable reserves. Wildcatting continues in Japan, with a number of promising gas shows. The South Korean government has reported one oil discovery, but initial tests have not been encouraging. Some promising oil and gas discoveries in Taiwan have been publicized. In the Philippines, after years of exploration, several discoveries by U.S. companies are now producing 40,000 barrels per day of medium-gravity crude oil, with modest prospects for additional discoveries.[127]

China, on the other hand, has sizable proven reserves (approximately 20 billion barrels) and a current production level of 2.12 million barrels per day.[128] It is estimated that the production rate increased by more than 20 percent per annum between 1958 and 1974; the average annual rate of increase since then appears to have dropped to between 10 percent and 13 percent, and in 1979 it was only 1.9 percent. Hypothetically, China's proven reserves will be exhausted in about twenty-six years if production is maintained at a rate of 2.12 million barrels per day and no new fields are discovered.

A major question, then, is the amount of China's total proven and undiscovered onshore reserves. Of China's 9.56 million square kilometers, half is considered by Chinese geologists to contain sedimentary basins. Although seismic work has been done on only about 10 percent of this area, a number of estimates of total reserves have been made, ranging from 39.6 billion barrels to 68 billion barrels.[129] The wide range indicates how limited is Western knowledge of China's petroleum geology. Two factors have contributed to this lack of precision in estimating China's reserves. First, the Chinese have been quite secretive about oil-related activities. Rarely have they announced the discovery of an oil field, sometimes keeping the existence of a field hidden for as long as eight years after it has gone into production. Second, Western and Chinese geophysicists approach their data from quite different theoretical points of view, making it difficult to evaluate their statements without full access to the underlying data. As a number of Western and Japanese oil companies are now beginning exploration activities on China's continental shelf and large numbers of Chinese technicians are studying in the West, these problems may diminish.

There is general agreement that formidable obstacles hamper the discovery of future onshore fields. The largest known onshore reserves are believed to exist in rather inaccessible areas near the Soviet border. As much as 65 percent of China's potential onshore reserves may be located in such barren and distant regions as the Dzungarian, Tsaitam, and Tarim basins in Sinkiang province.[130] Such areas could be fruitfully exploited only after the Chinese have made substantial infrastructure investments, such as expansion of existing railroad systems or construction of costly pipelines. Beijing will be compelled to make some very difficult choices concerning the allocation of investment capital between eastern and western China and between onshore and offshore development.

In the northeastern fields alone, China's geological characteristics are such than any additional increase in productive capacity will be more expensive than in other areas of the world. There are two categories of geological "traps" in which petroleum can be found. Structural traps of the type generally found in the Middle East often contain large reservoirs and can be located readily by seismic surveys. Stratigraphic traps do not yield a surface reflection, are difficult to locate without drilling, and are less likely to yield large reservoirs. Most Western geologists believe that the oil found in the Tachin, Takang, and Shengli fields is being recovered largely from stratigraphic traps.

It is by now quite clear that the Chinese are focusing their efforts on the offshore areas. Eleven Western companies have signed agreements with the Chinese for geophysical surveys on the continental shelf, and the Japanese National Oil Company completed a joint venture agreement on February 8, 1980, for the exploration and production of the Chengbei oil field in the Po Hai Gulf. Oil has already been discovered in the Chengbei field, and during the mid-1980s there will probably be more discoveries and a gradual increase in total Chinese production.[131]

Even though China is the only country in the western Pacific region with a sizable amount of proven (onshore) and potential discovered (onshore and offshore) reserves, Chinese oil will have a minor impact in the 1980s on expected petroleum-import requirements of the East Asian area and of Japan in particular. Total Chinese crude oil production has consistently kept just ahead of consumption. In view of China's minimal increase in production rate in 1979 (1.9 percent compared to a targeted 5.7 percent), it seems likely that China will not be able to maintain its past rates of production increase. China is faced with a difficult choice: If it hopes to maintain even a modest level of petroleum exports to earn foreign exchange and gain some economic leverage, it must reduce the rate of increase of domestic petroleum consumption; but if it intends to achieve current domestic industrial growth targets, it will be little more than self-sufficient in petroleum production.[132]

The Continental Shelf Disputes

Japan's hopes of acquiring significant energy imports from the East Asian region are further clouded by the complex tangle of disputes concerning sovereignty and ownership of the seabed resources on the entire continental shelf area extending from Japan to Malaysia. Multiple conflicting national claims to different areas of the shelf have reduced the amount of exploration activity in all but the least promising potential oil basins. Any discovery of oil before firm boundaries have been agreed upon would seriously complicate international relations in the area.

In Northeast Asia, the Yellow and the East China seas are surrounded by China, Japan, Taiwan, and Korea. The entire seabed in this region consists of a unified continental shelf with a narrow trough located along the west coasts of Japan's Kyushu and Ryukyu islands. The boundary dispute over these waters surfaced in 1969 when the prospect of oil in the offshore areas prompted the coastal states to begin staking out claims in the area and to offer leasing blocks to their own nationals and to foreign companies.[133] China has on several occasions denounced the claims of Japan, Korea, and Taiwan and claimed the entire East China seabed for itself. The same rhetoric may apply to the Yellow Sea, but this is not clear.

It is very difficult to delineate shelf boundaries in the Yellow and East China seas.[134] The coastlines are highly irregular, and it is complicated to draw straight baselines, if it can be done at all. In addition, there are many uninhabited offshore islands, claimed by one or more of the coastal states, which do not really qualify as base points for the measurement of offshore territorial claims. The Okinawa Trough is sufficiently deep (3,000–6,000 feet, or 900–1,800 meters) and long (500 miles, or 800 kilometers) to eliminate claims that Japan would otherwise have to a good portion of the continental shelf. Japan may refuse to accept these dimensions as a limiting factor. Finally, the territorial dispute between China and Japan over ownership of the Senkaku (or Tiao Yu-tai) Islands north of Taiwan must be settled prior to solving any boundary problems. The 1958 Geneva Convention on the Continental Shelf is of limited help, as only Taiwan of the parties concerned has ratified the convention.[135]

Before the United States and Japan normalized relations with China, Japan, South Korea, and Taiwan made several attempts to agree on joint oil development, setting aside boundary issues for later negotiation. China's hostile reaction thwarted these attempts. In early 1974, Japan and South Korea agreed jointly to explore and heavily develop overlapping areas of the East China Sea, again leaving the boundary issue aside for further negotiation. Chinese objectives prevented the Japanese Diet from ratifying the agreement for four years. However, it finally did so in May 1978, and exploration under this arrangement got under way in the 20.5-million-acre (82-million-hectare) joint development area.[136]

A similar arrangement now seems possible between Japan and China. During the late 1970s the two countries have downplayed their territorial disputes, ranging from the Senkaku Islands to the southern Yellow Sea. In light of the August 1978 Peace and Friendship Treaty and the seven-year trade agreement signed in the same year, it is conceivable that the two countries might seek a face-saving arrangement that would permit the area to be explored.[137] If hydrocarbons are found, the two might agree to undertake production with some sort of sharing of the output, leaving the question of sovereignty to be resolved at a later date. Some Japanese even argue that it would be better for Japan to let the Chinese explore and develop any potential deposits, incurring the large costs and taking the risks, if Japan could purchase a reasonable share of the output.

Non-Oil Energy Supplies and Japan's Vision of the Future

In coordination with other government agencies and interested industry groups, MITI annually produces an updated five-year energy program (the Petroleum Supply Plan) as mandated by the Petroleum Industry Law of 1962. This plan provides the guidelines according to which MITI controls refining-capacity usage and expansion and the industry's output of petroleum products. The plan for 1979–1983, which was issued April 20, 1979, six months after the Iranian revolution, incorporates the government's evaluation of the current and prospective world energy situation and the actions Japan should consequently take.[138]

MITI Forecasts

Assuming a 5.9 percent average annual GNP growth rate, the 1979–1983 plan envisages that demand for petroleum will increase by 4.3 percent by 1983, after allowing for the 5 percent reduction in oil use Japan has pledged to its IEA allies.[139] This would mean an energy/GNP coefficient of 0.73, which compares very favorably with the 0.80 coefficient Japan experienced from 1968 to 1977. The plan foresees Japan's oil-import requirements during the period as follows, in thousands of barrels per day:[140]

Year	Domestic Production	Imports	Total
1979	12	5,017	5,029
1980	12	5,225	5,237
1981	19	5,457	5,476
1982	24	5,864	5,888
1983	29	5,839	5,868

As part of the five-year petroleum supply plan, MITI also issued the "Long-Range Energy Supply and Demand Forecast," the principal projections of which are shown on Table 2.12.[141] This forecast

TABLE 2.12
Long-Range Energy Supply and Demand Forecast for Japan

Demand for Energy (Thousand B/D)	Unit	Fiscal 1977 (Actual) Expressed in Individual Unit	Share %	Fiscal 1985 Expressed in Individual Unit	Share %	Fiscal 1990 Expressed in Individual Unit	Share %	Fiscal 1995 Expressed in Individual Unit	Share %
Energy demand before conservation		Actual Energy Demand 7,099.9		11,408.2		14,165.4		16,767.6	
Rate of energy conservation				12.1%		14.8%		17.1%	
Energy demand after conservation				10,029.5		12,063.0		13,906.9	
Supply by Primary Energy									
Water Power									
Hydropower	Million KW	18.1	4.8	22.0	4.7	26.0	4.6	30.0	4.6
Pumped-up	Million KW	8.05		19.5		27.0		33.5	
Geothermal Power	Thousand B/D	2.6	0.0	37.9	0.4	125.8	1.0	244.7	1.8
Domestic Crude Oil & Natural Gas	Thousand B/D	65.3	0.9	137.9	1.4	163.7	1.4	241.3	1.7
Domestic Coal	Million Tons	19.72	3.2	20.0	2.5	20.0	2.0	20.0	1.8
Nuclear Power	Million KW	8.0	2.0	30.0	6.7	53.0	10.0	78.0	14.3
Imported Coal (incl. steam coal)	Million Tons (Million Tons)	58.29 (0.95)	11.6	101.0 (22.0)	13.6	143.5 (53.5)	15.6	178.0 (80.5)	16.5
LNG	Million Tons	8.39	2.9	29.0	7.2	45.0	9.0	50.0	8.7
New Energies	Thousand B/D	5.3	0.1	89.6	0.9	663.5	5.5	1,051.2	7.6
Sub-total:	Thousand B/D	1,809.5	25.5	3,722.3	37.1	6,031.5	49.0	7,909.9	55.6
Imported Oil (incl. LPG)	Thousand B/D (Million Tons)	5,290.5 (7.39)	74.5	6,307.2 (20.0)	62.9	6,307.2 (26.0)	51.0	6,307.2 (33.0)	44.4
Supply Total:	Thousand B/D	7,099.9	100	10,029.5	100	12,338.7	100	14,217.1	100
Surplus/(Shortage)	Thousand B/D	-		-		(275.7)		(310.2)	

Source: MITI: Natural Resources and Energy Agency, December 15, 1979 (mimeo).

would seem to be highly optimistic and based on assumptions that, if taken seriously by the Japanese themselves, could be dangerously misleading. MITI forecast a reduction in dependence on imported petroleum from 74.5 percent of total energy supply in fiscal 1977 to 51 percent in fiscal 1990 and 44.4 percent in fiscal 1995. To support this forecast, the ministry projected significant conservation and important increases in nuclear, imported coal, LNG, and new types of energy, with the following implied annual growth rates: overall energy, 3.9 percent; nuclear, 13.5 percent; LNG, 10.4 percent; imported coal, 6.4 percent; and new energies, 34.2 percent.

There would seem to be no chance of meeting even the reduced 1976 goal.[142] The CIA predicted in August 1979 that Japan would, at best, have an installed nuclear capacity of 18,000 megawatts by 1985, which "if existing technical problems can be overcome and all the reactors operate at plant factors approaching 60 percent, could contribute the equivalent of 500,000 barrels per day of oil."[143]

Japanese reactors were frequently shut down during the late 1970s by a long succession of operating problems, and there were cancellations and delays in ordering new plants and in construction. These uncertainties were exacerbated by the shutdown of seven of Japan's eight light-water reactors following the accident at Three Mile Island in March 1979.[144] MITI and Science and Technology Agency (STA) have a long-standing dispute as to whether Japan should continue to use foreign technology in its nuclear program or should develop its own. During the late 1970s, Japanese research developed a heavy-water design that some Japanese scientists argue should replace in future reactors the U.S.-type light-water design used in most existing reactors. A prototype of the Japanese-designed heavy-water reactor, known as the JOYO reactor, which produces more plutonium than it consumes, has gone into operation in Oarai, and there is now widespread debate as to which direction the nuclear power industry in Japan should take.[145]

One critical question in this debate concerns the supply and enrichment of uranium fuel for these reactors. Japan is totally dependent on the United States and France for imports of enriched uranium. In 1975 the Japanese concluded enrichment contracts with the U.S. Energy Research and Development Administration sufficient to cover fuel requirements for an eventual fifty-eight power reactors with a total capacity of 51,645 megawatts.[146] The Carter administration, concerned about the proliferation of nuclear technology, reluctantly agreed to the construction of a reprocessing plant in Japan and an interim agreement under which spent fuel from Japanese reactors is being reprocessed in France and Britain.[147]

As part of a strategy for the development of important nuclear power capabilities, the Japanese are thinking through the possibility of Pacific Basin cooperative arrangements. The elements of such arrangements would seem to exist, given existing and planned large nuclear power capacities in Japan, Taiwan, and South Korea; at least two-thirds of the world's proven low-cost uranium reserves and production capacity are in Canada and Australia.[148] A regional enrichment and reprocessing facility, tied into long-term supply contracts and with appropriate safeguards, might ultimately be feasible.

Given the current state of technology in synthetic fuels and solar energy, the lead times and capital costs involved in developing these technologies, and the problems currently being experienced in the development of nuclear power, the MITI forecast must be considered wildly unrealistic and should be taken more as a goal than as a forecast. Even under this highly optimistic forecast, it is significant that MITI expects Japan's imports of oil to increase rapidly, from 5.3 million barrels per day in 1977 to 6.3 million barrels per day in 1985, and to remain at that level through 1995. Thus, by 1985 Japan would be importing 20 percent more oil than it did in 1977.

The Nuclear Power Program

Japan's plans for the development of nuclear power have been greatly scaled down, but the expansion projected in MITI's long-range forecast still seems unrealistic. The government once planned to have 60,000 megawatts of nuclear capacity in operation by 1985; it has now lowered its sights to 28,000 megawatts of capacity by 1986.[149] In 1980 Japan had an installed capacity of 7,430 megawatts in fourteen reactors and only 14,460 megawatts of capacity in sixteen reactors under construction.

The Sunshine Project for New Energy Sources

If the Japanese nuclear power industry seems bogged down and unlikely to achieve even scaled-down goals, the prospects for early development of other new energy sources seem even less bright. Perhaps the most accessible new source utilizing present technology is geothermal energy, which lies close to the earth's surface in Japan's volcanic geology. Future developments in technology could make it possible for geothermal to become a major indigenous energy source for Japan. With MITI's encouragement and financial assistance, Japex and three private companies (Mitsui Metal Mining Co., Idemitsu Kosan, and Geothermal Technology Development Co.) are working on geothermal projects. In 1980 168,000 kilowatts (kw) of electricity were produced from this source; its development was planned as follows:[150]

1983	275,000 kw
1985	1,000,000 kw
1990	3,500,000 kw
1995	10,000,000 kw
2000	48,000,000 kw

A 48-million-kilowatt target for the year 2000 compares to the 1978 installed hydroelectric capacity of 27 million kilowatts for the 1979 thermoelectric capacity of 90 million kilowatts.

In other new energy fields, Japan contributes to two coal liquefaction development programs in the United States, one by Gulf Oil and the other by Exxon. The Japanese plan to establish experimental plants in Australian coal fields to test these processes. Similarly, some work is being done on tidal, wind, and solar energy.

The government guides and provides financing for programs on new energy sources within the framework of MITI's innovative Sunshine Project, unveiled on July 1, 1974. Huge expenditures totaling more than 7 trillion yen were originally planned over the last quarter of the century, as shown in Table 2.13.[151] The program, predictably, got under way more slowly than planned, and only 8 percent of the anticipated expenditures had actually been spent by the end of 1980 (see Table 2.14). More than 40 percent of the actual 1974–1980 expenditures are budgeted for 1980. Expenditures projected for the 1990s are also greatly scaled down from the original plan. The experience of the first five years of the plan persuaded the Japanese that coal liquefaction, geothermal, and solar energy demonstrate the highest potential for early commercialization, so resources are now being focused on those three areas.[152] The Overall Energy Council forecast in 1980 that coal liquefaction, geothermal, and solar sources will provide 5 percent of Japan's energy needs in 1990 and 7 percent in 1995.[153]

The Sunshine Project is an important and farsighted program, but its vision extends into the next century. It will contribute little to the solution of Japan's energy problems for the rest of this century. In this respect, as in others, Japan shares the dilemma of other industrialized countries: Even after allowing for maximum development of all other energy sources and maximum conservation, Japan and the other industrial countries will for the foreseeable future be dependent on oil supplies from the OPEC countries. Therefore, if these industrialized countries are to assure a continuation of the

TABLE 2.13

Sunshine Project: Original Plan of Government Expenditures--1974

Unit: ¥ Million

Programs	1974–1980	1981–1985	1986–1990	1991–1995	1996–2000	Total
Solar Energy	80,000	200,000	250,000	200,000	200,000	930,000
Geothermal Energy	1,100	3,000	4,000	1,500	–	9,600
Coal Gasification and Liquefaction	140,000	300,000	300,000	100,000	–	840,000
Hydrogen Energy	60,000	150,000	200,000	250,000	300,000	960,000
Supporting Research	485,000	1,080,000	1,330,000	770,000	600,000	4,265,000
TOTAL	766,100	1,733,000	2,084,000	1,321,500	1,100,000	7,004,600

Source: Japan Petroleum and Energy Yearbook: 1978.

TABLE 2.14

Sunshine Project: Actual and Planned Government Expenditures--1979

Unit: ¥ Million

Programs	Actual[1]						Cumulative 1974-1979	Budget[2] FY 1980	Planned[1]	
	1974	1975	1976	1977	1978	1979			FY 1980-1985	FY 1986-1990
Solar Energy	850	1,100	1,450	1,450	2,050	3,800	10,700	9,550	70,000	30,000
Geothermal Energy	550	1,000	1,550	2,550	3,200	3,550	12,500	8,600	70,000	20,000
Coal Gasification and Liquefaction	400	850	900	1,050	1,450	2,900	7,500	8,600	400,000	820,000
Hydrogen Energy	350	450	450	500	600	700	3,050	950	10,000	50,000
Supporting Research	250	450	550	650	850	1,000	3,750	550	30,000	100,000
TOTAL	2,400	3,950	4,900	6,200	8,150	11,950	37,500	28,250	580,000	1,020,000

Sources: 1) "Strategy for Accelerated Implementation of Sunshine Project", Interim Report. New Energy Technical Development Sub-Committee of Industrial Technology Council (A quasi-governmental organ under jurisdiction of MITI), Tokyo, November 1979.

2) From Fiscal Year 1980 Budget submitted to Diet.

prosperity they have achieved, they must find a way to maintain the essential supply volumes during the next couple of decades.

New Approaches for New Problems

Since the end of the postwar U.S. occupation, Japanese economic and diplomatic strategies have dealt successfully, indeed brilliantly, with evolving international realities. Japan took full advantage of the opportunities presented by U.S. and producing-country policies during the late 1950s and the 1960s to fuel its historical economic growth with very low-cost imported oil. The Japanese recognized sooner than any other consuming country the dangers inherent in their dependence on those imports and undertook strenuous and far-sighted initiatives to attempt to diversify their energy sources — geographically, by supplier, and by type of energy.

However, despite their early understanding, their sustained and earnest efforts, and their large investments, the Japanese entered the 1980s more dependent on Middle East oil than they were twenty years before. Their need for energy has far outpaced the fruits of their diversification efforts. Under the most optimistic assumptions about conservation and the development of alternative energy sources, Japan's need to import oil from OPEC countries is expected to increase until at least 1975 before leveling off and will then continue for the rest of this century to be some 20 percent higher than it was in 1977. At the same time, the import requirements of OPEC oil of the industrialized countries of the West are also expected to increase, and the USSR is expected for the first time to become an oil importer. This increased demand coincides with a period when the large OPEC exporters increasingly believe it is in their interest to reduce their exports.

Under these circumstances, assuming there are no structural or directional changes in the nature of the world's petroleum markets, we would appear to be moving toward inevitable conflict and a major breakdown of the world economy. The oil-consuming countries will compete more and more frantically for fewer barrels of oil. Economic warfare, if not worse, will be an almost certain outcome, with economic stagnation in the industrial countries and despair in the developing world.

As much as any country's and more than most, Japan's future depends on a successful resolution of the world's energy problems. In the pursuit of its own survival, Japan is being forced to reexamine the approach to world economic and political problems that has been successful for so long. Following the disastrous failure in

World War II of an activist and interventionist approach to the outside world, Japan has maintained a "low posture" on the international scene, monitoring and reacting to external developments rather than trying to influence them to achieve a desired outcome. Under the umbrella of U.S. power and a relatively stable world economic order, that approach proved to be highly appropriate.

The changes in the postwar international order since 1973 have been of a nature and magnitude requiring a major reevaluation of the role Japan must play on the international scene. As these changes coincide with Japan's emergence as an economic superpower, Japan has been subjected to incessant and increasing pressure to play a larger role, one more consistent with its massive economic power and with the influence it cannot avoid exercising, whatever its intentions. Nowhere has this requirement been more evident than in energy policy.

The world energy situation requires the early construction of new arrangements to assure for the remainder of this century the supply of those minimum quantities of oil needed to sustain a viable international economic order during the long gestation period of supplemental alternative energy sources. In establishing the foundations of mutual interest on which such new international arrangements must be based, it will have to be understood by both the oil-producing and oil-consuming countries that both these groups need a stable international order if they are to survive. The consumers need to have certain minimum volumes of oil made available by the producers, and the producers cannot for long maintain their independence and stability if there is depression and chaos in the industrial countries.

A workable framework of action might include the following principal elements:

1. The industrial countries would firmly commit themselves to energy conservation programs and the development of alternative energy sources;

2. The oil producers would agree to scheduled volumes of production during an agreed planning period, the agreed volumes being adequate to maintain the world economy while the alternative energy sources are being developed and brought into production;

3. To produce these volumes, the oil-producing countries would require, and should be given, protection against the inflationary degradation of their oil revenues that they fear (this might be accomplished by substituting for monetary pay-

ment a newly created real-value instrument for some portion of the agreed-upon production volumes); and
4. Oil producers and consuming countries should convene an international conference—similar to Bretton Woods—on energy to develop the framework of such a program and reach agreement between the major producers and consumers.

Japan's interests are so dependent on the successful solution of the current international energy dilemma that it cannot avoid playing an active role in the search for such a solution. If the new era is not reached and the necessary cooperation between oil producers and consumers does not materialize, Japan can expect to suffer more than most other countries. There are hopeful signs that Japanese leaders have begun to recognize this new necessity. Two examples are especially interesting.

In a speech to the General Assembly of the United Nations on September 25, 1979, Foreign Minister Sunao Sonoda said: "Because the energy problem is an important matter that concerns countries throughout the world, I believe it would be useful for the United Nations to consider how it could be dealt with. Thus, I shall follow with interest the initiatives to be taken by Secretary-General Waldheim on this subject."[154]

A more pointed speech was given in Tokyo in January 1980 by Foreign Minister Saburo Okita in which he accepted without reservation the requirement that Japan adopt an active foreign policy by which it would influence, rather than react to, international developments. Observing that "the two oil crises have demonstrated all too plainly how closely oil is tied to the political situation in the Middle East," he continued: "Japan can no longer view international relations as external givens but must perceive them as conditions that Japan itself should participate importantly in creating."[155]

Notes

1. Data calculated from United Nations, Department of International Economic and Social Affairs, *World Energy Supplies 1973–1978* (New York: United Nations, Department of International Economic and Social Affairs, 1978), pp. 52–68.
2. Organisation for Economic Co-operation and Development, *International Energy Trends* (Paris: OECD, March 5, 1979), p. 2.
3. Kiyotaka Kurokawa, ed. *Japan Petroleum and Energy Yearbook: 1978* (Tokyo: Japan Petroleum Consultants, 1978), pp. C4–C5.

4. United Nations, *World Energy Supplies 1973–1978*, p. 60.

5. International Energy Agency, *Report Based on Tokyo Energy Summit Meeting* (Paris: International Energy Agency, June 1979).

6. *Oil and Gas Journal* 77, no. 53 (December 31, 1979):70–71.

7. Figures for total proven world reserves were calculated by the Aramco partners; they are found in "The Future of Saudi Arabian Oil Production," *Petroleum Intelligence Weekly Special Supplement* (April 23, 1979), pp. 1–11.

8. *Japan Petroleum and Energy Weekly* 14, nos. 17 and 18 (April 23 and 30, 1979), p. 6.

9. "Japan's Petroleum Stockpiles Soar," *Platt's Oilgram News* 58, no. 7 (January 10, 1980):1.

10. Kurokawa, *Japan Petroleum and Energy Yearbook : 1978*, pp. G38–G57.

11. Japanese National Committee of the World Petroleum Congress, *The Petroleum Industry in Japan 1978* (Tokyo: Japanese National Committee of the World Petroleum Congress, April 1979), p. 16.

12. Toyoaki Ikuta, "Future of Solar and Nuclear Energy in Japan," in Toyoaki Ikuta, *Energy in Japan* (Tokyo: Institute of Energy Economics, March 1979), pp. 9–11.

13. Masao Sakisaka, *1985–2000: Choice of a Long Term Energy Strategy* (Tokyo: National Institute of Research Advancement, 1977), p. 6.

14. "Recommendations of the Overall Energy Council—1975," in Kurokawa, *Japan Petroleum and Energy Yearbook : 1978*, p. C95. The Advisory Council for Energy, often called the Overall Energy Council, was formed in 1966 as an advisory body on energy to the Ministry of International Trade and Industry. The council published its first recommendations in February 1967. Subsequently, it published updated reports in 1971, 1974, and 1975. The texts of the 1971, 1974, and 1975 reports are available in English in *Japan Petroleum and Energy Yearbook : 1978*.

15. Japanese National Committee of the World Petroleum Congress, *Petroleum Industry in Japan 1978*, p. 21.

16. Organisation for Economic Co-operation and Development, *Quarterly Oil Statistics—Fourth Quarter 1978* (Paris: OECD, 1979), p. 276.

17. This assumes that Saudi Arabia will continue to allow Aramco to market the bulk of its crude oil, that the Aramco partners (Exxon, Mobil, Texaco, and Standard of California) continue to supply 80–90 percent of their Japanese affiliates' need, and that Shell manages to do the same.

18. These countries are Venezuela, Saudi Arabia, Kuwait, Iran, Iraq, Libya, Indonesia, Algeria, United Arab Emirates, Nigeria, Ecuador, Gabon, and Qatar.

19. For a detailed analysis of OPEC see Suad Rouhani, *History of OPEC* (New York: Praeger Publishers, 1971).

20. Robert B. Krueger, *The United States and International Oil* (New York: Praeger Publishers, 1975), p. 59.

21. *Oil and Gas Journal* 76, no. 52 (December 25, 1978):104–105.

22. *Petroleum Intelligence Weekly* 18, no. 51 (December 17, 1979):12;

Oil and Gas Journal 77, no. 53 (December 31, 1979):225.

23. *British Petroleum Statistical Review : 1978* (London: Britannic House, 1979), p. 10.

24. Robert S. Pindyck, *OPEC, Oil Prices and the Western Economies* (Cambridge, Mass.: Massachusetts Institute of Technology Energy Laboratory, 1978), p. 3.

25. *British Petroleum Statistical Review : 1978*, pp. 6–8.

26. *Japan Petroleum and Energy Weekly* 13, no. 7 (February 13, 1978):7.

27. Central Intelligence Agency, National Foreign Assessment Center, *The World Oil Market in the Years Ahead* (ER 79-10327U), August 1979, pp. 43–50.

28. Historical data are from *Oil and Gas Journal* 68, no. 52 (December 28, 1970):112–132. Projections for future years are calculated from various issues of the *Oil and Gas Journal, Petroleum Intelligence Weekly, Arab Press Service*, and *Platt's Oilgram News*.

29. "Ike OK's Imports Plan for Reduction to 1,031,000 B/D: West Coast Exempted; Text of Imports Conclusions," *Platt's Oilgram News* 35, no. 146 (July 30, 1957):1–4.

30. Although each producing country then controlled its own crude oil pricing, international competitive realities required the producing countries to maintain value differentials between the various crude oils in the traditional way, i.e., taking into account the product values of each crude in the consumers' refineries, as well as the different transportation costs involved in bringing each crude to the market.

31. Figures for 1973 and 1975 are taken from Henry D. Jacoby et al., *Energy Policy and the Oil Problem: A Review of Current Issues* (Cambridge, Mass.: Massachusetts Institute of Technology Energy Laboratory, 1979), p. 8; 1980 figures are taken from "PIW's Tally of Key World Crude Oil Price Increases for Early 1980," *Petroleum Intelligence Weekly* 19, no. 1 (January 7, 1980):11.

32. *Middle East Economic Survey* 22, no. 49 (September 24, 1979):2.

33. For a discussion of the economics of this type of market situation, see M. A. Adelman, *Producers, Consumers, and Multinationals: Problems in Analyzing a Non-Competitive Market* (Cambridge, Mass.: M.I.T. Press, 1977).

34. Figures for demand are taken from Sherman H. Clark, *The Petroleum Outlook* (Menlo Park, Calif.: Sherman H. Clark Associates, 1979); the forecast of production capacity is based on a report prepared by Gulf Oil's Crude Oil Economics Committee, "World Petroleum Outlook 1978–1995," Houston Tex.: Gulf Oil Exploration and Production Company, November 1978, Table 7a; the production goals of the producing countries represent an aggregation of individual countries' goals as publicly announced by the respective nations from 1976 to 1982.

35. A congressional study in 1977 estimated the 1980 figure would be 65 million barrels per day. See U.S. Congressional Research Service, *Project Interdependence: U.S. and World Energy Outlook through 1990*, no. 95–31 (Washington, D.C.: Government Printing Office, 1977), p. 69.

36. For a brief review of some of the factors contributing to declines of productive capacity in some OPEC countries, see Central Intelligence Agency, National Foreign Assessment Center, *The World Oil Market in the Years Ahead*, pp. 43–50.

37. *Japan Petroleum and Energy Weekly* 14, nos. 17 and 18 (April 23 and 30, 1979):6.

38. This was agreed at a regularly scheduled OPEC ministers' meeting held in Geneva, June 17–19, 1978. In mid-February 1978, the Saudi Arabian government had issued a directive to Aramco to the effect that output of Arabian light crude should not exceed 65 percent of annual average liftings for the year 1978. One purpose of this directive was to take a first step toward correcting a significant imbalance of reserves and capacity; another purpose was to decrease the crude surpluses being put on the market. See *Middle East Economic Survey* 21, no. 19 (February 27, 1978):1, for details of the Saudi decision.

39. Both data for reserves and actual production data to calculate reserve life come from *Oil and Gas Journal* 76, no. 52 (December 25, 1978):104–105. Proved reserves of crude oil are the estimated quantities of oil that are "reasonably certain' to be recoverable in the future under existing economic and operating conditions. Reservoirs are considered proved if economic productibility is supported by either actual production or conclusive formation tests. The area of a proved reservoir is based on geological and/or engineering data that define an oil-water contact or the lowest structural occurrence of oil. Information extrapolated from other fault blocks or deeper horizons can be used to estimate contacts. Immediately adjacent portions of a reservoir not drilled as yet are considered proved if judged economically productive on the basis of available technical data. Fluid injection and other enhanced recovery techniques produce proved reserves.

40. *Petroleum Intelligence Weekly* 18, no. 50 (December 10, 1979):4; *Petroleum Intelligence Weekly* 18, no. 49 (December 3, 1979):5; *Middle East Economic Survey* 22, no. 51 (October 8, 1974):4. Historically, the spot market has accounted for less than 5 percent of the international oil trade, and the producing governments have not, in the past, been sellers in that market.

41. Gulf Oil Corporation estimated worldwide demand for crude oil in 1980 to be 29.6 million barrels per day; Exxon has announced a figure of 29 million barrels per day. Other estimates are within the same range, e.g., see "Little Peril Seen if Iran Cuts Off Oil," *New York Times*, January 14, 1980, pp. D1, D3. The OPEC figure is calculated by an analysis of the annual budgets of the various OPEC countries, assuming a 20 percent increase in these budgets for the given period. Also incorporated within this analysis are the varying amounts of oil price increases expected by these OPEC producers.

42. *Middle East Economic Survey* 23, no. 51 (October 8, 1979):1, 7; *Petroleum Intelligence Weekly* 18, no. 46 (November 12, 1979):1, 6; *Petroleum Intelligence Weekly* 18, no. 51 (December 17, 1979):1–2.

43. Data from proceedings of *World Oil Sessions* (Cambridge, Mass.: Massachusetts Institute of Technology, November 1979).

44. Robert S. Pindyck, *Some Long Term Problems in OPEC Oil Pricing* (Cambridge, Mass.: Massachusetts Institute of Technology Energy Laboratory, 1979), p. 7.

45. It should be emphasized that the cost of producing synthetic oil in large quantities is not known at this time; however, much research is under way. Gulf Minerals Resources Company has provided the following estimates. These data represents capital cost comparisons (in 1979 terms) given as capital costs of new resources in 1979, i.e., dollars of capital investment per daily barrel of capacity developed.

Cost per daily barrel

New petroleum (conventional crude oil reserves in U.S.) $10,000
Synthetic liquids from coal $13,000
Shale oil (refined on site) $25,000

In the case of shale oil, the cost per barrel for a 100,000 B/D plant is approximately $30, excluding return on investment. In other words, $25,000 capital costs would yield shale oil at $30 per barrel. This $30 per barrel figure to produce synthetic oil from coal is also quoted in the October 8, 1979, issue of the *Middle East Economic Survey*. This figure only applies to developed industrialized countries that have the technical, financial, and human resources to manage these huge and complex projects. An MIT Energy Lab Report (No. MIT-EL 79-012 WP) of June 1979 states that "the total cost of producing upgraded shale oil (i.e., shale oil acceptable as a feed to a petroleum refinery) by surface retorting ranges from about $18 to $28/barrel in late 1978 dollars with a 20 percent chance that the costs would be lower than, and 20 percent higher than that range." Another point that needs to be kept in mind is that development of all of these alternative energy sources is constrained by the long lead times required for their physical implementation.

46. Studies made at the Massachusetts Institute of Technology Energy Laboratory suggest that a period of 12 to 14 years is required to achieve 75 percent of the ultimate reduction in demand resulting from an increase in the price of oil. The delay results from (1) the time lag in replacing oil-burning and/or energy-inefficient equipment and (2) the time and cost required to develop substitute fuels. See *World Oil Sessions*.

47. Figures for 1978 are from Gulf Oil Corporation Internal Document, Strategic Planning Group, "Environmental Forecast," December 1978. Figures for 1985 and 1990 are based on an updated, but not yet published, version of that study.

48. This figure is based on a crude and natural gas liquids (NGL) production forecast of 66 million barrels in 1980, increasing to 77 million barrels in 1990.

49. Free-world conventional petroleum production is expected to peak at about 61 million barrels per day. This figure is based on "January 1980 World

Petroleum Outlook Analysis" as calculated by the Crude Oil Economic Committee and Gulf Oil Exploration and Production Company and includes crude and NGL.

50. United Nations, *World Energy Supplies* (Series J), various issues from 1965 to 1978.

51. "Exxon Chief Calls for $700 Billion Outlay on Synthetics over 30 Years," *Platt's Oilgram News* 57, no. 236 (December 7, 1979):1.

52. Stanley Ragone, in *Current News: College of Engineering* (Virginia Polytechnic Institute and State University) (Fall 1979):1–4.

53. Government goals are spelled out in U.S. Department of Commerce, *Energy Sources for the Future* (Washington, D.C.: Government Printing Office, July 1975), p. 61.

54. Pindyck, *Some Long Term Problems in OPEC Oil Pricing*, p. 27, has used a somewhat different assumption and has arrived at a figure of 32–33 million barrels of oil per day.

55. Data for 1950 are from the Japanese Ministry of International Trade and Industry. Data for 1960–1975 are taken from the Japanese Ministry of International Trade and Industry, Kurokawa, Japan in *Petroleum and Energy Yearbook : 1978*, pp. C4–C5. Data for 1977 are taken from *Japan Petroleum and Energy Weekly* 14, no. 10 (March 15, 1979):4; 1978 and 1979 figures are from the Japanese Ministry of International Trade and Industry.

56. Figures on indigenous fuel usage in the late 1940s and early 1950s are from Edward A. Ackerman, *Japanese Natural Resources* (Chicago: University of Chicago Press, 1953), pp. 179–184.

57. Japanese coal is not only limited in quantity but poor in quality, with low heating value and high ash content. This condition increases the need for imports even to burn under boilers. In addition, only 25 percent of domestic production is suitable for coking, so that coking coal imports were needed even when overall domestic supply was plentiful.

58. Figure for 1960 is taken from Ministry of International Trade and Industry, quoted in Kurokawa, *Japan Petroleum and Energy Yearbook : 1978*, pp. C2–C3; 1978 figure is from Natural Resources and Energy Agency of MITI, *Comprehensive Energy Statistics for Fiscal 1979* (Tokyo: Tokyo Trade Industry Research Company, 1979).

59. Figure for 1945 is calculated from Ackerman, *Japanese Natural Resources*, p. 210. Figure for 1978 is calculated from *Japan Petroleum and Energy Weekly* 14, no. 10 (March 5, 1979):4.

60. Data for 1952 are found in *Electric Power in Japan* (Tokyo: Overseas Electric Industry Survey Institute, 1966); 1979 figure is from *Comprehensive Energy Statistics for Fiscal 1979* (Tokyo: MITI, Natural Resources and Energy Agency, 1980).

61. *Platt's Oilgram News* 57, no. 238 (December 11, 1979):3.

62. 1950 figure from Ackerman, *Japanese Natural Resources*, p. 171; *Comprehensive Energy Statistics for Fiscal 1979*.

63. The one indigenous energy source that remains to be developed is geothermal, a new technology that will be discussed later.

64. Ackerman, *Japanese Natural Resources*, pp. 190–191, 197, 218.

65. *Japan Petroleum and Energy Weekly* 14, no. 9 (February 26, 1979):2.

66. Current oil production figure is from *Oil and Gas Journal* 77, no. 53 (December 31, 1979):102; for reserve figure see ibid., pp. 70–71; current consumption figure is from *Petroleum Intelligence Weekly* 14, no. 3 (January 21, 1980):6.

67. *Japan Petroleum and Energy Weekly* 14, no. 9 (February 26, 1979):2.

68. Figures are taken from data provided by the Economic Planning Agency of the Japanese government and from MITI in Kurokawa, *Japan Petroleum and Energy Yearbook : 1978*, pp. B1, C2–C3. Percentage growth of Japan's GNP between 1950 and 1973 is calculated from the "Table of Japan's Gross National Product," p. B1.

69. Data for Figure 2.6 come from the following sources: for 1950–1960, Japan Tariff Association, *Japan Exports and Imports* (Tokyo: Japan Tariff Association, 1950–1960); 1960–1977, Kurokawa, *Japan Petroleum and Energy Yearbook : 1978*, p. 68; January 1978–September 1979, Petroleum Association of Japan, *Japan Oil Statistics Today*, no. 29 (October 1979):2.

70. U.S. Energy Information Administration, quoted in *Basic Petroleum Data Book* (Washington, D.C.: American Petroleum Institute, July 1979), Section VI, Table 1.

71. J. E. Hartshorn, *Politics and World Oil Economics*, rev. ed. (New York: Praeger Publishers, 1967), p. 274. A discussion of MITI's foreign exchange allocations appears on pp. 272–276.

72. The Petroleum Industry Law No. 128 of 1962 is quoted in *Japan Petroleum and Energy Yearbook: 1975* 2, pp. A13–A18.

73. *Oil and Gas International* 5, no. 8 (August 1965):50.

74. The exception is Fuji Kosan, a lube oil manufacturer, which supplies Mobil's lube requirements.

75. Between 1951 and March 13, 1978, Japanese refining companies borrowed a total of $1.6 billion from foreign sources. See Kurokawa, *Japan Petroleum Energy Yearbook : 1978*, pp. G27–G31, for a complete listing of these loans by borrower and lender.

76. *Financial Times*, December 12, 1965, quoted by Edith T. Penrose, *The Large International Firm in Developing Countries – The International Petroleum Industry* (London: George Allen and Unwin, 1968), p. 235.

77. Data for Table 2.10 come from the following sources: 1970, Petroleum Association of Japan, *Petroleum Industry of Japan : 1975* (Tokyo: Japanese National Committee of the World Petroleum Congress, 1976), Tables 3–5, p. 17; 1973 and 1975, Petroleum Association of Japan, *Petroleum Industry in Japan 1978*, p. 21; 1978 and 1979, compiled from Ministry of International Trade and Industry figures.

78. Data for Table 211 are taken from the following sources: 1960, Petroleum Association of Japan figures; 1965, *Tokyo Petroleum News* 18 (January 26, 1968):2–3; 1970 and 1975, Ministry of International Trade and Industry, found in Kurokawa, *Japan Petroleum and Energy Yearbook : 1978*, pp. 641, 649; 1977, 1978, 1979, *Japan Oil Statistics Today*, no. 31 (December 1979):6–7.

79. Ministry for International Trade and Industry figures cited in

Kurokawa, *Japan Petroleum and Energy Yearbook : 1978*, p. G39, show Middle East imports reaching 91.23 percent of total imports in fiscal year 1967.

80. Kurokawa, *Japan Petroleum and Energy Yearbook : 1978*, p. W3, W18, T81–T87.

81. Data are from the Petroleum Association of Japan, tabulated in *Japanese National Committee on Petroleum Industry in Japan 1978*, pp. 26–27.

82. This action was taken by the Energy Subcommittee of the Industrial Structure Research Committee.

83. Kurokawa, *Japan Petroleum and Energy Yearbook : 1978*, pp. W3–W4.

84. Penrose, *The Large International Firm*, p. 136; and Kurokawa, *Japan Petroleum and Energy Yearbook : 1978*, pp. T5–T7.

85. JPDC's name was changed to Japan National Oil Company (JNOC) in June 1978.

86. *Japanese National Committee on Petroleum Industry in Japan 1978*, p. 16.

87. *Petroleum Intelligence Weekly* 18, no. 47 (November 19, 1979):10; *Petroleum Industry in Japan : 1975*, p. 16; Petroleum Association of Japan, *Petroleum Industry in Japan 1978*, p. 21; "Japan Crude Oil Supply in 1979 by Supplier," *Japan Petroleum and Energy Weekly* 15, nos. 2 and 3 (January 14 and 21, 1980):10.

88. *Petroleum Industry in Japan 1978*, p. 7.

89. *Japan Petroleum and Energy Weekly* 13, no. 7 (February 13, 1978):7.

90. "Japan: Final Terms for Chinese Oil," *Petroleum Economist* 45, no. 3 (March 3, 1978):123.

91. Central Intelligence Agency, National Foreign Assessment Center, *World Oil Market in the Years Ahead*, p. 42.

92. *Oil and Gas Journal* 77, no. 53 (December 31, 1979):42.

93. Barry Kramer, "Report from Peking," *Wall Street Journal*, February 22, 1980, p. 46.

94. Reported to the author by executives of a Japanese refining company importing Chinese crude.

95. *Japan Petroleum News* 18, no. 4628 (February 6, 1978):1.

96. *New York Times*, January 30, 1975, p. 55; "Soviet Union," *Petroleum Economist* 46, no. 8 (August 1979):340.

97. Robert F. Ichord, Jr., "Pacific Basin Energy Development and U.S. Foreign Policy," *Orbis* (Winter 1977):1029.

98. *New York Times*, October 13, 1977, p. 9.

99. "Soviet Union," *Petroleum Economist* 46, no. 8 (August 1979):340.

100. Richard C. Hanson, *Financial Times*, October 27, 1979, p. 2. For an update on the recapitalization that has occurred since the original agreement, see Sodeco Shareholders List, August 24, 1979, and December 7, 1979.

101. *Oil and Gas Journal* 77, no. 6 (February 5, 1979):39.

102. *New York Times,* January 24, 1978, p. 49.

103. *Soviet Oil, Gas and Energy Databook* (Stavanger, Norway: Noroil Publishing, 1978), Table 39, p. 50.

104. *Platt's Oilgram News* 57, no. 83 (April 30, 1979):4.

105. "Soviets Expect to Prove One Trillion Cubic Meters of Yakutsk Gas," *Platt's Oilgram News* 57, no. 191 (October 2, 1979):3.

106. Ichord, "Pacific Basin Energy Development," pp. 1028–1029; David I. Hitchcock, Jr., "Joint Development of Siberia: Decision-Making in Japanese-Soviet Relations," *Asian Survey* 11, no. 3 (March 1971):285.

107. Ichord, "Pacific Basin Energy Development," pp. 1028–1029.

108. *Petroleum Intelligence Weekly* 18, no. 47 (November 19, 1979):10.

109. For further discussion of this trend, see Christopher Tugendhat and Adrian Hamilton, *Oil: The Biggest Business* (London: Eyre Methuen, 1975), pp. 196–213; and Joe Stork, *Middle East Oil and the Energy Crisis* (New York: Monthly Review Press, 1975), pp. 222–255.

110. Tugendhat and Hamilton, *Oil: The Biggest Business,* pp. 206–212; Stork, *Middle East Oil,* p. 255.

111. Stork, *Middle East Oil,* p. 228.

112. Tugendhat and Hamilton, *Oil: The Biggest Business,* p. 228.

113. For further details of these industrial projects, see the following issues of the *Middle East Economic Survey*: 14, no. 39 (July 19, 1976):8; 14, no. 41 (August 2, 1976):7; 20, no. 11 (January 3, 1977):5; and 20, no. 45 (August 29, 1977):7.

114. This figure is calculated from data in *Economic Cooperation of Japan-1978* (Tokyo: Jetro, 1978).

115. *Middle East Economic Survey* 14, no. 50 (October 4, 1976):4; *Platt's Oilgram News* 55, no. 14 (January 20, 1977):3; Ministry of International Trade and Industry, *MITI Petroleum Preliminary Report* (Tokyo: MITI, January 24, 1980.

116. *Middle East Economic Survey* 23, no. 12 (January 7, 1980):6. The five major companies working on this project are: Mitsui and Co., Mitsui Petrochemical Industry, Ltd., Mitsui Toatsu Chemicals, Inc., Toyo Soda Manufacturing Co., Ltd., and Japan Synthetic Rubber Company, Ltd. Mitsui hoped to include as many as seventy companies and the Japanese government. However, the private sector was reluctant to commit funds given Iran's political instability.

117. *Middle East Economic Survey* 14, no. 47 (September 13, 1976):3; ibid. 22, no. 48 (September 17, 1979):3.

118. *Middle East Economic Survey* 22, no. 15 (January 29, 1979):4. The Saudi Petrochemical Development Company, Ltd., was established on January 22, 1979, in Tokyo with participation of fifty-four Japanese firms, including fifteen Mitsubishi group companies, eleven utility companies, thirteen oil refining petrochemical companies, and four banks.

119. *Platt's Oilgram News* 57, no. 232 (December 3, 1979):3.

120. *Oil and Gas Journal* 77, no. 34 (August 20, 1979):3. Additional data supplied by the Mexican Petroleum Importing Company, a consortium of

thirty-six Japanese refiners, banks, and trading companies organized to receive the Mexican crude. The Japanese loan was made at 8 percent over ten years.

121. *Platt's Oilgram News* 57, no. 205 (October 23, 1979):4; *Japan Petroleum News* 20, no. 5124 (February 6, 1980):2.

122. *Oil and Gas Journal* 77, no. 53 (December 31, 1979):70–71.

123. Michele T. Halbouty and John D. Moody, "World Ultimate Reserves of Crude Oil," paper presented to the 10th World Petroleum Conference, Bucharest, Romania, 1979.

124. There are two different ways to calculate development costs. The $500–$7,000 range is based on "peak daily barrel" production, where the denominator is the highest production attained by a field for a year. On the other hand, "average daily barrel" development costs are based on the daily production averaged for the life of the producing field. Peak daily barrel production is usually *twice* as high as the average daily production for a field; when development costs are given in terms of peak daily production, the cost range is usually about *half* that found for average daily production. For example, the Forties field in the North Sea has averaged 500 MB/D during its peak years of production (1978 and 1979), but during the whole production life of the field, it should average no more than 250 MB/D. For a further breakdown of development costs in the North Sea, see *North Sea Report* (Edinburgh: Wood Mackenzie and Co., Erskine House, January 1978–January 1980). For the low range, the Middle East development cost analysis is based on costs associated with onshore production primarily in Kuwait and Saudi Arabia. Other Middle Eastern production would have slightly higher associated costs because of the mountainous terrain and smaller fields.

125. The ranges shown here are based on Gulf Oil Exploration and Production Company estimates as of January 1978 and on estimates derived by Selig Harrison, quoted in Central Intelligence Agency, *China Oil Production Prospects* (ER77-100 30U), (Washington, D.C.: Central Intelligence Agency, June 1977), p. 8.

126. All data and estimates are from Gulf Oil Exploration and Production Company.

127. *Petroleum Intelligence Weekly* 18, no. 31 (July 30, 1979):11; *Oil and Gas Journal* 78, no. 4 (January 28, 1980):42.

128. *Oil and Gas Journal* 77, no. 53 (December 31, 1979):42; see also Table 2.6.

129. Central Intelligence Agency, *China Oil Production Prospects*, p. 5.

130. Ibid., p. 838.

131. Under the terms of the agreement, JNOC will operate and fund exploration of the field; China will share the cost of developing the field; and after commercial production begins in 1982, the field will be under Chinese control, with the two countries receiving approximately equal shares of the crude oil for fifteen years. See *Japan Petroleum News* 20, no. 5128 (February 13, 1980):1.

132. For a further discussion of this topic, see *London Oil Reports* 2, no. 1 (January 14, 1980):10–11.

133. *Harvard International Law Journal* 14, no. 1 (Winter 1973):213, 218.

134. For a full exposition of seabed and fishery disputes in Asia, see the various works of Choon-ho Park, particularly "The Sino-Japanese-Korean Sea Resources Controversy and the Hypothesis of a 200-Mile Economic Zone," *Harvard International Law Journal* 16, no. 1 (Winter 1975):28–29.

135. Park, Choon-ho, "Oil Under Troubled Waters: The Northeast Asia Sea-bed Controversy," *Harvard International Law Journal* 14, no. 1 (Winter 1973):224–225.

136. *Platt's Oilgram News* 56, no. 116 (June 16, 1978):4.

137. *Petroleum Economist* 45, no. 10 (October 1978):441.

138. *Japan Petroleum and Energy Weekly* 14, nos. 17 and 18 (April 23 and 30, 1979):2.

139. Ibid., p. 3.

140. Energy/GNP coefficients are calculated from data in *Japan Petroleum and Energy Weekly* 12, nos. 13 and 14 (March 28 and April 4, 1977); and ibid. 14, nos. 17 and 18 (April 23 and 30, 1979).

141. MITI Natural Resources and Energy Agency, "Long-Range Energy Supply and Demand Forecast (Provisional)," in *Comprehensive Energy Statistics for Fiscal 1979* (Tokyo: Trade Industry Research Co., December 1979). Table is a Gulf Oil Corporation translation of the original Japanese data.

142. Susumu Awanohara, "Japan Tries to Plug the Gaps," *Far East Economic Review* 99, no. 1 (January 6, 1979):59.

143. Central Intelligence Agency, National Foreign Assessment Center, *World Oil Market in the Years Ahead*, p. 56.

144. "Government Orders Reactor Shut Down—Check," *Japan Times*, April 15, 1980, p. 1; "Another Nuclear Plant in Japan Closed for Now," *Asian Wall Street Journal*, April 17, 1979, p. 5.

145. Richard C. Hanson, "Japan's Energy Programme—Search for Nuclear Independence," *Financial Times*, September 12, 1979, p. 4.

146. U.S. Energy Research and Development Administration, *U.S. Nuclear Export Activities* (1542), April 1976, pp. 3–103, cited in Ichord, "Pacific Basin Energy Development," p. 1040.

147. Awanohara, "Japan Tries to Plug the Gaps," p. 59.

148. Ibid., pp. 59–62; *Petroleum Intelligence Weekly* 17, no. 3 (January 16, 1978):7.

149. Central Intelligence Agency, National Foreign Assessment Center, *World Oil Market in the Years Ahead*, pp. 55–56.

150. *Nikkan Kogyo Shinbun* [Daily Industrial News] (Tokyo), February 8, 1980.

151. Kurokawa, *Japan Petroleum and Energy Yearbook : 1978*, pp. C51–C58. An English text of the Sunshine Project appears on pp. C51–C57.

152. New Energy Technical Development Subcommittee of Industrial Technology Council (MITI), "Strategy for Accelerated Implementation of

Sunshine Project: An Interim Report," November 1979.

153. MITI Natural Resources and Energy Agency, "Long-Range Energy Supply and Demand Forecast (Provisional)."

154. *Japan Report* 25, no. 20 (October 16, 1979).

155. From text of speech given by Dr. Okita on January 23, 1980, at the Foreign Correspondents Club of Japan, Tokyo.

3
Internationalizing Japan's Financial System

Eric W. Hayden

Introduction: The Domestic Financial System

At the beginning of the 1980s, major changes were under way in the Japanese financial system. These changes, which started in the closing years of the previous decade, have been slow and uneven. Nevertheless, they do point to the increasing liberalization, flexibility, and sophistication of the financial system of the free world's second largest economy. On the one hand, many of the changes initiated in the late 1970s specifically affected the domestic financial market—for example, the liberalization of interbank rates, the issuance of certificates of deposit, and the introduction of an open bidding system for national bond sales. On the other hand, many changes, such as further foreign exchange liberalization, increasing offshore activity by Japanese banks, and the expanded access of foreign borrowers to the domestic yen bond market, have encouraged Japan's emerging role as a major international capital market. Changes of the latter type are of particular interest to a broad and diverse community: scholars of monetary policy, exchange-rate movements, and capital flows; international bankers eager to benefit from the dynamics of greater competition; monetary authorities from the OPEC nations, concerned about protecting their oil revenues; and financial centers such as Hong Kong and Singapore, whose positions as maturing international financial centers could be jeopardized if the transition under way in Tokyo is allowed to reach its logical conclusion.

Although the focus of this chapter is an assessment of the changing international role of the Japanese financial system, some consideration of the powerful domestic confines within which it operates

A glossary appears at the end of this chapter.

is appropriate. To appreciate the extent of the transition occurring in the Japanese financial system, it is helpful to recognize how the system differs from that of the United States.

Perhaps the fundamental difference is the institutional structure of the two systems. In contrast to the more than 14,000 private commercial banks in the United States, Japan has only seventy-six roughly comparable (although legally different) regular commercial banks.[1] Another important distinguishing feature of the Japanese system is a higher degree of specialization of banks. For purposes of this discussion (and the later consideration of the growing international activities of the Japanese banks), there are four principal types of Japanese banks, frequently referred to in local banking circles as "ordinary banks": city banks, regional banks, long-term credit banks, and trust banks.

The thirteen *city banks* are headquartered in the principal metropolitan centers and serve the country's major industrial and commercial firms. As the city banks are typically in an "over-lent" position, they depend heavily for their funding base on a combination of rediscounting at the country's central bank, the Bank of Japan (BOJ), and borrowing in the interbank market from the sixty-three *regional banks.* These regional banks, headquartered outside the major metropolitan areas, lend mainly to regional firms and governments and typically earn a major part of their profit from the on-lending of their broad deposit base (household and corporate) to the fund-short city banks. While the loan assets of the city and regional banks are short-term (less than a year maturity), reflecting the short-term nature of their liabilities, most of their working capital loans are routinely renewed upon maturity, serving in effect as long-term loans and a source of ever-green funds for Japanese corporations. Unlike the city and regional banks, which depend on deposits and the interbank market, the three *long-term credit banks* are permitted to raise funds through the issuance of one-year and five-year debentures, sold widely to both institutional investors and at the retail level.[2] This more stable funding base allows them to provide fixed-rate, long-term loans to corporations, principally for capital expansion. As their name suggests, the last major category of ordinary banks, the seven *trust banks*, engage primarily in trust activities for individuals and institutions. Because of their strong term-deposit base (from issuing "loan trusts," or term savings accounts), they hold a significant share of the domestic long-term bank lending market.

Another major difference between the financial systems of the two countries is the greater degree of regulation in Japan over the entire credit-extension function of the private banks. The major means of managing the country's money supply has typically been through the rationing of credit by the Bank of Japan via its moral suasion, or "window guidance." Open-market operations of the kind engaged in daily by the Federal Reserve of the United States are unknown in Japan — a reflection (and a cause) of the relatively underdeveloped domestic bond market.[3]

In addition to the monetary dimensions, an equally important function of this system of administered credit allocation has been to ensure a sufficient supply of funds to the corporate sector, thereby providing the impetus to the postwar "interlocking triad" of growth, investment, and exports.[4] The importance of this aspect is underscored by the predominant role of indirect finance (as opposed to direct financing by equity or bond issues) in postwar Japan, the result of which has been to delay the development of a meaningful alternative to the banks for either corporate borrowers or household investors. Indeed, the principal function of the households in this corporate-oriented banking structure has been to deposit their legendary high savings with the banks, to be re-lent to the country's major corporations.[5] However, just as slower growth at home in the late 1970s propelled Japanese corporations and, therefore, Japanese banks to look abroad, so did the changing environment help redirect the domestic focus of the banks, presaging the thrust into the largely untapped consumer finance field that will be a principal area of expansion for local banking in the 1980s.[6]

A concomitant to official control over the credit-extension process in Japan has been the tight official regulation of interest rates. On the one hand, the net impact of this regulation has been to thwart the "efficiency" of the domestic financial market — that is, the extent to which the interest-rate mechanism determines the supply and cost of funds. On the other hand, it has been an inherent part of the strategy of ensuring sufficient and low-cost funds to priority corporate borrowers in a postwar Japan that has been generally short of funds. By way of example, the Bank of Japan, by controlling the interbank market and keeping the call money rate above the short-term prime lending rate, has typically channeled funds from the highly liquid regional banks to the "over-lent" city banks. They, in turn, have been enabled to on-lend to their customers, the country's major industrial enterprises. In such cases, the on-lending city banks usually circumvent the interest-rate controls to some extent by requiring substantial "compensating balances" of anywhere from 20 to 40 percent of the loan.

The interest-rate mechanism has been interfered with for another reason, namely, to contain the costs of government borrowing. Until the mid-1960s, fiscal deficits were unknown in Japan. The growth in the level of government debt was one of the major features of the 1970s for Japan, particularly in the wake of the 1973–1974 oil *shokku*, which gave rise to an era of slow growth and the assumption of a progressively larger role by the national government in order to propel economic growth. The amount of annual government borrowing in the late 1960s averaged only 550 billion yen (or less than $2 billion at then prevailing exchange rates): that level had doubled by the early 1970s, jumped quickly to nearly 5 trillion yen in the recession year of 1975, and then soared progressively over the next five years to reach some 14 trillion yen (approximately $60 billion) in each of fiscal 1979 and 1980. As the decade ended, the ratio of outstanding government bonds to GNP was an unhealthy 25 percent. One major local bank forecast that this ratio could jump by 1985 to 33 percent, assuming introduction of a general consumption tax to help government revenues, or as high as 44 percent if the government continued to rely on bond issues to finance its revenue shortfall.[7]

Whereas in the United States the federal government is obliged to price its debt instruments at competitive interest yields in order to sell in the open market, commercial banks in Japan are required to purchase and hold for specified periods the major share of government bonds. The amount of each issue of national bonds to be purchased and held by individual banks is determined by the Ministry of Finance (MOF) in accordance with the size of the particular institution.[8] However, the city banks collectively are generally obliged to acquire about 38 percent, the regional banks some 18 percent, the long-term credit banks about 9 percent, and the trust banks 6 percent. Together the banks finance more than two-thirds of the government's deficit. As a result, by the end of the 1970s, the amount of government debt being carried by the thirteen city banks had gone from 1 trillion yen in 1970 to 35 trillion yen in 1979; in the course of the decade, the ratio of bonds to total assets of the city banks had jumped from 6.5 percent to 8 percent, while the ratio of bonds to their deposits had skyrocketed from 5 percent to 40 percent.[9] In such a system of captive market and regulated interest rates, the Ministry of Finance has been understandably reluctant to accommodate the growing pressures in Japan to establish a more efficient market for government bonds comparable to the U.S. Treasury bills market.

Another closely related factor behind the government's tight control of interest rates is the desire to ensure that bank deposit rates do not compete with those offered by the postal savings system, itself a major source of government funding, accounting for about 30 percent of all savings deposits in Japan. Within Japanese banking and finance circles, the existence of more than 22,000 postal savings branches throughout the country has become an increasing source of frustration, particularly in view of (1) restrictions on new branching by commercial banks, (2) the interest-rate premium permitted postal savings accounts on time deposits, and (3) the effective tax exemption on interest earned by postal savings accounts.[10]

The tight control over domestic interest rates notwithstanding, major steps toward interest-rate liberalization occurred in the closing years of the 1970s. Naturally, these steps were piecemeal, and in the early 1980s, many vestiges remained of the rigid control of interest rates. For example, most bank deposit rates are adjusted by the Bank of Japan in tandem with changes in its official discount rate; the same holds true for long-term lending rates and for interest on government bonds. An open bidding system on certain of those bonds was initiated in June 1978, but the system is not universally applied. Similarly, although all controls over the bills discount and call money market rates were "officially" removed in 1979, the single major distinguishing feature remains the influence of the Bank of Japan, an influence exercised through the medium of the six dealers who operate the market under the close supervision of the central bank. Hence, although rates are more flexible (as they no longer are posted daily by the dealers, they move more often than before), they are still not truly determined by the forces of supply and demand.

Despite these remaining rigidities, two major steps were made in the latter half of the 1970s toward freeing domestic interest rates: the legitimization of the *gensaki* market and the introduction of negotiable certificates of deposit (NCDs). Both these events have been important in encouraging a greater role for market forces in determining the price and flow of funds in Japan. In the early 1980s, positive signs pointed to further changes in the traditionally rigid financial system. Although liberalization will result in major changes in the domestic financial system, it will also have a major influence on the internationalization of the Japanese capital market. For this reason, some elaboration of the *gensaki* and NCD markets is useful.

The *gensaki* market consists of the conditional purchase (or sale) of a government or corporate bond for a fixed period with a resale (or repurchase) agreement at a specified price. The price difference represents the yield to the investor or, inversely, the cost of funds to the borrower. Reflecting the extended time frame for the transactions involved, the word *gensaki* is a combination of two Chinese characters meaning present (*gen*) and future (*saki*). The origin of the market goes back to the 1950s, when securities firms, short of ready cash, would conditionally sell bonds from their portfolio against future repurchase.

Until the mid-1970s, the *gensaki* market remained a gray market outside the regulation of the Ministry of Finance. Fully legitimized in 1976 by a series of standardized rules and reporting procedures issued by the Ministry of Finance, the market has expanded significantly in recent years as slower domestic investment left corporations increasingly liquid. Simultaneously, local securities houses have actively promoted the market among their corporate and institutional clients. Until the introduction of NCDs in 1979, the yield on *gensaki* transactions was the only free-market rate available to local money managers.

Since their introduction in May 1979, NCDs have proved to be a useful instrument in fostering the intermediation function of the banking system. As such, they have been an important addition to the funding capability of the banks while also providing useful outlets for the surplus funds of investors. To the outside observer their introduction was long overdue (similar instruments were introduced in the United States in the 1960s), and the battle behind their introduction provides some insight into the operation of the Japanese financial system.

There were two major proponents of the introduction of NCDs in Japan: city banks, which nervously watched their deposit base erode as increasingly rate-conscious household savers transferred their money to the higher-yielding postal savings accounts and as corporations shifted their excess funds to the more attractive *gensaki* market; and foreign banks, whose small local deposit base has always been a major constraint on their operations in Japan. The initial opposition to the new funding instruments came from monetary authorities concerned about the possible dilution of their clout over the banks. However, some change of personnel in the Ministry of Finance, particularly in the banking bureau, in the mid-1970s resulted in a new perspective on the usefulness of NCDs for modernizing Japan's financial system.

Adamant in its opposition, however, was a united front composed of the long-term credit banks, the regional banks, the trust banks, and the securities houses. The long-term banks saw NCDs as strong competitors to the debentures that only they and the Bank of Toyko are allowed to issue. Likewise, regional banks feared a runoff of their lucrative local industry and government deposits, and trust banks saw a potential threat to their own loan trusts. Aligning themselves with the noncity bank forces were the securities houses, who argued that NCDs would drain money from the growing *gensaki* market.

Given the strong arguments pro and con, the complexion of the NCDs that were ultimately authorized was a compromise. They fell far short of the proponents' wishes, particularly in terms of tenure, minimum size, allocation per bank, and transferability. Nevertheless, by the end of the first year, the NCD market had already grown to more than 2 trillion yen, or roughly half the size of the more mature *gensaki* market.[11] Furthermore, the authorities promised eventual major modifications in the tenure, size, and allocation of NCDs to accommodate the wishes of the city banks. Most significant, however, in view of the strong opposition and the major shift in financial policy implicit in the introduction of NCDs is the fact that the authorities permitted them at all. In part, the decision was an expression of gratitude by the Ministry of Finance to the city banks for the ballooning quantities of national bonds they have been forced to purchase and hold in recent years. One can be hopeful, however, that the decision was in greater part a long-overdue recognition by Japanese officialdom of the need for interest-rate liberalization and the development of a full-fledged money market.

Lending support to this view was the fact that the Ministry of Finance in early 1980 permitted the nation's leading securities firm, Nomura Securities, to sell open-ended trusts to the public. Competing directly with bank fixed-rate deposits, the trusts offer higher interest rates plus greater liquidity than do the bank instruments. Presumably one reason the ministry granted approval was that a major portion of the trusts (reportedly 60 percent) is to be invested in national bonds. Despite their initial opposition to the innovation, many of the banks soon realized that Nomura's gain was potentially a gain for everyone in the uphill battle to establish a more competitive and liberalized money market in Japan.[12]

Offshore Banking Expansion

In turning to the internationalization of the Japanese financial system, perhaps the best place to begin is by reviewing the nature and extent of offshore activities of Japanese banks. Although the Sumitomo Bank has been in California since the 1920s, Japanese involvement in overseas banking generally is largely a phenomenon of the 1970s. The earliest postwar branches of Japanese banks were es-

tablished in London and New York in 1952, the year the U.S. postwar occupation ended. By 1970, offshore activity had expanded to
58 overseas branches and 6 subsidiaries; by the end of the decade,
Japanese banks had 127 branches scattered worldwide, along with
73 subsidiaries and 158 representative offices.[13]

As with most nations, the initial offshore forays of Japanese banks
were undertaken to accommodate the trade-financing requirements
of the nation's major corporations. As the total volume of Japanese
international commerce grew a hundredfold from 1952 to 1981 to
more than $200 billion, the financing of this expanded volume has
been a major growth sector of Japanese banking business. Likewise,
a significant concomitant dimension of the country's international
corporate business activity — and thus that of the banks — has been
the dramatic increase in offshore direct investment, with the
amount growing nearly tenfold in the course of the 1970s to more
than $30 billion.[14] The outgrowth of this investment has been that
Japanese banks aggressively compete abroad against local banks to
provide short-term working capital loans, bridge financing, me-
dium- and long-term loans, and a variety of advisory services, including project finance for offshore resources development. The initial thrust of the Japanese banks was servicing Japanese companies
and subsidiaries operating abroad. However, as the experience of the
banks grew and their reputation for quality service spread, they have
increasingly diversified their offshore portfolio to include an ever-
broadening range of non-Japanese multinationals, financial institutions, and foreign governments.

Indicative of this growing overseas involvement, the outstanding
balance of short-term loans from Japanese banks abroad amounted
at the beginning of 1980 to some $15 billion, while medium- and
long-term loans totaled more than $35 billion. One-quarter of this
amount was lent in yen and the rest in foreign currencies, primarily
U.S. dollars. In both 1978 and 1979, Japanese banks accounted for
more than 20 percent of total global commercial syndicated lending.

The development of this large overseas portfolio was not without
traumatic growing pains for the Japanese banks. The Ministry of
Finance generally exercises the same degree of close supervision
over offshore activities of the banks as it does over their domestic
activities. Notwithstanding the need for government regulation,
particularly given both the balance-of-payments impact of offshore
lending and the dollar-funding problem of Japanese banks, such supervision nevertheless has been frustrating for them. This frustration has arisen in particular at the apparent "on-again, off-again" approach to offshore banking taken by the regulatory authorities.

The periods of restriction interspersed with relaxation have been necessitated in large part by the country's balance-of-payments position. At the time of the current-account deficits of the first oil crisis of 1973–1975, the banks were severely curtailed in the amount of offshore lending they were permitted. With the return to surplus in 1976 and 1977, the curb on medium-term and long-term loans was relaxed and replaced in mid-1977 by an automatic validation system, subject to certain liability-matching requirements on foreign currency loans. By 1979, however, as the country's current-account surplus plunged into deficit following the second great oil crisis of the decade, the authorities once again restricted the offshore lending activity of the banks. This time, however, the authorities were motivated by more than just the current-account deficit and resultant downward pressure on the yen. At least three additional reasons lay behind the move to curb the activities of the banks.

First, Japanese banks had become so aggressive in the Eurolending market in 1978 and early 1979 that many competitors accused them of gaining business through vicious undercutting of interest rates; certain deals were dubiously termed "kamikaze loans." Unfortunately for Japan, this uproar in international financial circles coincided with the accumulation of massive trade surpluses and mounting accusations that Japan was dumping export products abroad at the same time that it was purportedly dumping dollar loans.

Second was the matter of country risk. On the one hand, the authorities were pleased that overseas activity permitted the banks an offset against both slower domestic economic activity and the negative drag on back earnings from their growing portfolio of national bonds. Bond prices fell steadily as the government sought to contain worsening inflation and support the softening yen by raising domestic interest rates. On the other hand, as the Japanese competed head-on with more experienced Western banks, fears rose in the Ministry of Finance and the Bank of Japan about the ability of domestic banks, so long protected in their own market, to assess country risk accurately, particularly on loans to non-oil less developed countries (LDCs). The fear was heightened with the fall of the shah of Iran in early 1979, when even the Western banks became concerned about their ability to judge risk.

Third, as U.S. monetary policy tightened in the second half of 1979 in an effort to contain spiraling domestic inflation and protect the tottering dollar, the Ministry of Finance and the Bank of Japan became increasingly concerned about whether the banks could continue to raise short-term dollars to fund their fixed-rate, long-term offshore loans. Painful memories lingered of the premium of up to two percentage points ("Japan rate") that had been forced upon the Japanese banks at the height of the first oil crisis.

Despite the gravity of these problems, the authorities also appreciated the arguments of the Japanese banks, namely, that too much restraint on their offshore lending activities would ultimately jeopardize their reputation for reliability and dependability. Therefore, although the concerns that mounted through 1978 and 1979 obliged the authorities to suspend all offshore yen lending in late 1979 (pending a reversal in the deterioration of the yen and an improvement in the country's current-account position), offshore foreign currency loans were restricted but not completely suspended. Priority was given to lending that was linked to Japanese trade, that was for natural resource projects (particularly those related to oil), or that was tied to loans from such international agencies as the World Bank.

In the early 1980s, although official Japanese policy toward offshore foreign currency lending remained unarticulated, certain features of official policy could be deduced. First, unlike in the boom years of 1978–1979, in which Japanese banks accounted for more than 20 percent of total global commercial syndicated lending, in the future such activity will be limited to between 10 and 15 percent. The lower level reflects Japan's share of global GNP and trade, and the upper limit represents its share of the collective GNP of the OECD countries. A specific target within the 10 to 15 percent range is not likely to be set, but there appears to be an evolving official consensus about the range. Second, lending to individual countries will be restricted to less than 20 percent of any particular bank's capital and surplus. A similar rule covers lending to domestic borrowers. Third, reflecting concern over country-risk exposure, the proportion of LDC loans in the aggregate bank offshore portfolio will be reduced from the 60 percent that characterized lending in the late 1970s to no more than 50 percent.

The surge in activity of the Japanese banks in the field of international lending, particularly toward the close of the 1970s, constituted an important phase in their overall maturing process. Based on this experience, the banks have systematically diversified their sources and methods of raising foreign currency, mainly U.S. dollars, in offshore markets. Ever mindful of the risk of another "Japan rate," most have significantly lengthened their dollar deposit maturities. Whereas in 1974 only about 10 percent of their Eurofunds had an average maturity of more than one year, the percentage had increased to between 20 and 25 by the turn of the decade. Besides actively expanding their offshore branch network as one means of raising funds, the banks have aggressively concentrated on selling certificates of deposits in all major offshore dollar centers. Japanese banks, for example, account for an estimated 90 percent of all certificates of deposit (CDs) sold in Singapore. They have also been responsible for pioneering a variety of innovations in the offshore CD market: the mixed-maturity floating rate in Singapore, five-year issues in New York, and the introduction of SDR-based CDs in the Euromarket. Furthermore, although the banks are not now permitted by the Ministry of Finance to issue commercial paper through their overseas subsidiaries, they have begun to ask major U.S. debt-rating agencies to rate their U.S. CDs in preparation for the inevitable day when commercial paper becomes a permissible means for raising offshore dollars.

Another and considerably more controversial method by which the banks have pursued offshore funds has been the issuing of foreign currency bonds. The push in this direction has been important not only because of the funding ramifications but, perhaps even more important, because of the implications for the separation, heretofore carefully defined, between Japanese banks and securities companies. Like the Glass-Steagall Act in the United States, Article 65 of the Japanese Securities and Exchange Law carefully differentiates between the banking and brokerage businesses, specifically forbidding banks from engaging in the underwriting business. Accordingly, while the long-term credit banks and the Bank of Tokyo are permitted to issue their own domestic yen debentures, no Japanese bank has been legally able to engage in overseas underwriting activity, whether for its own funding purposes or to accommodate the direct financing needs of its corporate clients.[15] Recognizing that strict adherence to this law would hinder their international competitiveness, particularly in Europe, where banks are able to manage and underwrite bond issues while also doing commercial banking business, the Japanese banks have subtly yet decisively stretched the letter of the law to the limit. This practice is of major significance to the banks and will have a positive impact on the future dimensions of the Japanese financial system.

As the Japanese banks expanded overseas, the Ministry of Finance, through its well-known system of "guidance," modified in 1975 the strictures of Article 65, specifying that a European subsidiary of a Japanese bank could comanage a Eurobond issue by a Japanese borrower, provided that the subsidiary of a Japanese securities company comanaged an equal share of the issue. In local parlance, this became known as the "both-or-nothing rule." In two specific instances in late 1979, two Japanese banks defied the rule and, in the process, paved the way for a major reinterpretation of Japanese banking procedures. Arguing that the both-or-nothing rule applied only to public issues, the wholly owned Swiss subsidiary of the Fuji Bank, one of the major city banks, took the lead role in managing a private Swiss franc issue for a Japanese construction company. Shortly thereafter, one of the long-term credit banks, the Industrial Bank of Japan (IBJ) led another Swiss franc Japanese placement. For the Japanese banks, concerned about the steadily shifting trend from indirect to direct financing by their customers, the actions of Fuji and the IBJ were refreshing and welcome steps, as was the tacit approval of the Ministry of Finance. To the Japanese securities houses, however, the move by the banks was a bold and hostile step to undercut their own growing offshore activities.

Nor has the breaking of tradition stopped there. In late 1979, Fuji Bank, again through its Swiss subsidiary, floated its own Swiss franc issue — this time as a means of funding its local lending portfolio. While the issue again proved highly controversial and elicited sharp attacks from the Japanese securities houses, the Ministry of Finance nevertheless gave its approval and, in so doing, set a major precedent by which Japanese banks might henceforth relieve their foreign currency funding problems, to the consternation of the securities companies.

The growing competition abroad between the Japanese banks and securities houses can be expected to be a major feature of the 1980s. The securities houses are concerned that the banks, as they expand their role in underwriting their Japanese clients' convertible bond issues in the Euromarket, will convert a large portion of their underwriting share. In the process, this practice would increase not only the equity of the banks in the companies but also their influence over the companies' management. Lacking the financial resources of the banks, the securities companies feel especially vulnerable to this strategy of the banks. This issue between the banks and the securities companies was in a highly fluid stage, but it is of major significance that, as of early 1982, at least two major securities houses were seeking Ministry of Finance permission for certain of their European branches to engage in banking business. Although such a step would further contravene the spirit of Article 65, the securities companies consider it only natural that the ministry, having tacitly approved the entry of the banks into the offshore securities business, would grant them similar permission to move into overseas commercial banking.

Another area in which innovation is likely to characterize Japanese international banking in the 1980s will be in offshore yen lending. The enthusiasm of the Japanese banks to expand this activity has been tempered by the desire of the authorities to limit the extent to which the Japanese currency is internationalized (used outside of Japan). As its international role has expanded in recent years, the exchange value of the yen has become increasingly a function of factors beyond the control of the monetary authorities. As a result, for example, in periods of strong speculative pressure on the currency, the Bank of Japan has had to intervene in the foreign exchange market by selling yen and buying dollars. The consequence has been to complicate domestic monetary management by increasing the supply of yen in the local money market.

The problem of money-supply control has been further compounded by innovative efforts of the banks to make the interest rate on offshore yen loans a function of the domestic cost of money. A case in point occurred in 1978 when the Mitsubishi Bank extended a loan to Mexico tied to the three-month bills discount rate. However, because the central bank uses the bills discount market (along with the other purportedly "free" interbank market, the call money market) as an instrument of monetary policy, it has expressly forbidden any subsequent efforts to tie the overseas yen lending rate to the domestic interbank rate.

A second effort to integrate the domestic and international yen markets was initiated in early 1980 by the Tokyo branch of Germany's Deutsche Bank when it received approval from the authorities to extend a medium-term offshore yen loan with a floating interest rate tied to the yen NCDA rate. However, the viability of this or any other floating-rate formula for offshore yen loans remains moot. In part, it will depend on the ability of the city banks to overcome the inevitable resistance of both the long-term credit banks and the trust banks to such an incursion into their traditional dominance of the yen term lending business. Of more importance will be movements in Japan's current-account position and the value of the yen, for it was problems in these interrelated areas that prompted the virtual freeze on nonresident yen lending in late 1979.

Perhaps the major factor, however, will be the extent to which interest-rate liberalization is permitted to run its logical course in Japan. As discussed earlier, funding is a major problem of the Japanese city banks, heavily dependent as they are on short-term deposits and interbank borrowings. The continued development of innovative funding instruments whose rates are free to move according to market forces rather than administrative fiat will be decisive in determining the ability to accommodate the yen loan demand of foreign borrowers. Development of these instruments, in turn, hinges

on the evolving attitude of Japanese officialdom toward the proper
role of Japan and the yen as major participants in the international
financial market.

Yen-Denominated Foreign Bonds

Reflecting the slowly expanding international financial role of
Japan and its currency is the country's market for bonds denominated in yen and floated by foreign borrowers, nicknamed the
"Samurai" market (just as a similar U.S. market for foreign dollar-
issuers is called the "Yankee" market). This market opened in December 1970 with a seven-year issue by the Asian Development
Bank for the equivalent of about $17 million at the prevailing ex-
change rate. By the end of the decade, particularly in the heady days
of 1978 as the exchange rate of the yen against the dollar breached
the 200 level, issues as large as $375 million equivalent with matu-
rities up to fifteen years were being offered in what had become one
of the world's most rapidly growing international bond markets. In
its peak year of 1978, the number of Samurai issues totaled 827 billion yen, the equivalent of some $3.8 billion, putting this market in
the same league as the other major world money markets of 1978:
London ($7.3 billion), New York ($5.8 billion), Switzerland ($5.7
billion), and West Germany ($3.8 billion).

Through most of the 1970s, a major feature of this bond market
was that only issues of international financial institutions (e.g., the
World Bank, Asian Development Bank, European Investment Bank)
and foreign governments were eligible for flotation. A major obstacle to broadening the market to include corporate borrowers was the
long-standing Japanese requirement that corporate issues be secured
by collateral such as a factory or real estate mortgage. Under
pressure from the domestic securities houses acting on behalf of
overseas firms, who saw in the market a means of acquiring yen liabilities to hedge local assets, the Japanese authorities modified the
rigid securities requirement, permitting Sears Roebuck and Co. in
1979 to float the first unsecured public corporate yen bond in more
than fifty years. At the time, the Sears issue was seen as the forerun-
ner of other foreign companies' tapping the Tokyo market. However, more realistically, the main reason the local securities houses
lobbied so intensively for the change in the collateral requirement
was the desire to develop the narrow base of Japanese companies
eligible to float corporate bonds in the local bond market.[16]

Besides the restricted eligibility requirements of the Samurai
market, its other principal distinguishing feature has been the re-

quirement that issuers convert their yen proceeds into foreign currency for offshore remittance. The growth of the market in the 1970s was very much a function of Japan's official policy toward capital outflow. In times of mounting current-account surplus, such outflow has been actively encouraged, resulting in an expansion of the Samurai market and renewed attention in global financial markets to Japan as an emerging capital market. At other times, however, as the country's current surplus turned to deficit, official policy shifted and the future of Japan as a capital market became less certain.

A major reason for the surge in foreign borrowers' interest in the Samurai market in 1978 was the yen's low interest rate. Most of the bonds were quickly oversubscribed, however, thanks to the frenzy of foreign investors attracted by the gains to be made on currency appreciation. The authorities, meanwhile, despite their inherent bias against subjecting the yen to such speculative pressure, were only too happy to encourage as many Samurai issues as possible as a means of exporting the country's embarrassing but nevertheless ballooning current-account surplus. As pressure mounted abroad for Japan to reflate, increase imports, and export more capital, the Japanese found their options increasingly limited. The already gigantic fiscal deficit acted as a built-in barrier to any meaningful pump-priming, while internal economic and political forces combined to minimize any significant change in either the composition of imports or the impenetrable distribution system. Therefore, the only immediately viable option for dealing with the chronically sticky eternal account was capital outflow.

By the end of 1978, however, the future of the Samurai market was far less bright than it had appeared six months earlier. The dollar defense package of November 1, 1978, took much of the glitter off the yen and forced many of the foreign purchasers of the Samurai issues to retreat. The next year, the Iranian collapse, followed by the second oil crisis, rapidly reversed the Japanese trade dilemma and forced the authorities to reconsider their capital-export strategy. A similar reassessment had impinged on the growth of the Samurai market in 1974, when a strong external position was also quickly eroded by an oil crisis. However, whereas in 1974 the authorities had suspended all Samurai issues as a means of defending the yen and stabilizing the country's external position, in 1979 their reaction was more moderate. Just as the country's bankers were arguing that a complete freezing of all Japanese offshore lending in the wake of the oil crisis would do irreparable long-term damage to their international reputation, the securities houses successfully maintained that another shutdown of the Samurai market would raise serious doubts about the credibility of the Tokyo capital market. Accordingly, while the Ministry of Finance decided to limit the number of monthly issues, it demonstrated by its actions an acceptance of the fact that the Samurai market had become too large and too much a part of the international financial system to be frozen because of a sudden change in the country's external accounts.

Like the matter of continued Japanese offshore yen lending, the future of the Samurai market will depend in no small measure on the continued ability of Japan to respond successfully to future threats to its external balance and the value of the yen. Given the proven resilience of the economic system in the face of both oil crises of the 1970s, however, one can be reasonably optimistic about this ability and, consequently, the continued evolution of Japan as an international financial market. A major factor affecting the speed of this evolution will be the extent to which the yen is further internationalized.

Internationalizing the Yen

The internationalization of the yen has lagged behind Japan's postwar evolution as a major global economic power. This lag has been occasioned not so much by the reluctance of foreigners to hold yen assets or to use the yen in international settlements as by the determination of the local authorities to restrict the currency to a principally domestic financial role. This official reluctance to see the yen assume a more active international function has been predicated on the related desire to minimize (1) the extent of outside speculative pressure on the currency and (2) the disruptive impact of such fluctuations on domestic monetary management. One means by which the authorities have sought to contain these outside pressures has been through tight foreign exchange controls. Another has been through perpetuation of an "inefficient" domestic financial market in which the proper functioning of the interest-rate mechanism has been thwarted. The net result has been not only to deny the yen the role it would otherwise have had in view of Japan's global economic position but also to delay the emergence of a sophisticated financial system commensurate with the country's industrial might. However, as changes under way in the Japanese financial system point to a more flexible domestic financial structure and a more active participation in international financial affairs, the yen has begun to assume a gradual but unmistakably increased international role as a settlement currency, a finance (or investment) currency, and a reserve currency.

This emergence of the yen was a phenomenon of the 1970s, particularly of the last three years of the decade, and is likely to be given added thrust in the 1980s. One major factor contributing to the growing yen internationalization in the 1970s was the expanded use of the currency in the offshore lending activities of Japanese banks, an evolution that has already been discussed. Another major cause has been the steadily enlarged role of the yen in Japanese trade.

In the early 1970s, yen-denominated exports accounted for only 2 percent of total Japanese exports. By 1980, this share had jumped dramatically to 30 percent. On the one hand, this figure remained low relative to most other major industrial countries; for example, the United States denominates all its exports in its own currency, and the United Kingdom, West Germany, and France rely on their respective currencies to finance anywhere from 60 to 85 percent of their exports. On the other hand, what is important for Japan and the yen is not only the increase from 2 percent to 30 percent over a decade but also the fact that, over this same period, the annual value of Japanese exports surged from less than $20 billion to well over $100 billion. As a result, some $35 billion equivalent worth of Japanese exports were being financed in yen in 1981, up from less than $500 million only a decade previously. Given even a modest nominal 10 to 15 percent annual growth in Japanese exports in the 1980s, that $35 billion will double within only a few short years; and if, as is likely, the share of exports denominated in yen increases further, the expansion will be even faster. This points to a growing need for buyers of Japanese products to increase their access to yen, a development that can only further expand the international role of the Japanese currency.

One reason behind the expanding use of the yen in the invoicing of Japanese exports has been the understandable need of Japanese exporters to minimize the risks of exchange-rate gyrations. The ability of Japanese traders to pass this risk on to overseas buyers has been largely a function of the high quality of Japanese products and the reliability of Japanese delivery.

Another factor that has fostered the expanded use of the yen in trade finance is a more recent but potentially more important occurrence, namely, the trend of overseas buyers of Japanese products to disassociate themselves from the U.S. dollar, which heretofore has been the major international settlement currency. Although the dollar is likely to remain the major international settlement currency for the foreseeable future, largely because of the preeminent global economic position of the United States, many major dollar holders have begun to diversify into currencies that offer greater prospects for stability and/or appreciation and, at the same time, are seen as less vulnerable to politically induced asset freezes of the type imposed against Iran in late 1979. Reflecting this trend toward diversification of assets is the growing tendency of overseas buyers, particularly from the Middle East, to request that their purchases from Japan be invoiced in yen.

An aspect of yen internationalization far more crucial to determining the ultimate international role of the currency will be the extent to which it pays for Japanese imports; its expanded use in this area will inevitably mean an expanded supply of yen in the hands of overseas sellers of goods and services to Japan. However, in contrast to its growing role in financing Japanese exports, the yen has scarcely been used to finance the country's imports—2 percent throughout the 1970s, a figure that pales in contrast to the comparable 25 to 40 percent for most major Western nations and that may remain static for at least the foreseeable future. Use of the yen has been influenced by two major factors. First, trade financing comes under the category of "general domestic loans" on which the Bank of Japan sets ceilings, including limitations on loans to a single borrower. Consequently, there exists little incentive for Japanese banks to provide yen trade financing; in some instances importers have simply been unable to accommodate the demands of foreign exporters for yen settlement.[17] Second and related has been the lack of any bankers' acceptance (BA) market in Japan. Unless such a local refinance market develops, Japanese importers will continue to be obliged to depend on the New York–based U.S. dollar acceptance market.

Within Japanese business and banking circles, however, there is concern over the continued ability of the U.S. acceptance market to provide sufficient funding for Japanese imports, a concern that has been heightened by the upward movement of international oil prices. The value of oil imports into Japan, which is dependent on foreign oil for some 98 percent of its oil needs and for about three-quarters of its total energy needs, ballooned from roughly $3 billion in the early 1970s to more than $60 billion in 1980.[18] In this situation, Japan's need for an increasing supply of dollars will remain acute (even with increased conservation measures), assuming continued oil price hikes at or above global inflation rates. For the Japanese banks, this fact raises the fear that their trade bills may overwhelm the New York market, particularly as the oil-related trade bills of other heavy oil importers like Korea and Taiwan also increase. This concern was recently intensified when the U.S. credit-restraint program of early 1980 caused some Japanese bankers to worry in addition about a resulting squeeze of U.S. bank lending to foreign banks.[19] Although the restraint program has since been lifted, the Japanese remain sensitive to the potentially negative effect of another such program on their own dollar-raising capability.

An indication of the problem Japanese banks have in trying to finance oil imports with a nonindigenous currency is that their short-term dollar liabilities have regularly exceeded their short-term dollar assets since 1973, with the biggest discrepancies occurring during both oil crises. In 1979 alone, for example, short-term dollar liabilities increased by nearly $14 billion to surpass the $50 billion level, putting the net excess of dollar liabilities over assets at more than $20 billion, or about the same size as Japan's foreign exchange reserves. Accordingly, although it remains "unofficial," there is growing discussion within both the Ministry of Finance and the Bank of Japan of the need to reduce Japan's overreliance on the U.S. dollar for import financing by encouraging a multipolar monetary system in which the yen assumes a far greater settlement role than at present. If the oil producers agree, such a system could reduce Japan's dollar dependence by letting it finance some, if not all, of its oil imports in local currency. Like all changes in Japan, however, any major alteration of the present system is likely to take place slowly and unevenly as policy makers weigh all the possible implications. Nevertheless, the pressures induced by the oil-importation problem are likely to ensure that the policy of gradualism will be implemented more quickly than might otherwise have been the case.

As noted earlier, the related concerns about the value of the yen and domestic monetary management have kept the authorities from letting the internationalization of the yen occur in tandem with the internationalization of the Japanese economy. These dual concerns remain important to both the Ministry of Finance and the Bank of Japan, but there is also the realization within official Japanese monetary circles that the different international economic environment of the 1980s—slower growth, higher inflation, and an uncertain oil-price and oil-supply situation—will require a considerably different approach to currency management than that which prevailed in the previous postwar decades. For example, events of 1978 (when the yen soared from 240 to 175) and then 1979–1980 (when it plummeted at one point below 260) have demonstrated convincingly to the authorities that regulation of the value of the yen is beyond their direct control. Another related lesson of the late 1970s has been that, in contrast to the 1960s and early 1970s, Japanese exports tend to perform better when the yen is strong rather than weak, thanks to the impact a strong yen has on containing domestic inflation (and hence export competitiveness). Finally, in an era of rising oil price costs and worsening global inflation, the authorities have seen that the nation's international reserve levels are better maintained when the yen is strong, prompting yen selling and hence dollar buying to contain upward yen pressure. As a result of such lessons, both the Ministry of Finance and the Bank of Japan accept the need for a strong currency (as opposed to the soft-currency bias that characterized official thinking in the 1960s and much of the 1970s).

This change of thinking at the official level is not unique to Japan. In the wake of the currency turmoil of the late 1970s, the West Germans, too, have come to appreciate the inflation-controlling features of a strong currency (and, conversely, the inflation-aggravating features of a weak one). Both nations benefited from the capital inflow that buoyed their currencies in 1978, and both suddenly found themselves in the opposite position as the oil events of 1979 forced them to assess new means of encouraging the inflow of billions of dollars to finance their mounting trade deficits, stem the downward pressure on their currencies, and contain rising domestic inflation. Like the Germans, the Japanese have had to consider how to increase the attractiveness to foreigners of holding yen assets, which, in turn, will foster the increased internationalization of the yen.

A wide variety of factors can affect capital flows (e.g., interest-rate differentials, expectations about an economy's future performance, currency speculation, and central bank portfolio-diversification decisions); there have been two major factors in the case of Japan. One is the official policy toward such inflow (demonstrated through foreign exchange regulations), and the second is the availability of sufficient domestic financial instruments for the foreign investor.

With regard to foreign exchange regulations, critics frequently note that every large fluctuation in the yen has triggered a major reversal in official policy toward capital inflow and outflow. Although this tendency has certainly been a salient feature of Japanese policy, a more relevant fact is that in recent years several major liberalizations in the country's foreign exchange laws have decidedly reversed a series of major restrictions in effect since the end of World War II.[20] The effect of the various changes has been to alter the official attitude toward external capital transactions from "restricted in principle and free on approval" to "free in principle and restricted only in special cases," including major deterioration in the balance of payments or chaos in the foreign exchange markets. Much of the liberalization has been directed toward easing conditions for capital outflow (such as overseas direct and portfolio investment by Japanese residents), but several of the liberalizations have direct bearing on encouraging capital inflows. For example, nonresidents need no longer retain for six months in Japan proceeds from the sale of local securities, and they are permitted to participate freely in the *gensaki* market; similarly, limits on the size of residents' foreign currency accounts have been completely eliminated. At the same time that it has been easing official regulations on capital inflow, Japan has also been increasing the variety of domestic financial instruments available to the offshore investor. Both the *gensaki* market and the newly established NCD market were opened to nonresidents in 1979.[21]

The impact of these changes, namely, the liberalized exchange regulations and expanded investment instruments, has been a dramatic increase in yen assets held by nonresident investors. Accordingly, in the five-and-a-half-year period ending September 1980, such assets had increased almost twelvefold and amounted to the equivalent of some $60 billion. Of particular note for Japan is that this growth occurred during a period of sharp gyrations in the value of the yen and the country's external position.

Of the substantial foreign capital finding its way into Japan in the early 1980s, some 60 percent is estimated to have gone into Japanese stocks and bonds. Among the major investors have been the OPEC oil producers, interested in diversifying away from the volatile and politically risky (post–Iranian asset freeze) U.S. dollar instruments. Nor are petrodollar holders the only outsiders attracted to yen investments. Surveys of the major securities houses in Japan indicate that institutional investors from the United States and Europe have been increasingly active buyers. Like the petrodollar investors, they seem to be expressing their confidence in the continued resilience of the Japanese economy to withstand future oil shocks as well as in the stability and/or further appreciation of the yen. In neither instance, however, is it reasonable to expect that the foreign investors will attempt management takeovers. Instead, they are far more likely to prefer leaving management control to the Japanese (whose ability is proven), content to reap dividends, capital gains, and currency appreciation. However, if this judgment proves incorrect and foreign investors do seek such management takeovers, the Japanese authorities can be expected to move to limit the extent to which outsiders can invest in local companies.

The second largest type of yen assets held by nonresidents has been bank deposits—free yen accounts at domestic Japanese banks, NCDs, and, especially, Euroyen deposits (yen deposits in banks outside Japan, typically in Europe, where deposit rates are not affected by artificial domestic interest-rate ceilings, withholding taxes, or reserve requirements). Most of the depositors are the monetary authorities of nations of the Middle East, Southeast Asia, and Latin America, again interested principally in diversifying their assets into a portfolio broader than the traditional bastion of the U.S. dollar. Indicative of this shift in official investment preference is that, as the decade of the 1980s began, an estimated 5 percent of total international reserves were carried in yen—a paltry percentage compared to the U.S. dollar's still dominant 75 percent and the German mark's 12 percent, but a significant increase from the less than 1 percent of the mid-1970s.[22]

Despite the variety of changes in the yen's role as an international currency, there is little likelihood in the foreseeable future (barring a major international financial collapse) that the dollar will be substantially dislodged from its premier global role. Any major expansion in the use of yen, particularly in a settlement or reserve function, is more likely to occur within the Asia-Pacific region. But it is important to stress that any formal currency linkage among Asia-Pacific nations similar to the European Monetary System but based on the yen is unlikely. A currency arrangement of the EMS type is realistic only for countries that are similar to one another in economic structure and stage of development and are mutually interdependent for the free movement of goods and capital. The members of the European system are economically homogeneous: the countries of the Asia-Pacific region are not. They range from industrial giants like Japan to predominantly subsistence economies such as Papua New Guinea. Likewise, the degree of interdependence in trade as well as financial transactions is far greater within the European community than it is within the Asia-Pacific region. Therefore, although an integrated monetary system is possible in Europe (and even there it suffers from major disruptions due to significant inflation differentials between members), a similar system is not feasible in the Asia-Pacific region.

However, what may be feasible is a yen bloc, reflecting the predominant economic role of Japan within the Asia-Pacific region, where it accounts for one-quarter of total intraregional trade, provides more than half of all private foreign direct investment and three-quarters of total regional official development assistance, and is represented by 74 of the top 100 indigenous banks.[23] Such a bloc will become more feasible if the world of the 1980s is subjected to a repeat of the dollar instability that characterized the late 1970s. In such an environment, it is a matter of economic self-preservation to defend one's own currency and, ultimately, economy. Accordingly, the linking of currencies to the yen through a basket formula becomes especially attractive, given the increasing use of the yen in the invoicing of Japanese regional trade, the continued growth of Japanese investment and official development assistance to Asia-Pacific nations, and the expanding role of the yen as an official reserve asset in the region. Indeed, as the 1980s began, many of the Asia-Pacific countries had already moved in the direction of establishing baskets, although the share of the yen in any of them is presumably still small relative to that of the dollar. Nevertheless, as further economic expansion in this most dynamic of geographic areas brings about further economic association with Japan, and as the yen assumes an ever greater intraregional role, its enlarged share in a growing number of currency baskets is highly probable—all of which points to its expanded role in an emerging multipolar international currency system.

Tokyo as an International Financial Center

There are two distinct aspects to the consideration of Tokyo as an international financial center, namely, as a yen-based center and as a dollar-based center. On the one hand, Tokyo has many of the essential prerequisites for an international financial center for both yen and dollars. It has a highly efficient communications and transportation network linking it with all the major financial and industrial centers of the world. Its interbank market is active (with an average net outstanding balance in recent years of more than 9 trillion yen, or some $40 billion),[24] as is its foreign exchange market (with daily turnover of spot, forward, and swap transactions of well over $2 billion).[25] It has a wide range of highly professional domestic financial institutions and bankers, and its foreign banking community is also well established, with sixty-four foreign banks operating a total of 186 branches and another eighty-five maintaining representative offices; in addition, sixty-five foreign securities firms are located in Japan, with three of them operating branches.[26] Finally, Tokyo is further advantaged by having sufficient financial backup services, such as accountants and attorneys, as well as a central bank whose officials are widely regarded as among the best in the world.

On the other hand, the nation's financial capital suffers from a variety of constraints that have restricted its evolution to date into either a yen-based or a dollar-based international financial center. For purposes of clarification, and because of the different factors affecting each, it will be useful to consider separately the potential for Tokyo as a yen-based and as a dollar-based center.

The constraints affecting the development of Tokyo as a yen-based international financial center, noted throughout the preceding pages, range from the lack of a truly market-oriented domestic financial system to the variety of officially imposed restrictions on the offshore yen lending activities of the Japanese banks and the internationalization of the yen. However, major progress continues to be made in the liberalization, flexibility, and sophistication of the domestic and international financial activities of the free world's second largest economy. The pace of this evolution has been slow and uneven, but its direction cannot be disputed. A major factor behind the gradual changes under way has been the force of outside events, particularly the development of Japan as a global economic power. Accordingly, in spite of resistance by authorities, the financial system has had no option but to follow pace, even if at a distance. Furthermore, this momentum will continue, propelled by such forces as the growing international activities of the Japanese banks, the expansion of the Samurai market, and the increased use of the yen as an international currency of settlement, investment, and reserve holding. One additional force is the Euroyen market.

As any currency becomes internationalized, one effect is for an offshore market in that currency to develop. For example, like the Eurodollar market, the Euroyen market comprises yen held outside Japan. According to unofficial estimates by informed sources at the Bank of Japan, the Euroyen market has doubled in size, from about $5 billion equivalent at the end of 1978 to some $10 billion equivalent by mid-1980. Despite its relatively small size (vis-à-vis the net $650 billion Eurodollar market), the rapid recent growth of the Euroyen market is a reflection of two factors: (1) the increased interest of nonresidents in holding yen assets and (2) the fact that as an offshore market it is free from the domestic controls that, despite the growth in nonresident bank deposits in Japan, still discourage many potential investors from maintaining yen accounts in Japan (namely, restrictions on most interest rates and the 20 percent withholding tax on interest payments). As long as such artificialities prevail, the Euroyen market will continue to thrive and expand.

Although its small size is unlikely to pose any near-term threat to Japanese domestic monetary policy, the potential for long-term destabilization cannot be ignored by the authorities, particularly in light of the complications that the ever-expanding Eurodollar market have caused U.S. monetary officials.

To counter this potentially destabilizing effect, it is in the interest of Japan to permit the further liberalization of domestic interest rates in order to provide nonresident investors with yields commensurate with those being offered in the offshore yen market. Within the confines of the Japanese system, this process will no doubt continue to be slow and convoluted. Besides the normal lethargy and reluctance for change inherent in any bureaucracy, there is the more pressing problem of the country's substantial fiscal dilemma, described in the first section of this chapter. Not only will its size keep the tax authorities at the Ministry of Finance from rushing to waive the interest withholding tax, but the growing debt-service burden continues to be the major obstacle in permitting the evolution of a truly free domestic financial market dictated by the forces of supply and demand.

Despite the strength of the forces pushing to maintain the present system, concerns over the implications of the growing offshore yen market are an equally compelling offsetting force. As even the authorities reluctantly admit, the yen's internationalization is proceeding irrespective of their preferences. In order to maintain as much control as it can over the situation, it is only logical that Japan seek to ensure that the nonresident yen market be centralized in Tokyo rather than, say, London.

The opening of both the *gensaki* and NCD markets to foreigners constitutes an important step in this direction, but these are only first steps. What the country needs is greater depth and breadth of money instruments that can be offered to offshore investors. The challenge from the Euroyen market suggests that the *gensaki* and NCD markets alone will not be sufficient for this purpose over the long haul. Similarly, although petrodollar holders are attracted to certain offerings of the Tokyo Stock Exchange, any viable money market needs more than the appeal of a few dozen attractive stock investments. Ultimately, what must be established in Tokyo are two free international money markets of the type existing in other major international centers like New York, namely, a market for national bonds (like the U.S. Treasury bills market) and a local-currency bankers' acceptance market.

If the dollar remains the major currency for financing Japanese imports in the 1980s, one of the major problems facing local importers will be to minimize the foreign exchange risk. Similarly, in their financing of ever-costly oil imports, one of the major challenges for the country's banks will be to ensure adequate supplies of dollars. This dual dilemma could be neatly solved by the combination of (1) a change in those Japanese banking regulations that presently discourage the use of yen in import financing and (2) a decision by OPEC to accept yen in payment for oil shipment. Even if both conditions are met—an optimistic scenario—Japan will not necessarily have solved its problems unless it can provide its trade partners with a sufficient range of yen money instruments by which they can effectively manage their yen funds. Again, the need for greater depth and breadth of the local market is obvious—both as a means of helping the country reduce its own external foreign currency liabilities and risks and of keeping the yen's internationalization within the monitoring capability of the Bank of Japan.

If the development of Tokyo as a yen-based international financial center appears, at least to the foreign observer, as inherently logical, so does the city's emergence as a dollar-based center. Indeed, one foreign author has even compared the latent potential of such a market to that of a Japanese sumo wrestler.[27] However, although the argument for becoming the world's major yen-based center has a certain appeal to even the most conservative officials (the yen is, after all, the Japanese currency), the argument that it should also develop into the major dollar center for Asia finds a far less sympathetic audience in Japanese officialdom.

One recurrent objection focuses on the potentially adverse impact of "leakages" from the offshore center on the management of the domestic money supply. Although offshore banking facilities are theoretically separable from domestic financial activities, the ending of Japanese foreign exchange rules is seen by the authorities as a factor weakening the "membrane" that they would like to maintain. Authorities are also concerned that the necessary incentives for attracting Eurodollar business, namely, an end to the withholding tax on interest earned and an appreciably reduced corporate income tax for financial institutions engaged in offshore dollar business, would complicate their already sizable fiscal problems. Finally, given Japan's sensitivities to how it is viewed abroad, particularly in its Asia-Pacific backyard, another difficulty frequently cited within Japan is how to establish a Tokyo dollar market without undermining the competition among Hong Kong and Singapore (and to a far lesser extent, Manila) to become *the* Asian offshore currency market.

These potential obstacles notwithstanding, there are equally compelling arguments on behalf of Tokyo's realizing its latent potential. It is of considerable importance, particularly in the Japanese context, that discussion on the subject was becoming more frequent in local financial circles in 1980.[28] It was reported that both the Ministry of Finance and the Bank of Japan were exploring the possible ramifications.[29]

The logic of Tokyo's role as a major international dollar-based financial center is at least three-pronged. First is Japan's economic size, business activity, and banking strength—all of which make it the economic center of the Asia-Pacific region and presumably should also make it the financial center, whether for dollars, yen, or any other freely convertible currency. Second is the relief that such a role would afford local banks as they seek to increase their supply of dollars to fund the country's mounting oil-import bills. This need would be drastically reduced if oil were even partially denominated in yen, but such a fundamental shift will occur only gradually. Even if it were to occur immediately, however, the Japanese need for dollars would not disappear, which points to the third factor supporting the evolution of Tokyo as a major dollar-based financial center.

This is the major alteration under way in the country's economic structure stemming from the two oil crises of the 1970s. Traditionally, the country has been able to finance its large invisibles deficit through buoyant export earnings. Indeed, it has persistently run a trade surplus every year since 1964.[30] However, the continuation of trade surpluses for Japan becomes increasingly uncertain, given the changing international environment reasonably likely in the 1980s, including (1) slower global economic growth, increased Western protectionism, and, hence, reduced world trade expansion; (2) higher oil prices, meaning steadily growing import costs for the non-oil-producing nations; (3) rising export competition from the "new Japans"; and (4) steadily upward pressure on the value of the yen, assuming that Japan continues to prove resilient in the new environment. Under these conditions, Japan will need a viable alternative to the traditional export surplus if it is to avoid major dislocations in its external accounts. That alternative is the invisibles earnings attendant on the country's becoming a major creditor nation, when more funds would flow in from offshore investments and loans than would flow out from such investments and loans within Japan. With projections of total offshore direct investments from Japan increasing fivefold to more than $155 billion by 1990,[31] one source of invisibles earnings will be dividends from these investments.

Another major source could be the offshore earnings of Japanese banks. The yen funding base of these institutions is relatively stable, but their ability to raise dollars remains problematic under present circumstances. Given the assumption that the dollar will remain the world's major currency for at least the foreseeable future, the dollar shortage of Japanese banks will be a continuing major constraint on their overseas activities. In short, the viability of offshore dollar lending requires the development of a secure source of dollars in Tokyo. If the current attraction of Japanese equities and bonds to OPEC dollar holders proves to be a long-term phenomenon, such inflows will contribute to the broadening of the local dollar base, whether as a source of funds for the Japanese banks' offshore lending or for their financing of dollar-denominated imports. However, petrodollars are potentially too volatile—being vulnerable to sudden reversals of sentiment and, hence, flight out of Japan as a result of a future oil crisis—to form the basis of a viable dollar-based funding source. Far more secure from Japan's point of view would be to develop a stable dollar deposit base in Tokyo, thereby guaranteeing local banks the supply of funds they need for offshore lending and trade financing. Without such a secure funding base, the nonyen activities of the Japanese banks will remain dependent upon such outside currency sources as the U.S. bankers' acceptance market or the London CD market, thereby remaining vulnerable to external factors like another "Japan rate" or capital (or credit) controls imposed by the United States to defend the dollar against a future crisis.

Conclusion

As a new decade opens, Japan's financial system is poised for further transition. The foremost aspect of the transition will be the acceptance by Japanese authorities that the system of controlled low interest rates has outlived its function of stimulating investment and, ultimately, growth and exports. The need for a more liberalized interest-rate mechanism has been necessitated by an external environment significantly altered by two major oil crises and the end of the system of fixed foreign exchange rates. For example, slower domestic growth means that businesses no longer depend as heavily as before on bank borrowings.[32] In addition, if government spending is to be a viable surrogate for corporate investment as a vehicle of economic growth, the deficit must be fundable in the open market through means other than the continued forced sales of low-yielding instruments to the nation's banks. Finally, managing the country's payments position through regulating the availability of credit is no longer sufficient to ensure a positive external balance; what is required by the new global environment is a system conducive to capital inflows and a strong currency.

Although factors such as these point to the obvious conclusion that the low-interest-rate policy is no longer tenable, the policy lingers and leaves Japan with a variety of distortions, most especially the inefficient allocation of financial resources. Nevertheless, the growing international economic role of Japan is bound to push the hesitant bureaucracy into accepting the continuing transition of the domestic financial system. As it unravels, the process will seem to the outside observer as painstakingly slow, even at times retrogressive. Within the Japanese context it is likely to proceed quite rapidly as the country struggles to adapt to the challenges of slower domestic and global economic growth together with increasingly costly oil imports. In the process, the already growing international activities of the Japanese financial institutions will continue to diversify. We can also anticipate that the yen will emerge as a major participant in an increasingly multipolar global currency system and that Tokyo will further mature into an international financial center. These developments will reflect the growing importance of Japan within the context of an increasingly vibrant Asia-Pacific region.

Notes

1. Besides the seventy-six banks—thirteen city banks (including the specialized foreign exchange banks and the Bank of Tokyo) and sixty-three regional banks—there are a variety of specialized institutions, such as the long-term lending banks (i.e., the three long-term credit banks plus the seven trust banks), a variety of financial institutions for small businesses (including the seventy-one *sogo* or mutual banks and some one thousand credit associations and cooperatives), as well as approximately eight thousand seven hundred agricultural, forestry, and fishery cooperatives. In addition, the Japanese financial system has six interbank money market dealers, more than forty insurance companies (divided equally between life and nonlife), more than two hundred and fifty securities companies, and a handful of housing finance companies. Besides these domestic banks, more than sixty foreign banks have branches in Japan, as do a handful of foreign securities houses.

2. The only other bank besides the long-term credit banks permitted to sell debentures is the Bank of Tokyo, one of the thirteen city banks. Because of its special charter as the country's principal foreign exchange bank, the Bank of Tokyo has been restricted in the number of domestic branches it

may maintain and is, therefore, allowed to raise local funds through the sale of its own bonds.

3. As discussed later, various financial institutions are required to purchase government bonds and hold them for a certain period of time. After the obligatory holding period, the banks may resell the bonds to the Bank of Japan (or to securities companies or private buyers). In repurchasing the bonds, the Bank of Japan does so on the basis of an allocation procedure among the various banks and in accordance with its management of the money supply. Although this sale and repurchase of government bonds may appear to be similar to the Federal Reserve's open-market operations, they really are quite different, as the bonds are purchased initially under duress. Instead, the system is more akin to the central bank's changing a particular bank's required reserve ratio. Otherwise, reserve levels per se play only a limited role in implementing Japanese monetary policy.

4. Gardner Ackley and Hiromitsu Ishi, "Fiscal, Monetary, and Related Policies," in *Asia's New Giant: How the Japanese Economy Works*, edited by Hugh Patrick and Henry Rosovsky (Washington, D.C.: Brookings Institution, 1976), p. 159. This chapter and that by Henry Wallich and Mable Wallich, "Banking and Finance," describe in excellent detail the crucial role and operation of the banking system in fostering the realization of postwar economic policies in Japan.

5. The percentage of average savings in Japan in relation to disposable income is among the highest in the world (more than 20 percent) due to a variety of factors, including the inherently conservative nature of the people; the limited availability of consumer and housing credit; aggressive savings campaigns conducted by the banks and postal savings institutions; corporate promotions of savings through payroll savings plans; the limited variety of alternative investment vehicles; relatively low individual tax rates (reflecting the relatively high proportion of government spending financed by borrowing); and the tax advantage of postal savings accounts discussed later in the text. However, I am not persuaded that the reason often cited for this high savings rate—the low level of social security equivalent benefits—is still valid, given the significant improvements in those benefits in recent years.

6. The relative importance of the consumer sector has grown. In the latter half of the 1960s it accounted for the same approximate share of the country's financial assets as the corporate sector—one-quarter. A decade later, the household share had increased to almost one-third, while that of the corporate sector had fallen to well below one-fifth. Calculated from the Bank of Japan, *Flow of Funds Accounts in Japan 1964–1971* (Tokyo: Ministry of Finance, 1972) and *Flow of Funds Accounts in Japan 1970–1977* (Tokyo: Ministry of Finance, 1978), and *Economic Statistics Monthly* (issues of May 1979 and May 1980).

7. Sanwa Bank, Ltd., "The Japanese Financial System in the 1980's," *Sanwa Economic Letter*, February 1980, p. 3.

8. Until recently, the minimum period during which the purchasing banks were obliged to hold the bonds was one year. By the end of the 1970s,

this system of national debt management had become particularly onerous for the banks in view of the higher interest rates and consequent deterioration in bond prices that characterized late 1979 and early 1980, when the average purchase price dropped to 85 percent of par. Accordingly, in mid-1980, the one-year holding period was reduced by the requirement that the bonds be held only until such time as they could be listed on the Securities Exchange, typically seven to nine months. However, as the rates offered by the government on its bonds remained below the market rates, the position of the banks was not materially improved by this policy change. Meanwhile, as a further palliative, the banks were permitted, as of the March 1980 accounting period, the option of valuing their government bond holdings at cost rather than market prices.

9. Sanwa Bank, "Japanese Financial System in the 1980's," p. 6.

10. Legally, interest earned on a depositor's postal savings accounts is tax-exempt provided the total amount of such deposits does not exceed 3 million yen. A similar exemption applies to bank deposits. However, although a bank depositor is required to sign a statement attesting to the aggregate amount of bank deposits, there is no such formal requirement for postal deposits. The result is that most Japanese avoid paying taxes on all interest earned on their postal deposits. In an effort to overcome this laxity, by 1984 each resident will be required to present a green identification card at banks and postal offices as a means of proving that deposits do not exceed the legal limit for the tax exemption.

11. Of this 2 trillion yen, the city banks accounted for about 55 percent, followed by the foreign banks (15 percent), regional banks (11 percent), long-term credit banks (9 percent), trust banks (6 percent), and other financial institutions (4 percent). Despite their initial opposition to the introduction of NCDs, the need to accommodate their customers forced the regional, long-term credit, and trust banks into offering the new financial instruments.

12. "Nomura Fires New Weapon in Bank War," *Asian Wall Street Journal*, 9 February 1980, p. 3.

13. Even these figures do not reflect the actual interest of the banks in expanding overseas, as the Ministry of Finance has deliberately restricted overseas expansion to one branch every three years and one representative office every year. In an effort to push the internationalization of the Japanese banks, the Ministry of Finance in early 1980 altered the regulations, permitting each city bank to open one overseas branch every two years and two overseas representative offices annually.

14. This expanded offshore direct investment results from a variety of factors that became increasingly acute during the latter half of the 1970s and that are likely to intensify in the years ahead: rising local land and labor costs; the need to guarantee offshore raw material resources, particularly energy, in which Japan is so poor; and a combination of international marketing considerations, particularly intensifying protectionism in the West, continued appreciation of the yen, and the growing competition from the "new Japans" of Asia.

15. The trend toward increasing offshore direct financing by Japanese companies is suggested by the figures. In 1979, for example, Japanese corporate issues abroad totaled almost $4.2 billion, having grown steadily from $1.9 billion in 1976, $2 billion in 1977, and $2.7 billion in 1978. Along with the value of issues, the number also increased appreciably, from 24 in 1977, to 95 in 1978, and to 145 in 1979. As a result, approximately one-tenth of all international corporate issues came from Japan in 1981. Besides interest-rate advantages, another major reason for this trend toward offshore funding by Japanese companies is their growing offshore direct investment and the concomitant need for foreign currency hedging. See Yoshio Terasawa, "Bigger and More Sophisticated," *Euromoney*, March 1980, p. 79.

16. As an illustration, by the end of the 1970s, of the more than $100 billion worth of public placements offered annually on the domestic bond market, corporate issues accounted for only about 5 percent; the vast majority of issues were various types of government bonds (more than 50 percent) and bank debentures (about 45 percent). Parenthetically, Samurai issues are the smallest factor, roughly 2 percent.

17. Yusuke Kashiwagi (president, Bank of Tokyo), "The Outlook for the Japanese Economy and the Internationalization of the Yen," speech before the Sydney (Australia) Chamber of Commerce, 31 July 1980.

18. Despite this twentyfold increase in the value of oil imports over the decade, the actual volume of oil imported has increased only about 25 percent.

19. Atsuko Chiba, "Seeking Dollars for the Lamps of Japan," *Institutional Investor*, May 1980, pp. 129–130.

20. Legislation eliminating the remaining restrictions on foreign exchange transactions except in times of emergency was implemented in late 1980.

21. Although these changes were unrelated to the defense of the yen, the easing of interest rates on government free yen accounts undertaken in early 1980 was a pure capital inducement measure that is likely to be reversed should upward pressure on the yen increase.

22. Despite the predominance of the U.S. dollar as the global reserve currency, its share of central bank reserve assets is considerably reduced (to about 50 percent) if we exclude both the OPEC countries (who are unique in view of their inordinately huge dollar receipts) and the other "Group of 10" countries (many of whom have involuntarily accumulated dollars in recent years through dollar defense intervention activities).

23. Based on total assets. "Asia-Pacific's Top 200," *Asian Banking*, June 1980, pp. 30–39.

24. Statistics Bureau, Prime Minister's Office, *Monthly Statistics of Japan*, April 1980.

25. This $2 billion-plus figure is a tenfold increase over the size of the market at the time of the 1973 oil crisis. Despite this dramatic increase, however, 90 percent of the local foreign exchange market is concentrated in dollar-yen transactions, reflecting the still-predominant role of the dollar in financing Japanese trade.

26. As of the end of fiscal year 1979 (31 March 1980).

27. Andreas R. Prindl, "The Latent Power of a Sumo Wrestler," *Euromoney*, March 1978, pp. ix–xiii.

28. For example, a much-publicized proposal to establish such a center was made in early 1980 by a former vice minister of finance and present adviser to the Industrial Bank of Japan, Takashi Hosomi.

29. "Forming 'Tokyo Dollar Market' Is Becoming Subject of Talk," *Japan Economic Journal*, 22 July 1980, p. 3.

30. On an f.o.b. basis.

31. Projection by Japan Economic Research Center, as reported in "Japanese Multinationals Covering the World with Investment," *Business Week*, 16 June 1980, p. 94.

32. Banks accounted in 1981 for 40 percent of total corporate funding, down from approximately 55–60 percent in the mid-1970s.

Glossary

Article 65. Banks are prohibited under Article 65 of the Japanese Securities and Exchange Law from engaging in the underwriting, dealing, brokerage, or distribution of negotiable securities, except public bonds and debentures. The underwriting business had been performed mainly by the banks before the war, but it was seen by the postwar U.S. occupation authorities as a major contributing factor to the prewar expansion of the interlocking relationships between banks and manufacturing entities (*zaibatsu*). Accordingly, in 1948, following the example of U.S. legislation, the "commercial" and "investment" functions of banks were separated.

Bankers' acceptance. A bankers' acceptance is an order in the form of a draft addressed by one party (drawer) to a bank (drawee) and accepted by that bank to pay a third party (payee) a certain sum at a specified future date. The underlying commercial transaction in such financing is typically between exporters and importers and amounts to much the same thing as obtaining a direct bank loan. However, the draft bearing the bank's commitment (or acceptance) becomes a marketable instrument that, when offered for sale by the bank at an appropriate discount from the face amount, is an attractive short-term investment for a corporation or other holder of temporary excess liquidity.

Currency basket. In order to reduce a currency's volatility (as when it is tied to such a widely fluctuating base as the U.S. dollar), a country often opts to peg its currency to a "basket" comprising the currencies of its major trading partners. The relative weight of each currency in the basket is a function of its respective country's trade share with the nation establishing the basket. In this way, the undue influence of one currency (e.g., the U.S. dollar) is reduced, thereby helping to ensure that the country's currency moves more in accordance with its relative economic strength (or weakness) vis-à-vis that of its major trading partners.

European Monetary System (EMS). Established in 1979 by the nine members of the European Economic Community, the EMS is aimed at creating a zone of monetary stability in Europe by imposing fixed (but adjustable) currency values free to fluctuate around narrow margins. If the currency of a member country reaches the upper or lower margin against another EMS currency, intervention by each country's monetary authorities to correct the position is compulsory. If pressure continues, the central rate can be changed, but only after consultations among the nine members. The EMS has also established a monetary unit of account (called the European Currency Unit) and international credit facilities for assisting members in balance-of-payments difficulty.

Gensaki. This term refers to the conditional purchase (or sale) of a government or corporate bond for a fixed period of time with a resale (or repurchase) agreement at a specified price.

Japan rate. In 1974, at the height of the first oil crisis, many Japanese banks found themselves in the position of trying to fund long-term dollar loans with short-term funds. Because Japan was initially so hard hit by the escalation in oil prices, many dollar holders, doubting the credit-worthiness of Japanese banks, forced them to pay a premium of up to 2 percent—dubbed the Japan rate—above the market for short-term funds.

Negotiable certificate of deposit (NCD). A certificate of deposit (CD) is a receipt for funds deposited with a bank, payable to the holder at some specified date (typically not less than thirty days after issuance, but presently in Japan not less than three months or more than six months) and bearing interest. A negotiable CD (NCD) may be transferred from one party to another by endorsement.

Samurai market. This is the term used for the Japanese market for long-term bonds denominated in yen and issued by foreign borrowers, most typically international agencies such as the World Bank and governments.

SDR-based CD: The Special Drawing Right (SDR) is a currency basket created by the IMF in 1968 to serve as a reserve asset supplementing the main international reserve currencies and gold. The SDR currency basket initially comprised sixteen currencies, but on January 1, 1981, it was simplified to five currencies (the U.S. dollar was 42 percent; the German Mark, 19 percent; and the pound sterling, French franc, and Japanese yen each 13 percent). Whereas a typical CD is denominated in only one currency, an SDR-based CD is made up of the currencies composing an SDR. As such, it affords both the depositor and issuer the opportunity to reduce the currency risk involved in buying or selling a CD denominated in only one foreign currency.

4
Cyclical and Macrostructural Issues in U.S.-Japan Economic Relations

Gary R. Saxonhouse

Introduction

This chapter seeks to assess the character of the macroeconomic interdependence between the Japanese and U.S. economies from 1965 to 1980. How has this interdependence contributed to the economic instability in both these economies and in these economies' relations with the world economy? Special attention has been given to the demand-management policies pursued in the United States and Japan over this period. What burdens have monetary and other demand-management policies in both countries placed on U.S.-Japanese economic interdependence even as other policy goals were being pursued, sometimes effectively and sometimes ineffectively? Given evolving financial and commercial institutions, will the current structure of U.S.-Japanese economic interdependence be maintained throughout the 1980s? To the extent that the present structure persists, what potential is there for successful, coordinated, countercyclical stabilization policies in the United States and Japan? What lessons may be culled from the experiences of the late 1970s? To the extent that financial, commercial, and political forces will considerably alter the character of interdependence, how may emerging institutions and relationships be shaped to mitigate the problems of the past? To this end, the first half of this chapter will review cyclical performances of the Japanese and U.S. economies. The second half will examine the possibilities for coordination.

This paper draws on work done in association with Eisuke Sakakibara.

Past Cyclical and Structural
Changes and Interdependence

Between 1967 and 1980, in only two years—1974 and 1975—did the Japanese and U.S. balances on current account fail to move in opposite directions. This negative relationship between changes in the flows of Japanese and U.S. current transactions, while varying greatly in size and scope, is not accidental. Japanese data identified $77 billion in current transactions between Japan and the United States in 1979; there is no larger overseas economic relationship in the world. The opposite and balancing movements in current international transactions of two of the major loci of economic activity in the world are potentially stabilizing influences on the world economy. At the same time these opposite movements can be a source of tremendous friction in bilateral U.S.-Japanese relations. This conflict between bilateral and global needs is most evident when it is recalled that 1974 and 1975, the so-called no-problem era in U.S.-Japanese relations, were the two worst years for the global economy since World War II!

The Late 1960s

The late 1960s saw for the first time in the postwar period the emergence of a strong Japanese merchandise-trade balance that overcame continuing Japanese deficits in invisible transactions and led to a persistent Japanese current-account surplus. At the same time that Japan was having its first sustained exposure to merchandise-trade surpluses, the U.S. economy, strained by the war in Vietnam, was experiencing its first merchandise-trade deficits in decades. Larger increases in Japanese exports to the United States helped alleviate some of the inflationary pressure created by war-related aggregate demand even as they also created the first postwar bilateral U.S.-Japanese merchandise surpluses for Japan.

In the late 1960s there also occurred the now unusual phenomenon of a major industrialized economy growing at a feverishly rapid pace even as it accumulated larger balance-on-current-account surpluses. Between 1966 and 1972, the Japanese current account improved by almost $7 billion while the Japanese gross national product grew at an unprecedented average annual rate of more than 10 percent. Such a coincidence could occur under the Bretton Woods system of fixed exchange rates.[1] An undervalued Japanese yen and an overvalued dollar led to enormous increases in the overseas markets for Japanese goods and fueled export-led rapid expan-

TABLE 4.1
Annual Balances in U.S. and Japanese Current International
Transactions ($ millions)

	Japan		United States	
	Current Balance	△ In Current Balance	Current Balance	△ In Current Balance
1967	-190	-	2,584	-
1968	1,048	△ 1,238	611	- △ 1,973
1969	2,119	△ 1,071	399	- △ 212
1970	1,970	- △ 149	2,340	△ 1,941
1971	5,797	△ 3,827	-1,419	- △ 3,759
1972	6,624	△ 827	-5,744	- △ 4,325
1973	-136	- △ 6,760	7,141	△ 12,885
1974	-4,693	- △ 4,557	4,851	- △ 2,290
1975	-682	△ 4,011	18,339	△ 13,488
1976	3,680	△ 2,998	4,605	- △ 13,734
1977	10,918	△ 7,238	-14,092	- △ 18,697
1978	16,534	△ 5,616	-14,300	- △ 200
1979	-8,754	- △ 25,288	-800	△ 13,500
1980	-13,250	- △ 4,500	+5,000	△ 5,800

Source: OECD, Main Economic Indicators; Bank of Japan, Balance of Payments Monthly; U.S. Department of Commerce, Survey of Current Business.

sion and restructuring of the Japanese economy. The disequilibrium in the yen-dollar exchange rate also led to more rapid structural adjustment in U.S. industries than was either desirable or necessary.

The responsibility for coping with the yen-dollar imbalance became a major issue in the early 1970s. Changing the exchange rate was a politically difficult step fraught with significant distributional consequences for both economies. Neither the Japanese nor the U.S. government wished to shoulder the political consequences of initiating such a step. Rather, many Japanese stressed that Japanese hard work and thrift and U.S. sloth, self-indulgence, and mismanagement had created this imbalance and that, if difficult steps were now necessary, it was the United States's turn for abstinence. In response, many Americans stressed the lack of appropriate formal access to the Japanese market and the special responsibilities faced by key-currency countries under the Bretton Woods system. Because the dollar was an international currency, it was argued, the United States must play a passive role in international exchange markets. Changes in par-values must be initiated by the United States's trading partners. It was argued that the problems faced by the dollar were the result of an obvious asymmetry in the potentially self-regulating character of the Bretton Woods system. Economies persistently in deficit in international transactions had to change the dollar-denominated external value of their currency. When a persistent deficit sapped an economy of its reserves, a dramatic exchange-rate adjustment was necessary. By contrast, surplus economies faced no such natural limit on their ability to maintain an overvalued exchange rate.[2]

In previous episodes of balance-of-payments surplus, Japanese demand management had allowed domestic inflation rather than exchange-rate adjustment to restore external equilibrium. In the context of the late 1960s and early 1970s, the size of the domestic inflation required to remove this surplus was as politically intolerable as exchange-rate adjustment itself. Rather, Japan sought to deal with a structurally caused external disequilibrium by changing the country's economic structure. This strategy relied on a selective liberalization of Japanese trade and capital controls to diminish Japan's surplus. These steps, although they had potentially long-term beneficial consequences, proved largely ineffective.

The New Economic Policy of 1971

Initially, it had been the policy of the Nixon administration to reduce war-engendered inflationary pressures by the use of tight fiscal and monetary policies. These policies restored the U.S. current account to surplus in 1970. A slow recovery in 1971; a renewed larger deficit in U.S. current international transactions; persistent outflows of short-term capital; continuing, if reduced, domestic inflationary pressures; and renewed strength in Japan's current-account position, together with a perception of ineffective Japanese government countermeasures, however, set the stage for stronger U.S. action.

On August 15, 1971, the U.S. government finally acted. The Nixon administration's New Economic Policy (NEP) was designed to return the U.S. economy to full utilization of resources even as it restored external equilibrium and smashed inflationary expectations. Japan, among other U.S. trading partners, was finally forced to allow the yen to appreciate relative to the dollar; U.S. monetary and fiscal policies turned expansionary; and wage-price controls were instituted.

The NEP had a mixed impact, both domestically and on U.S. trading partners. As might be expected, the impact on foreign exchange markets was immediate, and the currencies of most U.S. trading partners, including Japan's, floated in relationship to the dollar until new parities were established by the Smithsonian Agreement of December 1971. The U.S. economy, also strengthened in the quarter following the announcement of NEP and stimulated by tax cuts enacted in late 1971 and an expansive monetary policy, commenced on a vigorous expansion that renewed the inflationary expectations of the late 1960s. Only real trade flows proved slow to change in the desired direction in response to the changed environment of NEP. It took almost a year before the U.S. balance on current international transactions began to improve and the Japanese deficit began to decline. In 1972 the Japanese current-account surplus and the U.S. current-account deficit both reached record levels.

The Synchronized Boom of 1972–1973

For whatever reason, the Nixon administration took the imposition of wage-price controls in 1971 as providing license for pursuing unexpectedly expansionary policies in late 1971 and 1972. In all likelihood, these policies surprised Japanese and European policymakers. It was expected that U.S. monetary and fiscal policy would help ratify the devaluation by remaining relatively tight.[3] U.S. aggregate demand was expected to shrink in relative terms to make room for greater exports. In consequence, in order to cushion the expected deflationary impact of the NEP, Japan and the European countries adopted expansionary policies. What resulted, however, was the simultaneous expansion of the three prime loci of global economic activity.

As might have been expected, the global inflationary impact of this great expansion was felt first in the commodity markets. The immediate impact of the dollar devaluation on grains and other U.S. agricultural exports, followed by soaring global aggregate demand, fueled inflationary expectations and led to extraordinary price increases. During 1972 and the first half of 1973 there was a sharp change in the terms of trade between agricultural and nonagricultural products. This change helped finally push the U.S. current account into the black in 1973, even as domestic economic demand was also accelerating. These same changes in relative prices also re-inforced a sharp overall decline in the Japanese current account and in the U.S. deficit in merchandise trade with Japan.

The inflationary pressures generated by the massive increases in domestic and foreign demand for U.S. production had by late 1972 and early 1973 made continuance of wage-price controls all but im-possible, and they were lifted shortly after the start of Nixon's sec-ond term. This even triggered a massive flight of short-term capital from the United States and ruptured the par-values set by the Smith-sonian Agreement. The Bretton Woods international system was finally dead; the managed international floating of currencies that began in February 1973 is still with us.

The Oil Crisis

In late 1973, demand in the global economy was straining at capacity. Inflationary pressures in both the United States and Japan were extreme. In the United States, a depreciating currency was fueling inflationary pressures, while in Japan, the continuing appre-ciation of the yen was helping to partially alleviate such pressures. From the perspective of most of the world's economies, OPEC's quadrupling of crude oil prices and the Arab oil embargo could not have come at a worse time. With demand straining capacity, the oil embargo effectively removed a portion of capacity in the United States, Japan, and other industrialized countries. With inflationary expectations already exaggerated for reasons having nothing to do with oil, this temporary removal of capacity and the subsequent sharp decline in the terms of trade of non-oil-producing economies made matters still worse.

In both Japan and the United States, the immediate aftermath of the oil crisis was an inflationary binge without parallel for the pre-ceding twenty-five years. In Japan, inflationary expectations were accelerated by the sharp depreciation of the yen and ultimately became so severe that widespread panic buying and hoarding en-sued. Given the tight labor market and relatively liquid corporate positions that prevailed at the onset of the oil crisis, both Japanese and U.S. employers granted large increases in wages that also mag-nified inflationary pressures.

The Massive Global Economic Recession

Although the initial impact of the sharp deterioration in the terms of trade of Japan and the United States and other non-oil-exporting economies vis-à-vis OPEC was to heighten inflationary expecta-tions, before long the very size of the financial losses implied by the new price of oil proved highly deflationary. In 1974, in Japan and Europe and to a lesser extent in the United States, current accounts became more negative than before. When the fiscal drag from the foreign sector combined with the tight fiscal and monetary policies being almost universally pursued to brake the enormous buildup in inflationary pressure that antedated the oil price increases, the result was the most serious global recession of the postwar period. In the United States, GNP growth rates were negative for a full five quarters, and in Japan, although growth was sharply negative for only two quarters, the barely positive growth that followed was far from the average annual increases of 10 percent so characteristic of the period 1960–1973.

It should be emphasized that it was not simply the foreign and government sectors that were responsible for the recession in Japan and the United States. The household and even the corporate sector in both economies sharply increased their rates of savings out of disposable income, thus diminishing the force of aggregate demand in both economies. This increase in savings was larger and persisted longer in Japan than in the United States. Savings increased cyclically in Japan because the inflation of 1973 and 1974 severely diminished the real value of the large liquid assets Japanese households maintained in savings accounts whose interest rates were fixed and did not respond to changes in inflationary expectations, and because of the grave uncertainties that the oil crisis had engendered regarding the future of the international economic order.

Unsynchronized Recovery

Once the full scope of the global recession had become entirely clear, and with inflationary pressures subsiding and the balances of current and capital transactions improving dramatically for both Japan and the United States, both governments began to give a higher priority to steps designed to promote economic recovery. In 1975 both governments adopted relatively expansionary fiscal policies. In Japan and the United States, personal tax rates were cut to compensate for the increase in the effective real rate of taxation that resulted when inflation pushed households into higher tax brackets than were justified by the increases in their real income. In the United States a liberalized investment tax credit was also instituted. In both countries, there were also significant increases in 1975 in public expenditures.

Both the Japanese and the U.S. recovery helped renew relatively rapid economic growth in 1976, but the international elements of this recovery proved to be dramatically different. For the United

States, there was a renewed vigorous increase in private domestic demand. The rate of household savings out of household income fell from 7.9 percent in 1975 to 5.9 percent in 1976, indicating a healthy increase in consumption expenditures. Complementing this increase in household expenditure, real private investment increased by 9.5 percent. By contrast, in Japan, household savings remained at a very high 22.5 percent, while investment remained stagnant.

Unlike in Japan, which added to capital stock in the early 1970s on the expectation of continuing real rates of growth in GNP of better than 10 percent, U.S. visions were much more modest. In consequence, in the period after the oil crisis, U.S. corporations, unlike their Japanese counterparts, were not as troubled by the overhang of large amounts of underutilized capacity and heavy debt, both of which greatly inhibited new investment. Similarly, the U.S. household, unlike its Japanese counterpart, relatively speaking, did not have large liquid assets but did nonetheless have access to a much wider variety of financial instruments by which it could maintain the real value of such assets. In consequence, less of an increase over normal saving was needed for the U.S. household to repair its balance sheet after the inflationary shocks of the mid-1970s.

Stagnant domestic demand, and the depreciation of the yen that followed the decline in Japanese terms of trade, resulted in 1976 in a continued dramatic improvement in the Japanese current account. Despite almost completely stagnant private demand, a 22.5 percent increase in overseas demand for Japanese products fed a renewed rapid 6.5 percent increase in the Japanese GNP. By contrast, buoyant U.S. domestic demand and the appreciation of the dollar of the oil-producing United States relative to the currencies of its major trading partners led to a negligible increase in export volume and a huge increase in imports. The very dissimilar structures of the U.S. and Japanese recovery from the global recession led to a reemergence of a large U.S. merchandise-trade deficit with Japan. By July 1976, the no-problem era in U.S.-Japanese economic relations was dead. Its short life was only a little better than two years.[4]

Despite the strong resurgence of domestic demand in the United States in 1976, unemployment remained at better than 7 percent of the total labor force, and it was generally believed that considerable slack remained in the United States economy. What was true for the United States was also assumed to be true for the other major industrialized economies.

Unemployment in all the industrialized economies in 1976 was much higher than had been characteristic of the early 1970s, and indeed, it was higher than had been characteristic for most of the

TABLE 4.2
Prices in Japan and the United States

	Changes in the GNP Deflator		Wholesale Price Index		Consumer Price Index	
			(1970=100)		(1970=100)	
	U.S.	Japan	U.S.	Japan	U.S.	Japan
1970	5.4%	6.7%	100.0	100.0	100.0	100.0
1971	5.1	4.7	103.3	99.2	104.3	106.0
1972	4.1	4.7	107.9	100.0	107.7	110.9
1973	5.8	10.9	122.0	115.8	114.4	124.0
1974	9.7	20.1	145.0	152.2	127.0	154.1
1975	9.6	8.6	158.4	156.7	138.6	172.4
1976	5.2	5.6	165.8	164.6	146.6	188.6
1977	6.0	5.6	175.9	167.7	156.1	203.6
1978	7.3	3.9	189.6	163.5	168.0	211.4
1979	8.8	2.0	213.3	175.4	186.9	219.0
1980	9.5	2.0	N.A.	N.A.	N.A.	N.A.

Source: Bank of Japan, Statistics Bureau, Kokusai hikaku tokei 1980,
pp. 25-29, 80-84.

TABLE 4.3
Growth Rates in Real GNP in the United States, Japan, and
West Germany (1967-1980)

	U.S.	Japan	West Germany
1967	2.7%	12.5%	-0.1%
1968	4.4	14.0	6.5
1969	2.6	12.2	7.9
1970	-0.3	11.8	5.9
1971	3.0	5.2	3.3
1972	5.7	9.5	3.6
1973	5.5	10.0	4.9
1974	-1.4	-0.5	0.4
1975	-1.3	1.4	-1.8
1976	5.9	6.5	5.3
1977	5.3	5.4	2.6
1978	4.4	6.0	3.5
1979	2.3	6.0	4.4
1980	-0.7	5.0	1.8

Source: Bank of Japan, Statistics Bureau, Kokusai hikaku tokei 1980,
pp. 25-26.

TABLE 4.4
Growth in Export and Import Volumes in Japan and the United States

	United States		Japan	
	Growth in Export Volume	Growth in Import Volume	Growth in Export Volume	Growth in Import Volume
1971	-1.2%	8.6%	19.5%	-3.4%
1972	9.7	13.4	6.9	13.1
1973	23.0	6.2	5.9	28.3
1974	9.0	-3.4	18.0	-5.5
1975	-2.1	-11.2	0.3	-11.5
1976	3.4	21.9	22.0	8.4
1977	0.2	10.3	8.9	2.4
1978	11.9	10.1	1.1	7.0
1979	11.2	10.2	-1.1	10.8

Source: Bank of Japan, Statistics Department, Keizai tokei geppo;
U.S. Department of Commerce, Survey of Current Business.

TABLE 4.5
U.S.-Japan Bilateral Merchandise Trade Balance ($ billion)

	U.S. Survey of Current Business Data	Japan Balance of Payments Monthly Data
1970	1.2	1.5
1971	3.2	3.4
1972	4.2	4.0
1973	1.4	1.3
1974	1.6	1.9
1975	1.7	1.0
1976	5.4	5.5
1977	8.0	8.6
1978	11.6	10.7
1979	8.6	7.6
1980	9.9	N.A.

TABLE 4.6
Unemployment Rates in Major Industrialized Economies (% of Labor Force)

	1970	1971	1972	1973	1974	1975	1976	1977	1978
United States	4.9	5.9	5.6	4.9	5.6	8.5	7.7	7.0	6.0
Japan	1.2	1.2	1.4	1.3	1.4	1.9	2.0	2.0	2.2
United Kingdom	2.6	3.4	3.7	2.6	2.6	3.9	5.3	5.7	5.7
West Germany	0.7	0.9	1.1	1.3	2.6	4.7	4.6	4.5	4.4
Italy	3.2	3.2	3.7	3.5	2.9	3.3	3.7	7.2	7.2

Source: Bank of Japan, Statistics Bureau, Kokusai hikaku tokei 1980, p. 130.

period since 1950. In addition to the persistence of politically unacceptable high unemployment rates, there was also the widespread fear that the deflationary impact of the large OPEC balance-of-current-account surplus with the major market-oriented industrialized economies would trigger another recession in the oil-consuming countries. In order to prevent this from happening, it was widely suggested that still more expansionary programs were required.[5]

The proposed expansionary programs were to be carefully targeted. Although both the declines in gross national product and the subsequent resumption in growth were quite similar, there were great differences among the industrialized economies in rates of domestic inflation and in the condition of their external accounts. These large differential rates of domestic inflation led to wide fluctuations in exchange rates. In order to promote both economic growth and price stability, it was suggested in 1976 that as Germany, Japan, and the United States had strong economies with current accounts in surplus or near balance and with relatively low inflation rates, these economies should further expand domestic demand faster than GNP. It was expected that countries such as Canada, France, Italy, and the United Kingdom, which at that time were experiencing current-account deficits and higher inflation rates, would not stimulate domestic demand but would rather allow their recoveries to be pulled along by an increase in their exports to the so-called three locomotive economies.

Unfortunately, this analysis did not entirely comprehend the full

TABLE 4.7
Balance on Current Account of Major World Groupings ($ billion)

	OECD	OPEC	Non-Oil Developing Countries	Other
1970	6.8	-0.5	-8.1	-2.9
1971	9.9	0.3	-9.8	-2.7
1972	7.8	1.3	-5.2	-1.9
1973	9.9	7.7	-6.2	-3.5
1974	-27.5	59.5	-23.3	-9.7
1975	-0.3	27.1	-37.5	-18.5
1976	-19.1	36.6	-25.5	-13.0
1977	-26.3	29.1	-23.0	-8.7
1978	6.4	5.9	-35.0	-10.4
1979	-35.0	68.0	-37.0	-3.0
1980	-73.0	116.0	-50.0	-5.0

Source: Organisation for Economic Co-operation and Development, Economic Outlook, 1981.

extent of the change in the U.S. external position. The U.S. current account had been deteriorating rapidly throughout 1976, so much so that by the latter half of the year the current account was negative. Thus, when the new Carter administration, taking office with a firm commitment to lower unemployment, embraced the locomotive approach, a major premise for the U.S. role as a locomotive had already dissolved. Of course, this problem became all the more serious when West Germany and Japan did not take up their designated roles as the other two locomotives in the global stabilization plan. In consequence, the U.S. economy sustained an enormous balance-on-current-account deficit, while Japan, its leading overseas trading partner, experienced an unprecedentedly large current trading-account surplus.

This Japanese surplus, the result of the interaction of the cautious policies of the Japanese government and Japanese households and businesses with the more stimulative actions of the U.S. government, put enormous pressure on the Japanese yen. During 1977 the yen appreciated by 25 percent. Unfortunately, neither this very large yen appreciation, nor the special public work programs the Japanese government initiated, nor the attendant, enormous Japanese government deficits had much impact on Japan's external position during 1977 or most of 1978. The Japanese current-account surplus increased by another $6 billion in 1978, while the U.S. current account showed no improvement at all.

The large disequilibrium of Japan's external sector during 1977 and 1978 was hardly surprising. During much of the period between 1960 and 1973, the very large savings of the Japanese household sector was absorbed by the almost equally large borrowing of the Japanese corporate sector. After 1973, the Japanese household savings rate increased. By contrast, Japanese corporate investment and therefore the demand for private savings experienced a sharp decline. Because available Japanese household savings were an unprecedentedly large share of GNP, even a Japanese government deficit, which was itself an unprecedentedly large share of GNP, proved noninflationary. Given the very high household savings and the very low corporate investment, a still larger government deficit, probably far in excess of the politically unacceptable 40 percent deficit on central government expenditures, would have been required for external equilibrium to have been achieved in 1978.

Government demand-management policies were inadequate during 1977 and 1978; developments in the foreign exchange market also proved slow to have an impact on the Japanese current account. The effective appreciation of the yen by 45 percent during 1977 and 1978 had a relatively quick effect on export and import volumes, but as these export volumes were now being sold at higher dollar prices abroad and as imports were at the same time cheaper in dollars, it was only at the very end of 1978 that the changes in trade flows were large enough to have the desired impact.

The Second Oil Crisis

In the last quarter of 1978 and the first quarter of 1979, domestic demand finally recovered sufficiently to bring the Japanese current account on international transactions into balance. The rapid growth in consumption expenditures, and particularly in business fixed investment, at this time went hand in hand with, even if it was not caused primarily by, the sharp decline in the Japanese rate of inflation due to the external appreciation of the yen. In the end it was only a change in the behavior of Japan's private sector, induced by higher profit margins, lower inventory, and higher capacity-utilization rate and by the more stable planning environment brought on by a markedly lower rate of inflation, that ended Japan's external disequilibrium. Only at the end of 1979 did Japanese businesses and households finally emerge from the lingering influence of the first oil shock. For example, it was only at this time

TABLE 4.8
Financial Balances by Sector in Japan (as a % of GNP)

Cal- endar Year	Public Sector	Corporate Business Sector	Personal Sector	Rest of the World Sector
1972	-2.6	-6.8	11.6	-2.2
1973	-2.8	-6.2	8.9	0.2
1974	-3.8	-4.6	7.7	1.0
1975	-7.3	-3.6	10.8	0.1
1976	-7.5	-4.0	11.5	-0.6
1977	-7.2	-2.6	11.1	-1.5
1978	-9.0	-1.0	11.0	-1.7
1979	-7.8	-3.0	9.1	0.9

Source: Bank of Japan, Keizai tokei geppo (various issues).

that Japanese nonresidential, nongovernment real investment recovered to the levels it had reached in 1973.

Ironically, just at the time that Japan had fully adjusted to the first oil shock, the second oil shock occurred. The successful Iranian Revolution in January 1979 led to renewed tightening of the oil market and a substantial increase in world oil prices. In the fifteen months following the Iranian Revolution world oil prices increased from $13.7 a barrel to $31.8 a barrel. In 1980, spot market prices reached $42. The impact of the second oil shock on the Japanese economy has been remarkably different from that of the first shock. The second oil shock came at a time when neither Japan nor the global economy was suffering from the burden of excess aggregate demand.

Given the absence of strong inflationary expectations in 1979 — the fruit of five years of cautious monetary and fiscal policies — the large increases in the price of oil had a relatively modest impact on the Japanese economy. Unlike in 1974, the effective loss of two or three percentage points of GNP due to oil price increases in 1979 and in 1980 did not lead to an immediate dramatic decline in either Japanese investment or Japanese consumption expenditure. Indeed, the absence of inflationary expectations also made possible, at the same time, relatively modest wage demands by Japan's workers.

The renewed sharp deterioration in Japan's terms of trade that began in 1979 came just at the time when the dramatic revival in

TABLE 4.9
Japanese Gross Private Non-Residential Investment

billion yen, 1970 prices		quarterly data at annual rates		
1969	13,293	1978	1Q	17,393
1970	15,430	1978	2Q	17,768
1971	15,179	1978	3Q	18,082
1972	15,730	1978	4Q	19,690
1973	18,656	1979	1Q	20,760
1974	17,527	1979	2Q	21,064
1975	16,326	1979	3Q	21,419
1976	16,559	1979	4Q	21,795
1977	17,070	1980	1Q	22,109

Source: Economic Planning Agency, Kokumin shotoku nempo.

Japan's private domestic demand, the earlier large appreciation of the yen, the U.S. government's emergency dollar-support programs, and even the Japanese government's emergency import programs were having a major impact on the Japanese current account. In consequence, during 1979, the Japanese yen depreciated by more than 25 percent, and there was an unprecedented deterioration in the Japanese current account on international transactions of more than $25 billion. This left Japan with a $9 billion deficit. This sharp depreciation of the yen resulted in a renewed growth in Japan's exports. The volume of Japanese exports, which had been stagnant since mid-1977, began increasing once again in the second quarter of 1979 and continued to grow through 1980.

While Japan in 1979 and 1980 benefited from its decision in 1977 not to pursue an aggressive expansion of its economy, the United States at the same time suffered the consequences of having pursued a rather different strategy. From 1970 through 1977, the U.S. economy had out-performed Japan on managing inflation. The over-expansion of the Japanese economy in 1973 created serious problems for economic managers in the mid-1970s. Since 1977 relative Japanese and U.S. performances have been quite different. The slack in the Japanese economy helped dampen inflationary expectations in Japan after 1976. By contrast, the rapid growth in U.S. domestic demand during 1977 and the first half of 1978 rekindled inflationary expectations. The massive deterioration of the current account of the balance of payments and the failure of the other industrial economies to take effective expansion steps led the U.S. government to recognize that it must give new priority to fighting infla-

TABLE 4.10
Recent Price Developments in Japan and the United States

	1977	1978	1979	1979 Q. 2	1979 Q. 3	1979 Q. 4	1980 Q. 1	1980 Q. 2
Japan Implicit GNP Deflator	5.6	3.9	2.0	3.0	−2.9	3.6	−3.5	3.6
U.S. Implicit GNP Deflator	6.0	7.3	8.9	9.3	8.5	8.3	9.5	10.4
Japan Implicit Private Consumption Deflator	7.2	4.2	3.1	2.0	0.6	1.1	1.5	3.0
U.S. Implicit Private Consumption Deflator	5.7	6.8	8.9	9.2	9.8	9.8	12.4	10.0
Japan Implicit Import Price Deflator	−3.6	−16.2	22.1	10.7	12.6	14.4	11.8	−2.4
U.S. Implicit Import Price Deflator	9.1	5.3	15.4	19.0	35.0	28.0	32.9	8.5

Source: U.S. Department of Commerce, Survey of Current Business; Bank of Japan, Keizai tokei geppo.

tion. This new resolve resulted in plans for a tighter fiscal policy, a significant tightening in monetary policy, and finally the dollar-support, anti-inflationary program of November 1978.

Unfortunately, before any of these programs could have much lasting impact on inflationary expectations, the second oil crisis began. The dramatic increase in oil prices was imposed on an economy with relatively little slack and continuing high inflationary expectations. And unlike in Japan, this increase in energy prices quickly spread to intermediate and finished goods and resulted in a substantial acceleration in inflation.

Despite the increasingly tight management of U.S. monetary and fiscal policy, the U.S. economy continued to expand for most of 1979, finishing in more robust health than at the beginning of the year. Growth in the economy continued during 1979 because consumption expenditure, fed by a decline in the personal savings rate, continued to grow; because high interest rates proved less effective than previously in restraining demand; and because of the very strong U.S. export performance.

During 1978–1979, U.S. external sector performance was a mirror image of the Japanese performance. The earlier substantial depreciation of the dollar finally had its impact on U.S. international trade in goods and services. This exchange-rate-induced improvement was supported during 1979 by tighter demand-management policies that weakened U.S. demand for imports while it freed resources for export.

Despite excellent Japanese and poor U.S. performance on inflation, Japanese trade performance deteriorated during much of late 1978 and through most of 1979, while U.S. trade performance improved. The second oil shock, unlike the first, did not impose parallel performance on Japan and the United States. We should also note that despite the improvement in the U.S. current account and the deterioration of the Japanese current account during 1979 and 1980, the bilateral merchandise-trade deficit the United States had with Japan was relatively unaffected.

Nonsynchronization and the Coordination of Macroeconomic Policy: an Evaluation

Linked Econometric Models

Evaluating the effectiveness of demand-management policies in Japan and the United States and assessing the need for and the possibility of coordinated countercyclical stabilization policy present numerous complex issues. Inevitably, both the evaluation of past demand-management policies and the consideration of past bilateral conflict are profoundly influenced by the general analytical framework held appropriate as well as that framework's particular empirical implementation.

In a general way, the United States is long past the era when a very small foreign sector, the absence of overseas dependence on critical raw materials and manufactures, and even the lack of an international capital market permitted the framing of macroeconomic policy without any regard to foreign consequences or feedback.[6]

With growing interdependence, nations that wish to formulate optimal economic policies must measure the use of any important policy instrument against the imperatives of all important policy targets.[7] This, in turn, implies the coordination of economic policies among nations, with a corresponding reduction in national sovereignty. From this perspective, if public housing policy in Japan has an appreciable influence on the price of wheat in the United States, then the legitimate interest of the United States in the framing of such policy must be considered.

Coordination of domestic economic policies in the interest of international economic stability requires a quantitative understanding of the relationships being stabilized. Until the turbulent international economic conditions of the late 1960s and early 1970s, it was not possible even to make a pretense of such quantitative understanding. Although working econometric models of national economies had been available since the early 1950s, in all these models the world beyond the domestic economy was treated as a noninteractive part of the environment. These models could not assess the specific consequences for one country of a policy initiated in some other country.

More recently a large number of internationally linked econometric systems purporting to capture most, if not all, of the major means by which economic disturbances are transmitted from one country to another have been developed. The possibility of an empirically based, internationally coordinated macroeconomic policy would appear to be tantalizingly close.[8] For example, with the software available from this econometric work, it is possible to examine what might have happened to the major industrialized countries and other actors in the global economy had the "three locomotive" coordinated fiscal and monetary policies been fully adopted.

Most of the extensive simulation work that has been done with linked world econometric models does suggest that at least some of the problems the U.S. and the world economy faced in the late 1970s might have been alleviated had synchronized, coordinated fiscal and monetary policies been pursued by the U.S., Japanese, and German governments. Such simulation work suggests that further expansion and possibly greater stability for the world economy could have been achieved during the period following 1976 at the possible cost of additional inflation for Germany and Japan. According to this econometric work, had the locomotive been run as planned, it would have had the strength to exert real pull on other economies.[9]

The Empirical Underpinnings of Coordination

Whether simulation work actually vindicates the locomotive approach and provides the basis for future coordination of macroeconomic policy remains a complex issue that needs to be discussed from a variety of perspectives. For example, how much information is there in the large-scale econometric models that are the intellectual underpinnings of an internationally coordinated macroeconomic policy? For all their complexity, such models, by and large, do not provide relatively accurate forecasts and simulations.[10] It is always possible to rationalize poor forecasts on the grounds of lack of accurate information on policy variables, but large-scale econometric models have been subjected to more fundamental criticism.[11]

Much of these discussions finally boils down to whether the global economy is viewed as primarily deterministic or primarily stochastic. A deterministic system suggests that policymakers know most relevant details of economic structure and therefore have the opportunity to successfully control the system. Most discussions of fine tuning or international coordination of demand-management policies are carried out under this assumption. Increasing numbers of economists and mathematical statisticians are beginning to question whether the state of knowledge in economics warrants the use of such deterministic models. There are so many aspects of the economic system that are not now known or that cannot be pinned down in sensible causal relationships. Under this view, the economic system is largely stochastic. As early as the 1930s, the Nobel Prize–winning economist Ragnar Frisch hypothesized that it is these unknown disturbances that generate economic cycles. By definition, these unknown disturbances cannot be predicted unless future disturbances are in some way related to present and past disturbances.

If these disturbances are correlated in some regular fashion, predictions can be generated, and to that degree the economic system can be manipulated. The degree of accuracy of forecast or feasibility for control, however, depends upon the degree of correlation of these disturbances. Research conducted for the Japan-U.S. Economic Relations Group suggests that the extent of control for the yen-dollar exchange rate, the U.S. and Japanese trade balances, and Japanese and U.S. production is relatively limited.[12] In other words, the movement of the exchange rate, the trade balance, and Japanese and U.S. production are largely dominated by disturbances that are relatively difficult to predict, and attempts to control them within a reasonable margin of error run a high risk of failure. Simulations conducted in the course of this research indicate that although the complete coordination of monetary policy and/or complete synchronization of cycles does dampen somewhat fluctuations in the exchange rates and trade balances, substantial swings in these variables are inevitable as long as the current free regime of international transactions is maintained.

The Perverse Consequences of Synchronization

It is not simply that the coordination of international macroeconomic policy is likely to be ineffective. Rather, there is the danger that attempts at such coordination may have perverse results. If coordination is understood to be movement in tandem of the Japanese, U.S., and possibly the West German economies in order to mitigate trade imbalances and exchange-rate fluctuations, such coordination might run the risk of destabilizing the rest of the world economy. A stable world economy rests on the absence of parallel movements in the major elements of the world economy. Notwithstanding the increasing interdependence of national economies, the natural transmission mechanism of economic shocks from one country to another will quickly dampen large disturbances emanating from any one country. By contrast, a growing replacement of internationally decentralized demand management by synchronized policies might work to enhance such shocks.[13]

It is a matter of debate whether suggesting parallel movements in the U.S., Japanese, and West German economies might further synchronize or de-synchronize the global economy. If the deflationary impact of a large increase in the nominal value of OPEC exports is met by an expansion of U.S., Japanese, and German domestic demand, then from a global perspective that includes OPEC, three locomotives running down the track might be thought of as globally stabilizing behavior. Of course, this was the perspective from which the locomotive policy was framed in 1976. As has been discussed earlier, this perspective did not fully incorporate the strength of underlying expectations still present in the major industrialized economies. The OPEC price increase, like all such large price increases, has had a three-pronged impact. At one level, such increases are deflationary because they reduce real income and hence demand. At another level, by rendering a portion of production capacity economically obsolete, they reduce supply as well as demand.[14] Finally, and only loosely related to their other supply-and-demand effects, OPEC price increases can significantly alter expectations regarding the underlying rate of price inflation. In the context of the original debate regarding the appropriateness of a locomotive approach to global stabilization in 1976–1977, the character of expectations regarding the underlying rate of inflation, and how the unknown but possible inadequacy of effective supply might affect such expectations, could be only dimly understood.

The unpredictable and possibly uncontrollable character of the world economic system seems to stem in some measure from the

effects and the erratic nature of expectations held by economic decision makers, whether in the household, the corporation, or the government. The influence of such expectations has been particularly
conspicuous in foreign exchange markets. Expectations had been
relatively stable in the 1950s and 1960s when the world trade and
financial system was more solidly anchored. As the Bretton Woods
system began to exhibit weaknesses in the late 1960s and early
1970s, the changing expectations of private transactors began to
play a more central role. Such expectations became crucial in the
determination of exchange rates, but they also played a more and
more important role in trade and production decisions as well.

Private transactors closely watch the moves of policy authorities
and form their expectations on the basis of the authorities' expected
moves and other information available to them. To this extent, both
fiscal and monetary policies can have profound effects on the
economy. It may be difficult, however, to assess the impact of these
policies because it is possible that they operate mainly through expectations and not through the traditional channels specified by
demand-oriented econometric models. There are not yet analytical
frameworks that adequately capture the generation and aggregate
economic role of such expectations.[15] Substantively, all that can be
done at this stage is to make some conjectures about the effects of
policies on expectations and to draw some qualitative implications.
The poor predictive performance of large-scale econometric models
stems at least partially from their failure to incorporate expectations
in an appropriate manner.

Expectational elements may make the global economic system
relatively unpredictable and uncontrollable, but this does not
necessarily imply that policies are unimportant. On the contrary, as
the previous analysis indicates, they may have been quite instru-
mental in generating the current acceleration in world inflation. Expansionary monetary and fiscal policies in the United States during
the 1976–1979 period may have generated expectations of permanent price inflation, which have been difficult to counteract by the
subsequent tightening of policies. The experiences of the United
Kingdom and Italy subsequent to the expansionary monetary and
fiscal policies they employed during 1974 and 1975 are also perti-
nent. By contrast, the cautious policies of Japan and Germany immediately following the first oil crisis, although delaying recovery,
did successfully damp inflationary expectations and seem to have
laid the groundwork for subsequent solid economic growth. Ever
since the first oil shock, inflation has become a major concern for all
economic decision makers, and expectations regarding inflation

have become a prime determinant of the character of the economic
system. Policies not placing a major emphasis on this aspect of the
system seem ultimately ineffective in one way or another. Traditional concern for unemployment remains most important, but
unless policies succeed in damping price expectations, they do not
appear to be effective in reducing unemployment. Synchronization
of fiscal and monetary policies among the major industrialized economies surely runs the risk of frustrating this objective.

Economic Diplomacy for Decentralized Economies

Even if enhancing the international business cycle were not a consideration, there are other reasons why even the very process of
coordination, let alone synchronization, might turn out to be destabilizing. In the absence of a shared view of economic reality — or
even with a shared view but in the absence of shared wishes with
respect to inflation, unemployment, exchange-rate movements, and
trade balances — international macroeconomic policy coordination
can quickly become the subject of high-level, and possibly high-
profile, diplomatic initiatives. At best, institutionalizing regular international consultations on macroeconomic policy can prevent
miscalculations of the sort that occurred in late 1971 and 1972,
when Tokyo apparently did not appreciate the extent to which
Washington was pursuing expansionary policies. Most likely,
however, given the continuing asymmetries in economic
diplomatic leverage, coordination could quickly lead to U.S.
pressure on Japan to change its macroeconomic policies. From the
Council on International Economic Policy through the more recent
economic summitry there is ample evidence that this is a habitual
outcome.

There is nothing illegitimate about resolving policy differences
among nations facing common problems with a measure of pressure. At the same time, it is necessary to understand that the international diplomacy of macroeconomic policy is different from the
diplomacy of international security policy and even the diplomacy
of international commercial policy. Governments do not command
economies. London and Bonn summiteers and Robert Strauss and
Nobukiko Ushiba can agree to a target rate of growth of GNP or
target current-account surpluses, but the ability of the governments
represented by summiteers and Strauss and Ushiba to accomplish
such objectives is relatively limited. As has been observed, this
powerlessness may spring from the limits of economic theory and
quantitative understanding. It may also spring from the very
character of the great noncommunist industrialized economies to-

day. Aggregate economic performance rests on the decentralized decision making of countless corporations, households, and even government entities. In nonhierarchical economies, agreement among international elites on targets and even instruments is not enough.

If, as has been previously discussed, policy works its influence through altering economic decision makers' expectations rather than through more traditional direct channels, then the character of diplomacy as well as the substance of policy needs careful reevaluation. An unstable policy environment can have an important impact on aggregate economic behavior through its influence on household and business decision making.[16] Macroeconomic policies that are exclusively informational and that do not presume further negotiation for achieving more concrete coordination doubtless enhance economic stability. Consultation that presumes a coordinated strategy toward achieving global macroeconomic objectives may have the opposite impact. Public wrangling between the United States and Japan over macroeconomic instruments and targets can also have perverse effects. The uncertainty generated by such diplomacy aimed at fiscal and monetary expansion in Japan, either through its impact on the exchange rate or directly, will undermine spending plans of households and corporations.[17]

Notes

1. The German experience in the 1960s, very similar to that of the Japanese, provided some of the stylized facts for the so-called monetary theories of the balance of payments. Such theories stress that economic upswings actually lead to surpluses by demanding accommodating money flows from abroad. This theory is discussed in M. Shirakawa, "Monetary Approach ni yoru kokusai shushi-kawase seito no jisoho bunseki—waga kuni no kesu o chushin ni" [An analysis of the foreign exchange rate system through a monetary approach], *Kinyu kenkyu shiryo* 3 (August 1979).

2. The issues of this period are discussed in more detail in G. Saxonhouse, "Employment, Imports, the Yen and the Dollar," in H. Rosovsky, ed., *Discord in the Pacific* (Washington, D.C.: Columbia Books, 1972), pp. 79–116.

3. R. Komiya and Y. Suzuki, "Inflation in Japan," in L. Krause and W. Salant, eds., *World-wide Inflation: Theory and Recent Experience* (Washington, D.C.: Brookings Institution, 1977), pp. 303–354.

4. As early as February 1975, in a paper supplied for the Commission on Critical Choices for Americans, it was suggested that the "no-problem era" would have a short life. See G. Saxonhouse and H. Patrick, "Japan and U.S.:

Bilaterial Tensions and Multilateral Issues," in D. Hellman, ed., *China and Japan: A New Balance of Power* (Lexington, Mass.: D. C. Heath, 1976), p. 107.

5. Paul McCracken et al., *Towards Full Employment and Price Stability* (Paris: Organisation for Economic Co-operation and Development, 1977); and Organisation for Economic Co-operation and Development, *Economic Outlook* (July 1976 and December 1976).

6. At a theoretical level, this fact has been appreciated at least since the classic rendering of the international implications of the Keynesian theory of income deterioration by Machlup, Metzler, and Meade in the early 1940s and 1950s: L. Metzler, "Underemployment Equilibrium in International Trade," *Econometrica* 10, no. 2 (April 1942):97–112; F. Machlup, *International Trade and the National Income Multiplier* (Philadelphia: Blakiston Company, 1943); L. Metzler, "A Multi-Region Theory of Income and Trade," *Econometrica* 18, no. 4 (October 1950):329–354; and J. E. Meade, *The Balance of Payments* (London: Oxford University Press, 1951). See also R. N. Cooper, "Macro-Economic Policy Adjustment in Interdependent Economics," *Quarterly Journal of Economics* 83, no. 1 (February 1969):1–24.

7. There are, of course, many examples in the theory of economic policy where such coordination is shown to be unnecessary. Indeed, the early development of this literature by Tinbergen and Mundell suggested that decentralization of policymaking could be effective. Policies, they argued, should be paired with the objectives on which they have the most influence. See R. Mundell, "The Appropriate Use of Monetary and Fiscal Policy Under Fixed Exchange Rates," *IMF Staff Papers* 9, no. 1 (March 1962): 70–79; and Jan Tinbergen, *On The Theory of Economic Policy* (Amsterdam: North-Holland Publishing Company, 1952).

8. These systems include among others, Project Link, initiated by the Wharton School; the Mini-Meteor Model, by the Central Plan Bureau in the Netherlands; the Multilateral Exchange Rate Model, by the International Monetary Fund; the Multi-Country Model, by the Federal Reserve System in the United States; the EPA World Economic Model, by Japan's Economic Planning Agency; the OER Linked Policy Impact Mode, by the Central Intelligence Agency's Office of Economic Research; and the OECD's InterLink Model. These models are described in K. N. Johnson and L. R. Klein, "Stability in the International Economy: The LINK Experience," in A. Ando et al., eds., *International Aspects of Stabilization Policies* (Boston: Public Information Center, Federal Reserve Board of Governors, 1974); Centraal Plan Bureau, *Mini-Meteor: A Simple Multi-Country Simulation Model* (The Hague, 1974); Howard Howe et al., "Assessing International Interdependence with a Multi-Country Model," International Finance Discussion Paper No. 138 (Federal Reserve Board of Governors); Economic Planning Agency, *Trade Linkage Sub-Model in the EPA World Economic Model* (Tokyo: Government Printing Office, 1980); M. C. Depple and D. M. Repley, "The World Trade Model: Merchandise Trade," *IMF Staff Papers* 25, no. 1 (March 1978):147–206; and OECD, "The OECD International Linkage

Model," *OECD Occasional Studies* (January 1979). Significantly, the OECD InterLink Model is used as a regular part of the OECD semiannual forecasting cycle for checking international consistency. Of course, the OECD was a major proponent of the locomotive policy.

9. In the absence of linked econometric evaluation, the pulling power of the impact locomotives might seem quite small. For example, it was recommended that West Germany, as a locomotive, should stimulate its economy by 1 percent GNP. Roughly speaking, West Germany's GNP elasticity of imports is 2. Assuming that import shares remain constant, German stimulation would result in an additional demand for United Kingdom GNP of 0.05 percent, an additional demand for French GNP of 0.07 percent, and an additional demand for Italian GNP of 0.06 percent. This arithmetic calculation, which is made by Wood and Jianakopolos in "Coordinated International Economic Expansion: Are Convoys or Locomotives the Answer?" *Federal Reserve Bank of St. Louis Review* (July 1978), may be contrasted with findings from the simulations conducted with the OECD InterLink Model. Such simulation indicates an increase in demand for French GNP of 0.4 percent, an increase in demand for the United Kingdom's GNP of 0.34 percent, and finally, an increase in the demand for Italian GNP of 0.46 percent.

10. J. Armstrong, "Forecasting with Econometric Methods: Folklore Versus Fact," *Journal of Business* 51, no. 4 (October 1978):549–564; C. Nelson, "Rational Expectations and the Predictive Efficiency of Econometric Models," *Journal of Business* 48, no. 3 (July 1975):331–343; Y. Oritani, "Money Supply oyobi zaisei shishutsu to meimoku GNP no kankei ni tsuite" [Money supply, income, and government expenditures: A Test of monetary hypothesis on the Japanese economy], *Kinyu kenkyu shiryo* [Journal of monetary studies] 1 (January 1979); M. Shirakawa, "Monetary Approach ni yoru"; M. Shirakawa, "Gaikoku kawase shiryo ni okeru kitai keisei ni tsuite" [Formation of expectation in the foreign exchange market: An empirical study of Japan], *Kinyu kenkyu shiryo* 3 (August 1979); and Y. Oritani, "Infure kitai to kinri—Fisher kika kensho to sono implication" [Expected inflation and interest rates: Empirical test of the Fisher effect and its implications], and "Applications of Akaike's Method to Economic Time Series," *Kinyu kenkyu shiryo* 4 (September 1979).

11. For example, it is argued that most large-scale econometric models are not statistically identified. Such models are typically specified one equation or one bloc at a time, with the result that the zero identifying restrictions appearing in any given model are artificially imposed. Full systemic treatment of such restrictions would make many of them appear most unreasonable. Furthermore, the necessary dynamics of such models presume a prior knowledge of exact lag length and orders of serial correlation. Finally, even on their own terms many such models fail identification because of model-builders' typically arbitrary distinction between endogenous and policy variables. Criticisms in this spirit have been made in R. E. Lucas, "Econometric Testing of the Natural Rate Hypothesis," in Board of Governors of the Federal Reserve System, *The Econometrics of Price Determination* (Washington, D.C.: Government Printing Office, 1972); R. E. Lucas,

"Macro-Economic Policy Evaluation; A Critique," in K. Brunner and A. Meltzer, eds., *The Phillips Curve and Labor Markets* (Amsterdam: North-Holland Publishing Company, 1976), pp. 1–22; C. Sims, "Macro-Economics and Reality," *Econometrica* 48, no. 1 (January 1980):1–48; and Z. Griliches, "The Brookings Model: A Review Article," *Review of Economics and Statistics* 10, no. 2 (May 1968):1–48.

12. E. Sakakibara, "Structure of U.S.-Japanese Economic Interdependence and Feasibility for Policy Coordination" (mimeographed paper), May 1980.

13. B. Hickman and S. Schleicher, "The Interdependence of National Economics and the Synchronization of Economic Fluctuations: Evidence from the LINK Project," *Weltwirtschaftliches Archiv* 114, no. 4 (1978):4.

14. R. Raasche and T. Tatum, "The Effects of the New Energy Regime on Economic Capacity, Production and Prices," *Federal Reserve Bank of St. Louis Review* 59, no. 5 (May 1977):2–12; and J. R. Artus, "Measure and Potential Output in Manufacturing for Eight Industrialized Countries, 1955–1977," *IMF Staff Papers* 24, no. 1 (March 1977):1–35.

15. B. Kantor, "Rational Expectations and Economic Thought," *Journal of Economic Literature* 17, no. 4 (December 1979):1422–1441.

16. Ibid.

17. G. Saxonhouse, "Helping the Japanese Economy," *New York Times*, 11 January 1978.

5
The Economic Dimensions of the U.S.-Japan Alliance: An Overview

Hugh T. Patrick

The relationship between the United States and Japan was in serious trouble between mid-1977 and mid-1979. Economic problems became highly visible and politicized on both sides of the Pacific. In both countries, substantial negative feelings about the other emerged, although public utterance was considerably more muted in Japan. Both Americans and Japanese felt a crisis of confidence, and neither government was very adept at managing this crisis.

The immediate cause of this unhappy and potentially perilous situation was the United States's very large trade and current-account deficits from early 1977 to mid-1979 and Japan's concomitant very large trade and current-account surpluses, both with the world as a whole and with each other.[1] Indeed, many Americans saw the U.S. balance-of-payments problem as emanating almost entirely from Japan. Substantial, if complex, bilateral causal forces were at work, and this image of a "Japan problem" is much more extreme than the realities would warrant. Japan's immense global current-account surpluses of 1977 and 1978 rapidly turned into large

This is an updated, expanded, and revised version of a lecture entitled "United States–Japan Political Economy: Is the Partnership in Jeopardy?" presented at the Graduate School of Business Administration, University of Washington ITT Key Issues Lecture Series, published in Kermit O. Hanson and Thomas W. Roehl, eds., *The United States and the Pacific Economy in the 1980s* (Indianapolis: Bobbs-Merrill, 1980). The effective cut-off date for this analysis is fall 1979, prior to the Iran and Afganistan crises, although some data are provided for calendar 1979. I have benefited from comments by Stephen Krasney, Edward Lincoln, Kazuo Nukazawa, Daniel Okimoto, and Ezra Vogel, among others, none of whom can be held responsible for the views presented herein.

deficits in 1979 and 1980, making it appropriate to view this recent situation in the long-run perspective of both past and future.

The extent of the recent and current trade imbalances is symptomatic of long-run economic forces at work. They are fundamental determinants of the viability, durability, comprehensiveness, and depth of the U.S.-Japan alliance. Thus, recent difficulties can best be assessed in the long-run perspective of the forces that shape the evolving nature of the partnership. Accordingly, I first trace the evolving nature and significance of the partnership itself in light of these fundamental forces of change. In subsequent sections, I consider the overall pattern of the recent bilateral economic relationship, the policy options and choices each country had in trying to solve the balance-of-payments and the trade problems, and certain features of the politicization—the political economy, if you will—of these problems. In the final section, I identify certain major likely trends and potential problem areas in the bilateral economic relationship. This discussion focuses primarily on the economic aspects of the alliance; the security aspects are not treated.[2]

Three points are basic to this analysis. First, Japan is an extremely important partner for the United States, both economically and in terms of comprehensive national interests.[3] Second, how the United States resolves both short-run and long-run economic problems with Japan will be the major determinant of the future prospects for the partnership. Third, the way in which difficulties are resolved, or handled, is likely to have even greater global than bilateral impact on the credibility of U.S. leadership in this increasingly complex world. The United States may be, perhaps unwittingly and without full recognition, at a major turning point in its relations with the rest of the world, a turning point brought about by events in which Japan has been both a catalyst and an active force. At the same time, how Japan handles its trade and balance-of-payments problems with the United States and with the world will vitally affect its credibility as an advanced, industrial market economy committed to the principles of a multilateral, open, free-trade-oriented, international economic order. Without such credibility Japan may well be increasingly isolated from both Europe and the United States.

The Evolution of the Alliance

"Partnership" is too limited in meaning to encompass the comprehensive nature of the U.S.-Japan relationship. This relationship has been, is, and I anticipate will continue to be an alliance in the

broadest strategic terms—military and political as well as economic—between what are now the first and second largest capitalist
economies, the second and third most populous political
democracies (after India), and the strongest military power in the
world and perhaps the weakest military power among the major industrial nations. For some thirty years, ever since the culmination
of the Chinese revolution in the Communist accession to power in
1949, the keystone of U.S. foreign policy in Asia has been its
alliance with Japan. The initial, and growing, importance of this
alliance for U.S. national interests is difficult to overestimate.

For Japan, alliance with the United States has been more than
very important—it has been vital, the core of Japan's foreign policy.
In 1952, regaining independence following a period of U.S. occupation, democratization, and other profound changes in institutions,
values, and behavior, Japan was weak and vulnerable by virtually all
criteria—economic, political, military. In certain respects, weak
and vulnerable countries have a simple life: Options are few,
choices simple, the scope for action, even at the margin, limited. In
the early 1950s Japan needed a guardian and a patron; the United
States was the obvious choice. It might be noted that for a country
that is very strong but vulnerable, as Japan has become, life becomes
more complex and, although better, in some ways more difficult.
The range of options is wider, the choices are less clear-cut and obvious, and the opportunities at the margin are substantially greater.

In the beginning the alliance was highly asymmetric. Japan was a
client state, with a weak economy generating a per capita income
less than that of such countries as Brazil, Chile, or Malaya. Japan
was treated benevolently, generously, and on occasion patroniz-
ingly. Like Europe and the less developed countries at that time,
Japan was allowed to impose severe import and foreign exchange
restrictions on goods, services, and capital. With a lower per capita
income, the process of liberalization of its restrictions on foreign
transactions was allowed to lag behind that of Western
Europe—well into the 1960s, and in many respects, into the 1970s.
Indeed, it has been both the actual slowness of Japanese liberalization, and Western perceptions that it has been even more lagging,
that have constituted one of the main issues over the past decade
and certainly in this recent period of tension.

The partnership and alliance have proven immensely beneficial
for both nations by most economic, political, and security criteria.
The foundations of political democracy in Japan have deepened and
strengthened. Japan's outstanding economic growth performance
over the past quarter-century is well known;[4] it has brought Japan to

the forefront of the major industrial powers. Clearly it has been, and will increasingly be, in the United States's national interest to have a Japan that is prosperous and growing, that is opening up its economy and providing economic aid to developing nations, and that is democratic, politically stable, and aligned with the United States.

In this respect Japan has the same national interests vis-à-vis the United States—a prosperous, growing, open, politically stable U.S. society embodying and living up to its democratic values and allied with Japan. But the alliance has even deeper meaning for Japan. The United States has served Japan well. It was Japan's patron when one was needed in the 1950s and early 1960s, remains the country's military guardian with its nuclear umbrella guarantee, and on the whole has maintained a relatively free and open economy to which Japanese entrepreneurs, like other foreigners, have had substantial market access. The United States is the leader of the noncommunist world; the Japanese have appreciated and desired that leadership and would like it to continue.

However, the conditions, circumstances, and relative power relationships, global and bilateral, that shape the extent and nature of U.S. leadership have changed gradually but dramatically over the past twenty-five years. World political changes are well known: the rise in Soviet military power; the search for detente and for nuclear nonproliferation; the formation of the European Community; the emancipation of colonies and the growing economic success of many independent developing nations; the formation of OPEC, oil politics, and the traumatic series of increases in energy prices; the Sino-Soviet split and the dramatic recent changes in Chinese foreign policy; Middle Eastern instability and the recent events in Iran and Afganistan; and the growing sense of a power game in Asia involving a newly defined Big Four—the United States, the Soviet Union, Japan, and China.

Perhaps less well understood have been the nature, extent, and especially the implications of the global changes in economic power relationships. These changes have been extremely significant in themselves and to a considerable extent have underlain many of the changes in world political conditions. At the end of World War II the United States had hegemonic power, economically as well as militarily and politically. The United States welcomed and actively assisted in the reconstruction and rapid growth of Western Europe and Japan as well as the developing nations. Although foreign economic aid has been helpful, the major contribution has been the creation and maintenance of a multilateral, free trade, market-oriented international economic system. U.S. leadership was and will continue to be essential in this effort. The credibility of U.S. leadership in the economic sphere has been founded on its commitment to free trade.

The very success of U.S. foreign economic policy implied the decline and eventual loss of U.S. hegemonic economic power. The rise of Western Europe and Japan, the oil power of OPEC, the growing economic strength of the newly industrializing developing nations all bespeak a shift in relative economic power away from the United States. The United States economically is now the first among equals, still a leader (with substantial veto power) but no longer able virtually to dictate its own terms.

Success has brought with it need for structural adjustment in all major economies. In the United States, as elsewhere, rising incomes, population growth and migration, changing consumer demand, and technological innovations create investment and work opportunities for many, but they also force others — in a private-enterprise, market economy — to shift out of certain investments and jobs. The underlying principle is that of evolving comparative advantage, as reflected in the changing relative prices of goods and services. Analogies to the automobile's replacement of carts and buggy-whips are occurring all the time in a dynamic national economy; the same process is at work internationally. Indeed, rapid growth and industrialization, lower transport costs, and better communications have made the process more rapid and more pervasive than ever before. The benefits of dynamic change have risen, but so too have the costs of adjustment, domestically and internationally.

These needs for adjustment to changing trade patterns — an integral feature of the process of world economic growth — have been the fundamental cause of the breakdown of the Bretton Woods fixed-exchange-rate system, the depreciation of the dollar relative to European and Japanese currencies, and tensions in trade in certain specific goods. Some industries face growing, ever-tougher competition from imports; others are discovering and responding to rapidly expanding new export opportunities. In recent years these fundamental pressures to adjust, and the costs of adjustment, have been exacerbated by the oil crisis, world inflation at differential national rates, and differential national responses in degree and timing to the recession in the industrial world that began in 1974. Although the underlying structural forces of changing economic strength and trade advantage and disadvantage are the fundamental factors, certainly these cyclical factors and exogenous shocks are of importance in explaining the recent situation.

Japan, and the evolving nature of the U.S.-Japan partnership, fit centrally into this story. The very rapidity and immensity of Japanese economic success are not only important in themselves for the United States and the rest of the world. They also exemplify — as perhaps the most extreme case — the combination of mutual benefits and the generation of pressures for domestic economic adjustment that result from economic growth, and hence the tensions that are created in a structural sense and exacerbated in terms of cyclical difficulty such as recession, unemployment, and balance-of-payments disequilibria.[5] Put simply, the relationship has evolved — due mainly to Japanese economic growth — from that of Japanese dependence to one of mutual interdependence in economic and political domains.

Japan no longer needs a patron in world economic affairs, and the capacity, will, and desire of the United States to serve as patron rather than economic partner has probably come to an end. Nonetheless, a certain nostalgia for past relationships and slowness in psychological adjustment to the new economic realities on both sides retards the ongoing redefinition of the relationship. More important, Japan continues to need (and is coming to recognize this need ever more clearly) a patron for its military security, and that patron continues to be the United States. Thus Japan and the United States cooperate (and compete) essentially as equal partners in economic matters, while Japan remains very much the junior partner in the sphere of military security. Because of this substantial asymmetry in power, the relationship is a complex one, and this complexity is enhanced by two recent factors: a tendency to link (or think of trade-offs between) economic and military domains, and the emergence of crucial issues of economic security, notably access to stable supplies of energy and other essential basic materials.

Fundamental Forces in the Growing Economic Relationship

Over time, the bilateral economic relationship has become very important; the two-way exchange amounted to $55.8 billion in merchandise trade alone in 1980.[6] Interestingly, although the United States is still Japan's largest trading partner, its relative importance as a market and a source of supply for Japan has declined — from 30.9 percent of Japan's trade in goods and services in 1955 and still in 1965, to 25.0 percent in 1975, and 26.1 percent in 1978. In contrast, Japan has grown from being a modest market and source of supply for the United States to its largest overseas trading partner, second only to Canada in total U.S. trade. Specifically, Japan's share in U.S. trade in goods and services (exports plus imports), only 4.1 percent in 1955, had risen to 7.9 percent in 1965, 11.7 percent in 1975, and 12.2 percent in 1978.

All too often Americans think first of the difficulties this trade growth has brought for certain groups in the United States without adequately taking into account the benefits. *All* Americans as consumers have benefited immensely from the expansion of our trade relationship with Japan, and indeed with all countries. Brand names symbolize these direct benefits — Sony, Panasonic, Pioneer, Toyota, Datsun, Mazda, Honda, Canon, Nikon, Kikkoman, to name a few. U.S. firms have responded to greater Japanese competition with improved quality, new products, and lower prices. It is no accident that the prices of color television sets, apparel, and other imports have risen far less over the past decade than the general cost of living. Japanese consumers also have benefited from the expansion of trade, although on the whole perhaps less, and certainly less directly, than U.S. consumers.

Japan has become a particularly important market for certain U.S. producers. It is now by far the largest single market for U.S. agricultural exports, taking one-sixth of the total.[7] And yet about two-thirds of U.S. exports to Japan are nonagricultural. Japan's share of U.S. exports is particularly notable in such items as corn (17.1 percent), sorghum (36.4 percent), tobacco (19.3 percent), soybeans (18.1 percent), logs and lumber (62.3 percent), raw cotton (20.5 percent), coal (27.5 percent), chemicals (11.0 percent), computers (7.6 percent), commercial aircraft (9.6 percent), photographic supplies (12.7 percent), and toys and sporting goods (15.8 percent).[8]

Imports from Japan have put considerable pressure on U.S. producers of the same products. This pressure has resulted at times in substantial injury before adjustment could work itself out through the normal processes of the free-market mechanism, abetted by government adjustment assistance programs. Some U.S. producers, like those elsewhere, are quick to "cry wolf" as import competition becomes intense. Many of the recent and ongoing tensions in the U.S.-Japan partnership, and indeed U.S. economic relationships with many nations, emanate from the difficulties faced by certain specific import-competing U.S. industries — textiles, consumer electronics, and steel in particular.

Domestic problems of adjustment in specific manufactures to foreign competition have plagued Japan less thus far, for two reasons. First, most of the imports into Japan, a resource-deficient nation, have had to be oil, minerals, and other commodities not so directly competitive with domestic producers. One consequence of its lack of a natural resource base is that Japan has had broad com-

parative advantage as a processing economy, exporting manufactures—in direct competition with others—in order to pay for
raw material imports. Second, Japan has been able to protect its
farmers and certain other economically inefficient producers as an
inheritance of the earlier era of import restrictions, an inheritance
exceedingly difficult to overcome politically. In this respect, Japan
is, of course, by no means unique.

Nonetheless, the very fact of Japanese economic success has
meant that it too has been gradually losing comparative advantage
in certain manufacturing sectors. Wage rates have become so high
that Japan has lost its price competitiveness in many textiles and
other labor-intensive manufactures. Japan now imports a higher
proportion of its textile consumption than does the United States.
Land and water have also become more scarce, and industries—
notably pulp and paper—using those resources have also faced a
deterioration in competitive ability. This gradual erosion of comparative advantage has been aggravated by the sudden loss of competitive strength in petrochemicals, aluminum refining, and other
energy-intensive industries due to increases in oil prices.

Two additional factors of a fundamental, long-run nature, one
Japanese and one American, have an important effect on the bilateral partnership as well as the economic and political relations of
each partner with the world. The United States has become a major
oil-importing nation—and during a time when the price of oil rose
sharply. Despite the 1978 energy bill and long-run efforts to develop
domestic energy resources as well as to conserve energy, most
energy studies project an increase, not a diminution, in U.S. oil and
natural gas imports over the coming decade or longer.[9] This has
added a new dimension to the adjustment process. The large and
growing oil-import bill in dollar terms has had two interrelated consequences as the United States searches for ways to pay: pressure on
the dollar to depreciate vis-à-vis currencies of countries with
stronger balance of payments, and the need to generate more exports. Dollar depreciation eases the pressure on domestic industries
from competing imports and makes exporting more attractive. The
second point is, however, the more important in the long run. If the
United States is not to give up its world leadership, which requires a
liberal trade policy, it must become a much more export-oriented
nation.[10] These facts, although global in nature, have also underlain
the U.S. perception of the proper way to solve both short-run and
long-run trade problems with Japan: expand exports to rather than
restrict imports from Japan.

The second special factor is the dramatic change in Japan's fundamental balance-of-payments situation brought about by its successful economic performance. Japan, for twenty-five years a nation with a tendency for imports to exceed exports and hence for the balance of payments to constrain domestic economic growth, has in the last decade become a nation in current-account surplus. This is a secular, not just a cyclical, phenomenon. Japan's global current account on average is likely to continue in surplus for another ten to fifteen years, even though cyclical forces brought about especially by increases in oil-import prices will cause temporary deficits.[11] However, future surpluses at 1977 and 1978 rates will probably not be politically acceptable to the United States and Europe. Nonetheless, as a mature economy Japan will be a net capital exporter. This is natural and should not be surprising, as the economic history of England in the nineteenth century and the United States in the twentieth informs us.

How did this situation come about, and what are the implications for the U.S.-Japan partnership? As with most other nations in the 1950s and 1960s, under the fixed-exchange-rate system, Japan's potential import demand was greater than exports; demand was constrained both by import restrictions and by cyclical dampening of domestic growth booms when they caused excessive balance-of-payments deficits. However, Japan's rapid industrialization created many new industries, productivity grew rapidly, and costs and prices declined; many industries became increasingly export-competitive. Gradually the growth in export competitiveness outstripped import demand. In the 1950s and 1960s these export proceeds were used to raise the ceiling on GNP growth and to liberalize imports gradually; both policies raised the level of imports. In hindsight, by the late 1960s Japan had moved into a situation in which exports tended to exceed imports at the exchange rate of 360 yen per dollar; the balance of payments was no longer a constraint on growth. Japanese policymakers were cautious at the time, interpreting the 1970–1972 surplus as a cyclical phenomenon, particularly with the appreciation of the yen and ending of fixed exchange rates. The late 1973 oil shock and subsequent Japanese balance-of-payments deficit in 1974 and 1975 seemingly vindicated this cautiousness, but in fact they masked Japan's underlying export strength. Japan's quick responsiveness in policy and in export performance to its heightened oil-import bill and worsened terms of trade manifested itself in the extremely large current-account surpluses of 1977–1978, embarrassingly large for Japanese policymakers because the problems caused for the United States in particular were considerable and the backlash severe.

Inasmuch as a large share of Japan's trade has been with the United States, its growing export competitiveness and evolving comparative advantage have had a substantial direct impact on the bilateral partnership. On a commodity trade basis, the United States ran a bilateral surplus with Japan until 1965; U.S. policymakers explained to their concerned Japanese counterparts that that was all right and even efficient, because what really counted after all was multilateral, not bilateral, balance, and services and capital flows had to be taken into account as well. Since 1965 the bilateral surplus has been with Japan; Japanese policymakers have reminded their mentors of the lessons they were taught earlier. And indeed those lessons are correct: It is multilateral, not bilateral, balance that counts, and measurement of balance-of-payments equilibria must take into account capital flows as well as trade in both goods and services.

The U.S.-Japan partnership has been buffeted by several major crises since the alliance was formed in 1952. The last two[12] have had economic causes; they occurred over the period from 1971 to early 1973 and the period from mid-1977 to summer 1979. Both crises had the same immediate causes: an unacceptably large U.S. global balance-of-payments deficit and an overvalued dollar relative to the yen and West German mark; a very large and rapidly growing Japanese global trade and current-account surplus and buildup in foreign exchange reserves; and (inevitably, given the trade patterns) a very large Japanese trade surplus with the United States.[13] There were generally similar policy responses in both cases in each country; there were also notable differences. On the whole the U.S. policy approach in 1977–1979 was less unilateral and "shocking," with perhaps more emphasis on global than bilateral balance as its target.[14] Nonetheless, U.S. policymakers, congressmen, and the general public tended once again to see U.S. trade and balance-of-payments problems as caused substantially by Japanese intransigence.

It is worth noting that between these two periods of bilateral tension, the U.S. current account went into surplus and Japan's into deficit, and policymakers in both countries stated with considerable satisfaction that the bilateral partnership had never been better. It is somewhat ironic that in 1975 the United States considered Japan's trade system and behavior as reasonable and not a major problem; subsequently Japan further liberalized its imports without subsidizing its exports, and yet during the 1977–1979 crisis and even today Japan is perceived by many U.S. policymakers and the general public as behaving unfairly. This perception lends further credence to the argument that it is the combination of excessive U.S. balance-of-payments deficits and Japanese surpluses that brings fundamental difficulties of adjustment to the fore and causes the sorts of widespread tension the bilateral relationship experienced between mid-1977 and mid-1979.

The 1977–1979 Crisis and the Policy Responses of Japan and the United States

Explanation of the recent difficulties in the bilateral partnership involves a complex set of interrelated causes that are difficult to disentangle. As already noted, there were the fundamental forces of changes in the relative competitiveness of various industries in both nations concomitant with successful economic growth. Oil is only part of the story. By generating exports, Japan adjusted more rapidly to its higher import bill than did the United States. Between 1975 and 1978 the major increase in U.S. import expenditures was on manufactures, from the newly industrializing nations as well as Japan. Differential rates of inflation, especially Japan's greater success since 1977 in controlling inflation, were another factor. So too has been the depth of the 1974–1975 recession in each country, which required greater attention to the problems of general redundancy of labor, unemployment, and industry difficulties. The more rapid economy recovery in the United States than in Japan and Europe made the United States the major growing market in the world, a market to which all producers—domestic and foreign alike—aspired.

Both countries made mistakes in economic policy. In Japan especially those mistakes led to intolerable foreign trade surpluses. The first occurred in the summer and fall of 1976, when the Japanese government did little to stimulate the economy, still operating at 9 percent below capacity. The hope of policymakers was that the export boom of spring 1976, fed in large part by the recovery of the United States, would spill over sufficiently strongly, as in the past, to stimulate domestic private investment, consumption, and then import demand.[15] There were two mitigating factors in Japan's inaction: Policymakers were still deeply concerned about controlling inflation; and for one of the very few times in postwar Japan, economic policy was given short shrift by the political system, which had to cope with the Lockheed scandal, the replacement of Prime Minister Kakuei Tanaka, and heavy conflict within the Liberal-Democratic party. The Japanese economy did not really generate its own steam through private demand in 1976 (or indeed finally until the spring of 1979). Aggregate demand did not increase sufficiently to narrow significantly the gap between actual and full-capacity GNP.[16] Japanese exports continued to boom for two years while imports lagged.

Japan's second mistake, in 1977, was seriously to underestimate the extent and durability of its growing foreign trade surplus and to misjudge the foreign repercussions, especially in the United States and Europe. Policymakers were slow to react, and the surplus became larger and larger in 1977 and 1978, requiring ever-greater policy steps in correction. Japanese monetary authorities continued to peg the yen at an increasingly undervalued rate relative to the dollar until early 1977, and thereafter well into 1978 they reluctantly allowed the yen to appreciate more slowly than was required to restore balance-of-payments equilibrium.

Both countries faced the same policy choices, in terms of basic strategy and of policy instruments, to restore equilibrium globally and hence bilaterally. The basic strategy choice was whether to eliminate the trade imbalances through outward-looking, trade-expansion measures or by more domestic-oriented, trade-restrictive measures. Both opted essentially for an outward-looking strategy, and this identity of interests has become a basic underpinning of the partnership. For both countries an international economic system based on free trade meets their interests much better than a world of protectionism, which inevitably leads to the formation of rival economic blocs conferring favors on members and raising barriers against outsiders. Trade expansion in this context means that the United States must become a more export-oriented economy and Japan a more import-oriented economy.[17]

Thus, trade restriction has been eschewed in principle. In the 1977–1979 context of the bilateral partnership this meant that the United States should not impose import restrictions, while seeking ways to expand exports, and that Japan should not impose so-called voluntary or other export restrictions, while reducing existing import barriers. In the gray world of political economy the choices in principle may be mutually exclusive yet in practice involve a mixture of both U.S. import restrictions and Japanese export restraints. It is the direction and extent of the movement along the spectrum between protectionism and free trade that counts. The United States has indeed restricted certain imports, with a strong focus on Japan; import quotas for color televisions and the steel trigger-price mechanism are important examples. And Japan, through the Ministry of International Trade and Industry, engaged in export-restriction guidance to the U.S. and European markets, particularly in steel, automobiles, and ships. Nonetheless, the main thrust of policies in both countries was trade-expansive rather than trade-restrictive.

Both Japanese and U.S. policymakers, over time and not without tension-generating and rather destructive processes, came to agree on a general package of policies designed to correct the respective global and bilateral imbalances—although substantial differences in emphasis persisted with respect to the effectiveness of various specific measures. The package had three major components: (1) demand expansion in Japan and, in 1979, restriction in the United States; (2) changes in relative prices; and (3) liberalization of Japanese import barriers and expansion of U.S. export efforts. The first two policies relied primarily upon macro instruments, while the third embodied more specific, micro measures. It should be emphasized that the policy package, especially the aggregate demand-management and relative price components, was essentially multilateral in nature, although it inevitably had strong bilateral overtones because Japan's trade surplus with the United States loomed so large in the overall U.S. deficit.

By summer 1977 an important component of the solution had become an acceleration of Japanese growth, both to restore the economy to full capacity and to generate greater import demand. Only from late 1978 did U.S. as well as Japanese leadership consider that part of the immediate solution was for the United States to slow its own growth, not so much to restrain U.S. import demand as to slow the rate of inflation.

It was recognized—earlier in the United States than Japan—that U.S. exports and domestic goods competitive with Japanese imports had to become more price-competitive and foreign goods less so. The obvious solution, and the one strongly espoused by the U.S. Treasury and State Department, was a general reduction in U.S. prices relative to Japanese and European by allowing private-market forces to carry out the depreciation of the dollar relative to the yen and other strong currencies. This was the single most important policy action by the United States in trying to solve its balance-of-payments problem. Japan reluctantly went along and greeted with relief the U.S. decision in November 1978 to stabilize the dollar.

The third part of the package combined Japanese actions to open its markets to U.S. exports and an enhancement of U.S. business efforts to exploit opportunities in the Japanese market. The major U.S. effort concentrated on overcoming perceived Japanese trade barriers that were amenable to policy change: reduction of tariffs, liberalization of import quotas on agricultural products, ending of

"Buy Japanese" policies of the government of Japan and its various state-owned agencies, simplification and liberalization of inspection and other customs procedures, and the like.[18]

More recently, some within the U.S. government, particularly in the Congress and in the Departments of Commerce and Agriculture, argued that greater access to the Japanese and other markets and enhanced price competitiveness through depreciation of the dollar are not sufficient and that the government must take additional steps to encourage U.S. producers to seek export markets. Proposals included such actions as a stronger U.S. Export-Import Bank, expanded tax incentives for export activities beyond the present Domestic International Sales Corporation (DISC) (GATT-illegal) subsidy program, and a redefined mission for the Department of Commerce (or State, or both) or the creation of a new department to give greater weight to export expansion (along the lines of the MITI).[19] In effect a battle has been raging in Washington as to whether a generalized price-incentive approach through exchange-rate adjustment is the proper one, or whether more direct, specialized inducements to export should be utilized more strongly, in part as a complement to but in part as a substitute for exchange-rate adjustment ("to ensure the stability of the dollar").

Both nations made major efforts to implement this policy package. Japan was under very substantial pressure from the U.S. side, which in itself exacerbated the tensions.[20] Yet the results, as measured by global and bilateral trade balances in dollar terms, were disappointing. Japan's global current-account surplus, $10.9 billion in calendar 1977, rose to $16.5 billion in 1978 despite all efforts to reduce it. The U.S. global deficit, the highest ever in 1977, declined only slightly in 1978.[21]

Then, quite suddenly and unexpectedly, Japan's payments situation from spring 1979 began to move toward deficit. This was the consequence of the combination of underlying adjustment forces at work and the new round of sharply higher import prices of oil. Japan's initial official projection of a current surplus of only $7.5 billion in fiscal 1979 by mid-spring seemed reasonable, perhaps even high.[22]

However, as data from the first and second quarters of calendar 1979, showing a small but growing current-account deficit, became available, it became increasingly obvious that Japanese projections were too optimistic; significantly, these trends developed prior to any impact of the oil price increases. By summer 1979 it was obvious that Japan's 1979 current account would record a substantial deficit, although even then few anticipated that it would be Japan's largest ever and that the swing from 1978 surplus to 1979 deficit would amount to $25 billion. The 1979 improvement in the U.S. balance of payments was somewhat more expected, as a result of the global depreciation of the dollar and improved export performance, even though it too was hit in the latter part of the year by increases in the oil-import bill.

These major changes in both nations' balance of payments were reflected much less in changes in the bilateral current-account and merchandise-trade balances. Japan's trade surplus with the United States, $8.1 billion in 1977, rose to $11.6 billion in 1978 and declined in 1979 — but only to $8.7 billion.[23] However, the U.S. export performance, bilateral as well as global, was very good in 1979. Exports to Japan, which had increased 23.7 percent (in dollar terms) in 1978, rose a further 36.4 percent in 1979. The U.S. share of Japan's total imports increased despite the sharp rise in Japan's oil-import bill. At the same time U.S. imports from Japan, which had increased 31.9 percent in 1978, rose only 7.3 percent in 1979. The combination of major changes in the global balance-of-payments condition of both countries, the turnaround of the bilateral balance, and the sharing of the difficulties imposed by the spring and summer increases in world oil prices, caused the bilateral economic tensions of the previous two years to evaporate by mid-1979.[24]

Two broad questions arise naturally from this recent experience. First, what went wrong: Why didn't the adjustment policies work better and more quickly? Second, what caused the sharp turnaround in Japan's balance of payments in the first half of 1979? It is still too early to know with any certainty, but some conclusions can be suggested. First, Japan tried hard to reduce sharply the trade surplus; it proved to be more difficult, and to have higher domestic political costs, than anyone expected. Second, the United States also tried quite hard, also with less than satisfactory results, especially in controlling inflation. Third, it takes considerably more time than was earlier believed for changes in relative prices (exchange rates) to have their predicted impact on trade flows. Fourth, trade problems are not just cyclical; they incorporate the accumulation of some twenty years of past needs in both countries to carry out structural adjustments that are more difficult politically and economically in recession than in periods of full-employment growth.

Japanese Policies to Reduce the Current-Account Surplus

One should not minimize the policy steps Japan took between 1977 and 1979. In order to accelerate domestic growth, the central government since 1977 has engaged in massive deficit financing, so that government bond issue has been on the order of 35 percent of the budget—far higher than ever before in postwar Japan and far higher than in the United States.[25] Yet private demand did not respond as hoped to this stimulus until spring 1979, and economic growth, although good by international standards, lagged behind targets. Between early 1977 and late 1978 the yen appreciated about 35 percent vis-à-vis the dollar. Export volume actually declined in 1978 and import volume rose, signaling an eventual reduction in Japan's current-account surplus. However, the appreciation was so substantial and so rapid that in dollar terms Japan's current surplus actually increased in 1978, although it narrowed substantially in yen terms.

The length of the trade lags and other countervailing responses to exchange-rate changes proved disheartening, especially to those policymakers and economists (such as myself) who believe in the efficiency and effectiveness of private-market mechanisms. The phenomenon of short-run (J-curve) perverse responses came to be understood and accepted, although the time lags for adjustment were greater than had been (perhaps naively) hoped. There has been some perception (at times exaggerated) of the countervailing effects on rates of inflation, as yen appreciation somewhat reduced wholesale and consumer price indices in Japan and slightly raised them in the United States.[26] Less understood has been the power of oligopolistic industries to take actions that offset the benefits of exchange-rate adjustment. The Japanese were quick to point out the ineffectiveness of exchange-rate adjustments that pushed up the dollar prices of Toyotas, Datsuns, and Hondas in the United States by 25 percent when U.S. producers responded not so much by price competition as by raising their own prices 14–15 percent.[27]

The rapid shift in Japan's global current account from surplus to deficit in the first half of 1979 was impressive, particularly in light of the record surplus of 1978. However, the turnaround really began by summer 1978. It simply took time for the cumulative effects of the series of yen appreciations to work themselves out through the merchandise markets. Indeed, the excessive appreciation of the yen by September 1978 relative to long-run equilibrium, followed by the U.S. dollar-defense program announced at the beginning of November, resulted in a large subsequent depreciation of the yen: by April 1979, 17.0 percent on a bilateral basis, 20.4 percent on a real bilateral basis (adjusted for relative inflation rates), 13.3 percent on an effective exchange-rate basis (a weighted average of changes in fifteen currencies), and 13.9 percent on a real exchange-rate basis.[28] After adjusting for inflation, Japan's real effective exchange rate (a measure of global competitiveness) was back to the level it had reached at the end of 1977. In the short run this depreciation resulted in J-curve effects that further increased Japan's current-account deficit in 1979; in the long-run yen depreciation can be expected to result in renewed current-account surpluses once the oil price hikes are absorbed.

During 1978 the demand impetus to Japanese growth shifted strongly from foreign to domestic, mainly government, sources. By spring 1979 Japanese business confidence had revived; new plant and equipment investment, as well as inventory demand (which was seen sooner), expanded throughout the year. While real GNP growth in calendar 1979 was 6.0 percent, the same as 1978, the main sources of demand shifted from the public sector to the private, especially business fixed investment; the current-account deficit was a negative factor, reducing domestic demand by 0.8 percent.[29]

The extent of Japan's global current-account deficit in 1979 was due to the exogenous shock of the Iranian crisis and sharply higher prices of oil imports; by December 1979 the average landed (c.i.f.) price of crude oil imports was $25.36 per barrel, an increase of 85.2 percent over a year earlier.[30] These events worsened the U.S. balance of payments as well. The effects on U.S.-Japan bilateral economic relationships have probably been more indirect than direct, as well as quite complex, as a global, general-equilibrium framework of analysis is required. Moreover, the inflationary impact of oil imports is likely to evoke somewhat different policy responses in the two countries. Foreign exchange markets have signaled that, in the short run at least, Japan has been harmed more than the United States. It remains to be seen whether the dollar will eventually depreciate relative to other major currencies and whether this in turn will further enhance U.S. export consciousness and performance. Similarly, will reawakened anxieties in Japan concerning the ability to pay for oil imports blunt somewhat recent efforts to expand imports of manufactures? Certainly any new energy crisis will make predictions about the U.S.-Japan bilateral economic relationship difficult.

The problems of remaining Japanese trade barriers, and of U.S. business export efforts, continue to be the most difficult to analyze, in substantial part because of lack of comprehensive, hard data. The Japanese love to complain that U.S. businesses do not try to adapt products to the Japanese market, such as by putting steering wheels in cars on the right side or wiring electrical appliances for the Japanese 50-watt, 100-volt system, or even by translating labels,

packaging, or instructions. U.S. businessmen have their own horror
stories of Japanese trade barriers. The bilateral Trade Facilitation
Committee, set up in fall 1977 by the U.S. Department of Commerce and MITI to handle problems of access to the Japanese market, has nonetheless had only a few cases submitted to it by U.S.
businesses.

One must consider separately Japanese import barriers in
agriculture and in industry. Agriculture is an anomaly: Half is
liberalized, with large import flows, and half is highly protected. As
already noted, Japan is not only the world's largest importer of agricultural products, it is by far the largest national market for U.S.
agricultural products—notably wheat, soybeans, and corn; and the
United States is Japan's largest single supplier. Yet imports of certain products important to the politically powerful Japanese
farmers—especially rice, beef, and citrus fruit—are severely
restricted, and domestic prices are several times world levels.[31] The
government of Japan has set, and exceeded, a target of full self-
sufficiency in rice as the basic foodstuff, for reasons of national
security, among others; liberalization of trade in rice has not yet
been an issue in the partnership. The U.S. Department of Agriculture estimated in 1978 that complete liberalization of other
Japanese agricultural products could increase U.S. exports by about
$500 million annually after five years. Two implications stand out:
(1) Japanese agricultural liberalization will not do much to improve
the U.S. balance of payments; and (2) the projected increase due to
liberalization would be only 12–13 percent of 1978 levels of U.S.
agricultural exports to Japan.

Japanese import barriers in manufactures are both easier and more
difficult to assess: easier because the only import quota is on leather
goods (for reasons having to do with domestic minority groups);
more difficult because this is the area in which administrative practices at the individual commodity level may constitute real barriers.
It is one thing for top political leaders and elite bureaucrats to shift
policy to encourage imports; it is another to have this policy implemented by low-level bureaucrats whose lives, until now, have
been dedicated to helping Japanese industry and to making it more
difficult for competitive imports to enter Japan—it takes time to re-
educate the troops. At least this is my interpretation of why horror
stories on the practical difficulties of exporting to Japan persist;
such difficulties are not due to conspiracy or deviousness at high
governmental levels.

It should be recognized that neither the United States nor Japan is a perfectly free trader in manufactures, even excluding military goods. Both use import restrictions: tariffs, quotas, "buy American," "buy Japanese," other forms of subsidy of certain domestic industries, difficulties in import procedures. On average, tariff levels in the two countries are about the same, and will be low as the MTN (Tokyo Round multilateral trade negotiations) reductions take place over time. The United States applies implicit (or explicit) import restrictions for certain politically sensitive domestic industries in order to ease the process of adjustment, notably textiles, steel, and color television; the Japanese counterpart is agriculture. My judgment is that, overall, Japanese government restrictions on imports of manufactures from the United States are no more severe, and possibly less severe, than U.S. restrictions on imports from Japan. This judgment differs markedly from the prevailing, although incorrect, image of an "unfair Japan."

Two further points on Japan's import prospects should be made. First, the evolution of Japan's comparative advantage will benefit certain U.S. exporters, including producers of high-technology goods, luxury fashion goods, industrial chemicals, and coal as well as agricultural products. However, it will benefit the newly industrializing countries even more; they can produce labor-intensive goods of standard technology cheaply. Japan is in the same process of adjustment as the United States, losing competitiveness in the cheaper lines of textiles, black and white television, and similar products. The main growth in Japanese imports of manufactured goods is likely to be from the developing countries, not from the United States. One implication is that it is unrealistic and undesirable to expect bilateral balance in U.S.-Japan trade; but that is what the multilateral trading system is all about. U.S. concerns should properly be focused on global, not bilateral, economic competitiveness. Only when coal replaces oil as a major energy source, perhaps toward the end of the century, is the bilateral trade balance likely to shift once again in favor of the United States.

Second, given Japan's requirements for energy imports, minerals, and foodstuffs, an increase in the share of manufactures in total imports over the long-run will mean an increase in the ratio of imports to GNP. Although to some extent that would reduce Japan's current-account surplus, the export share in GNP would probably rise in order to pay for the imports. Such exports will also be manufactures; many will be competitive in the U.S. market. It seems likely, therefore, that an increase in the share of manufactured imports in Japan's total trade and GNP in a relatively free multilateral trading system will widen the U.S.-Japan bilateral trade gap, not narrow it. This outcome should not be feared. Indeed, it will be desirable for both countries by efficiency and welfare criteria.

Evaluation of U.S. export performance requires further, separate study at both macro and micro levels. Perhaps one should not be too pessimistic; the U.S. export performance in 1978 and 1979 was excellent. In 1978 exports of goods and services to the world rose by 20.6 percent ($37.8 billion); merchandise exports to Japan increased by 23.7 percent ($2.5 billion). In 1979 the comparable increases were 29.5 percent ($65.3 billion) and 36.4 percent ($4.7 billion). Part of the increase was due to price changes, but one study indicates that export volume rose between January and November of 1978 at an annual rate of nearly 25 percent in contrast to the miserable total increase of only 1.8 percent for 1974–1977, when rest-of-world import volume expanded by 13.6 percent.[32] It is estimated that about half the increase in nonagricultural exports can be traced to the improvement in U.S. price competitiveness since the beginning of 1976 through dollar depreciation; the other half was due to growing foreign demand and other factors. However, the U.S. balance of payments began to improve only in the final quarter of 1978 as imports continued to rise. Therefore one should not be overly sanguine; it will take continued and increasing emphasis on exports to generate the foreign exchange earnings both to maintain a liberal foreign trade (import) policy and to pay for expanding, higher-priced oil imports.

The Political Economy of the Partnership

The discussion thus far has been primarily at the macroeconomic level, focusing mainly on the overall balance of payments. But it can be argued that this is not the direct source of the negative feelings and tension on both sides of the Pacific. The politics of the economic partnership are influenced by those who feel, often quite correctly, that their interests are being hurt by imports from the other. As noted above, the problems of adjustment fall on the workers, management, and stockholders in specific import-competing industries. Tensions have been exacerbated by differences in culture, bureaucratic systems, levels of expertise and knowledge, policy-formation processes, and negotiating styles.

The domestic policies that shape and constrain the partnership are of great importance in both countries.[33] The first rule in any political democracy is that foreigners do not vote. The political systems in Japan and the United States are strongly influenced by interest-group politics. Consumer interests are not well represented relative to those of producers, particularly in Japan.[34] Consumer interests are too diffuse, lacking in intensity, and difficult to organize. Conflicts arise between those sectors producing for export and those facing import competition; each mobilizes its own legislative representatives and seeks to sway the legislature and the executive branch through broader appeals and other instruments of the political process. Those having to adjust to import competition are essentially protectionist; others benefit from a free-trade-oriented international economic policy.

In both countries protectionists have always been fairly powerful, but their power expands particularly in periods of domestic recession, when the adjustment process is more difficult, and in periods of balance-of-payments deficit, when their special interests can ride on the coattails of more general concerns. In Japan farmers have a particularly strong political voice because of the de facto gerrymandering. As the Liberal-Democratic party legislative majority declines, to stay in power it must hold vigorously onto the votes of farmers, of small business people, including wholesale and retail traders, and of other conservatively inclined interest groups. Similarly, in the United States the textile industry has long had great political clout, evidenced most clearly and negatively for the partnership in Nixon's "southern strategy" and the tensions generated in finally reaching a negotiated agreement with Japan in 1971.[35] More recently, the steel industry was very effective in mobilizing congressional support in fall 1977 to force the administration to devise some way to restrain steel imports, with Japan identified as the major source of difficulty; hence the creation of a new trade-restrictive device, the trigger-price mechanism.[36]

Domestic political realities and cultural styles affect the policy-making and negotiating processes in both countries. Detailed, comparative analysis of these processes is beyond the scope of this study, but a few important points should be noted.[37] In both countries, it is important to achieve considerable consensus on foreign policy issues. The process is usually more careful and time-consuming in Japan. U.S. policymakers are typically not very well informed on Japan, and for various reasons — including bureaucratic in-fighting and domestic policies — they concentrate their efforts on what on occasion appear to be the wrong economic issues. Certainly this has been true, for example, of the intensity of the U.S. effort to force liberation of Japanese imports of selected agricultural products. The payoff in U.S. export growth would be quite modest. And the political price paid in terms of the relationship has been high.

U.S. policymakers apparently had some difficulty in determining an effective strategy to press for the liberalization of Japan's import system. On the one hand they were heavily involved with Japan in the Tokyo Round of multilateral trade negotiations, a broad, systemic approach to reducing tariff and nontariff barriers to trade: It involved both the full range of commodities and trade practices and all market-oriented trading countries on a multilateral basis. Inevitably these negotiations were complex, necessitated substantive trade-offs, and required considerable secrecy from time to time. Accordingly, they were not highly visible in domestic political arenas in the United States and Japan.

U.S. policymakers evidently felt that more direct and visible bilateral negotiations were necessary to ensure liberalization of the Japanese import system. They accordingly proceeded with a series of specific demands for liberalization: easing of import restrictions on beef and citrus; the opening of purchases by government and public corporations, such as Nippon Telegraph and Telephone (NTT) and the producer and distributer of cigarettes, Japan Monopoly Corporation, to foreign sources of supply; the easing and simplifying of various import and payments procedures, including methods of payment and inspection of certain commodities; handling of specific complaints through the Trade Facilitation Committee; and the like. These were, and certainly appeared as, unilateral demands rather than negotiations in which a narrowly defined quid pro quo was involved. The basic justification was that a country in surplus should use that opportunity to reduce its trade barriers for the benefit of all, regardless of domestic political cost. Looming behind these demands were the increasingly common threats of U.S. protectionist actions against imports from Japan.

It was recognized on both sides (and stressed by the Japanese) that liberalization of specific items at this micro level was more symbolic than substantive; that alone would not solve the bilateral or global imbalance. Presumably the U.S. strategy was based on several interrelated lines of reasoning. The cumulative effect of successful negotiations for the liberalization of one Japanese import item after another would involve significant trade quantities. More important, the symbolic effects would be great—in both Japan and the United States. For Japan negotiations on specific items, such as NTT procurement practices, would serve as a model for changes in the import system as a whole by providing concrete illustration of both general problems and general solutions. For the United States, and especially for Congress, this approach would demonstrate U.S.

official concern as well as the willingness of its Japanese partner to respond.[38] Moreover, it would increase pressure on Japan for appropriate macro policies.

Although there was merit in this approach, it also raised a number of problems, especially for the long run. On balance, the case-by-case strategy was probably pushed too hard and too far, at increasingly high political cost to the partnership. It intensified the image in the United States of an "unfair Japan" and the Japanese image of a "bullying America."[39] Solution of specific micro issues led to U.S. expectations that the macro problem was also solved; these were inevitably frustrated. The strengths of various Japanese and U.S. interest groups were underestimated; political realities were not fully appreciated on the U.S. side; and the political difficulties and costs for Japanese leaders of making concessions were high. The way this strategy was pushed generated and heightened tensions on both sides. Economists, who can clearly see the benefits of trade liberalization, often are not used to, much less skilled in, estimating these costs.

The nature and style of Japanese policy responses to U.S. pressures unintentionally contributed to the image of an "unfair Japan." At the macro level the Japanese made promises that were difficult to keep and in fact were not kept: Prime Minister Takeo Fukuda at the July 1977 summit promised a 7 percent GNP growth rate for fiscal 1977 and a reduced current-account surplus in 1978; and again in 1978 he promised a 7 percent growth rate and a speedy solution to the balance-of-payments problem. Soon after accession to office in December 1978, Prime Minister Masayoshi Ohira repudiated the 7 percent growth target and issued a statement that seemed to say that Japan had done all it could to solve the bilateral trade imbalance and the rest was up to the United States.

On trade issues Japanese policy appeared to have been ad hoc, without demonstrating initiative in making changes in the import system as such. Systemic change — in procurement policies, inspection procedures, and the like — appeared to be forthcoming only reluctantly and under great pressure from the United States. Japan's excessive trade and current-account surpluses seemed to be regarded as temporary rather than structural in a world whose economic future appeared more uncertain than usual. In a contingent world why not take contingent policies? These attitudes probably underlay the special $4 billion emergency import program and the restraints on selected exports to the United States. Both could be terminated at any time — and indeed in late spring 1979 they were.

But such Japanese perceptions did little to allay the concerns of those Americans who saw the bilateral difficulties as embodying substantial structural features.

The cumulative effect of Japanese policies, each of which singly has its own reasonable explanation, has been to create an image of Japan as, if not "unfair," narrow and selfish rather than well-meaning and forthcoming. As James Abegglen put it, Japan is seen abroad as "a nation that defines its self-interest narrowly and takes advantage whenever possible for as long as possible."[40] Such an approach by Japan to its foreign economic policy is not only short-sighted but increasingly risky.

One consequence of the negotiating process, in substance and style, and the respective domestic political realities, was the rise in "scapegoatism" on both sides during the 1977–1979 crisis. Foreigners are sometimes useful scapegoats for unpopular or difficult domestic decisions. Protectionists recognize this point and attempt to simplify and emotionalize issues so as to win wide public acceptance, playing on fears of unemployment, national security concerns, and the like. U.S. industries, including their labor unions, that face vigorous import competition from Japan have been rather successful in the United States in creating and enhancing the image of an "unfair Japan," especially in Congress.[41] It is probably correct to say it was this negative image, as much as the balance-of-payments difficulties, that caused the strains on the partnership on the U.S. side during the 1977–1979 period.

In the United States, Japan has been used as a foreign scapegoat for domestic problems mainly by business and labor organizations—the private sector. In Japan, the United States has been used as a scapegoat by the public sector—politicians and bureaucrats—abetted by the mass media. This pattern may well be inherent in the combination of the ongoing bilateral trade deficit, Japanese export competitiveness in a small number of highly visible manufactured goods in U.S. markets, and the delicate balance of Japanese domestic politics.

Over the years the U.S. government has let itself be used as the excuse for the Japanese government to take controversial, difficult, or unpopular domestic decisions. In the 1977–1979 crisis in particular, U.S. officials cooperated with Japanese Foreign Ministry and MITI officials against the Ministry of Finance and Ministry of Agriculture in the Japanese domestic debate on how to solve its unacceptable trade surplus. For example, the domestic rationale for heavy deficit financing was that Japan had to grow fast in order to import more from the United States, not because it was in Japan's interest to restore the economy to profitable, full use of its labor and capital resources; that agricultural and other imports had to be liberalized because of U.S. pressure, not because liberalization would benefit Japanese consumers; that steel exports had to be restrained because of U.S. threats, not because in fact major Japanese steel producers favored a cartel-like arrangement that raised their export prices and total profits substantially. Making the "big brother" United States the scapegoat is a game Japanese politicians and bureaucrats have played, especially for issues of domestic economic policy, and U.S. policymakers have abetted it as a way of getting Japan to solve the trade problem.

This pattern of U.S.-Japan governmental negotiations on economic issues is reinforced by a variety of factors, political and cultural as well as economic. The trade imbalance means that it is almost always the United States that is taking the initiative, seeking Japanese changes in policy and performance. And almost always Japan is reactive, trying to determine "what the United States really wants" and to figure out how the U.S. requests (often seen as demands) can be met or blunted. Some Japanese — especially policymakers well aware of the complex balances of power within and among the politicians, the bureaucracy, and the relevant economic interest groups (e.g., big business, small business, and agriculture) — recognize the benefit of foreign, especially U.S., pressure in helping bring about desired domestic economic policy changes. Of course those hurt by those changes resent the foreign scapegoat.

One important implication of this process is that, on matters of bilateral economic policy at least, U.S. negotiators have learned that the most effective way to obtain their objectives vis-à-vis Japan is to apply pressure strongly, relentlessly, and with increasing severity. In the U.S. bureaucratic perception, the Japanese ask for these little "shocks," and the most effective approach is to provide them. As one senior U.S. official privately put it, "the only way to get the Japanese to do anything is to hit them over the head, if necessary repeatedly; their officials know it and ask us to."

This approach to the management of the economic relationship may have been useful in the past, but the 1977–1979 crisis provided signals that it has become increasingly dangerous. It was somewhat successful in the short run; it may well be very harmful in the long run. At some point, those being hit stop reacting submissively and start getting angry. The heavy-handedness of U.S. pressure in the 1977–1979 crisis, although almost certainly less extreme than in 1971–1973, began to generate considerable negative reaction in

Japan. The decline in U.S. popularity has been substantial among those who have considered the United States their friend—and not just among farmers.[42] Simply because, for cultural reasons, the Japanese mute their resentment, Americans should not be oblivious of it.

Perhaps a more serious cause of strains in the relationship on the Japanese side has been a decline of confidence in the capacity and will of the United States to exercise world leadership. Japan's increasing concern about U.S. leadership is in part the working-through of the long-run processes of differential growth rates, changes in relative economic power, and the adjustment problems created for a number of U.S. industries. But it has become more than that. Many Japanese fear that the United States cannot solve its own economic, much less social, problems in a constructive fashion.[43] From a Japanese perspective at the end of 1979, inflation had not been brought under control, and recession is an expensive way to go about trying. The long-run energy problems appear far from solved, the U.S. strategy still not fully articulated. Protectionist forces in the United States seem to have become increasingly powerful, threatening to undermine the international economic order from which Japan benefits at least as much as the United States. Despite the incentives of greatly enhanced price competitiveness brought about by depreciation of the dollar, U.S. producers have not responded as vigorously or competitively as expected or desired. They have increased prices at home rather than fighting to take market share away from imports, and they have not yet expanded export volumes sufficiently to solve the U.S. trade-deficit problem over the long run.

In this Japanese perspective, the burden of adjustment should be shared between nations with balance-of-payments-surpluses and those with deficits, and the United States has not been doing its fair share. The Japanese argue, with some persuasiveness, that U.S. balance-of-payments difficulties have been created more by U.S. than by Japanese policies and economic action, and it behooves U.S. policymakers to respond constructively by solving these difficulties without adopting protectionism in the process.

Just as U.S. images and perceptions of Japan are distortions of reality, so too in many respects are Japanese images and perceptions of the United States. The U.S. tendency toward self-criticism, analysis of its faults, and pluralistic sets of pressures and counterpressures may lead the Japanese to underestimate basic U.S. social, political, economic, and military strengths, as well to as feel confused as to which direction the United States might follow. Then too the nostalgia among many Japanese for the "good old days" of security under U.S. hegemonic power and leadership sometimes clouds realistic appraisals of present political realities.

Neither country has been adept in anticipating and thereby minimizing these occasional crises in the U.S.-Japan partnership or in handling them once they have reached serious proportions. This inadequacy is probably inevitable given the immense size of both countries' economies; their private, decentralized, market-oriented economic systems; and the complexities of the policy processes in each country involved in identifying problems, reaching decisions, and implementing them. The events of 1977–1979 were a combination of "too much too soon" and "too little too late." For example, Japanese exports to the United States increased too rapidly, especially in certain industries, such as color television, in which U.S. producers were seriously injured. The United States, once it moved, let the dollar depreciate sharply and rapidly, much to Japanese discomfort. But both policies were consequences, in part, of earlier policy inactions in both countries. Most important, the Japanese response to a burgeoning export surplus was slow and limited, necessitating far larger and more severe policy actions later.

The politicization of economic issues has generated crises in the bilateral partnership. To some extent this is inevitable, as one purpose of the political process in democratic societies is to solve income-distribution and other problems arising from the economic system. When the overall balance-of-payments position of the United States has been healthy, then those special interests facing import competition from Japan and those whose access to the Japanese market was restricted have had only a limited influence within the U.S. political system; their complaints can be handled, more or less adequately, without serious pressure on the partnership itself. However, when the U.S. balance of payments has been in difficulty and/or the U.S. economy has been in recession, then the politicization of issues has become much more general and widespread.[44] Protectionist elements in both countries were much more able to appeal to the general public; latent negative images came to the fore; and scapegoatism became all too easy for businessmen, bureaucrats, and politicians on both sides. It is through this combination of circumstances that the U.S.-Japan partnership came to be dominated by short-run but nonetheless intense tension. And this tension, I believe, proved to be costly: Each country drew down substantially on its stock of accumulated goodwill toward the other.

Perspectives on the Partnership's Future

Given the rather contradictory situation—the high degree of interdependence between the United States and Japan and the importance of the alliance to both, on the one hand, and the high degree of tension in the relationship during the 1977–1979 economic crisis, on the other—what are the prospects for the partnership? All the recent negative factors—scapegoatism, bad images, trade problems, difficulties in carrying out domestic sectoral adjustments, decline in the credibility of U.S. leadership, slow Japanese responsiveness to the implications of its position as a major economic power—have led some to argue that the United States and Japan are on a collision course. This is an exaggerated, excessively pessimistic view of the future and of U.S. and Japanese capabilities to solve problems once they are understood and defined. The more relevant, if more subtle, danger is that the two countries will gradually drift apart without being fully aware of what is happening.

The future economic problems and prospects for the U.S.-Japan economic partnership must be viewed in multiple perspectives. The time dimension is important; my focus here is on trends and issues for the 1980s. My central concern is with the bilateral economic relationship; however, that must be seen within the dual perspectives of the problems and policies each country faces on the one hand and the great importance of the world environment (the multilateral context) on the other. The purpose of the following discussion is not so much to predict as to identify certain major probable trends and potential problem areas in the bilateral economic relationship.

In the past, as discussed in earlier sections, U.S.-Japan economic relations have been handled predominantly within a purely bilateral context. This pattern evolved, for reasons of convenience and custom, from the earlier client-patron relationship. An extreme bilateral focus is certainly no longer desirable, and perhaps not even feasible. Rather, a multilateral approach has become essential for several reasons. First, each economy is much too large and important, to each other and to the world economy as a whole. Together, the United States and Japan produce about one-third of the world's GNP and engage in more than one-fifth of the world's trade. Bilateral (as well as unilateral) economic decisions have a substantial impact on other nations, especially those in Asia and the Pacific.[45] This is an important aspect of the interdependence each has, not just with the other, but with all its trading partners. Second, the bilateral trade imbalance is most appropriately judged in the context of the global balance-of-payments position of each country. Third, certain very important issues can most effectively be resolved in a multilateral rather than a bilateral framework, as is discussed below. First, however, it may be useful to examine prospects for the bilateral economic relationship itself.

The Bilateral Economic Relationship

Two-way trade between Japan and the United States, already huge, will continue to expand roughly in proportion to the growth in total trade of each. This point, although obvious, is of great importance, as both countries benefit immensely from the trade relationship. Indeed, the strength of this trade relationship is one of the foundations of the overall alliance. The growing market of each will provide opportunities for the exports of the other; at the same time, as discussed below, some exports of each will continue to produce problems for domestic producers in the other.

At the macro level the bilateral trade surplus of Japan will persist as a structural phenomenon, although its size will fluctuate cyclically. Essentially this phenomenon exists because Japan must import large amounts of raw materials and pay for them by exports of manufactured goods, while the United States cannot supply sufficient proportions of Japan's raw material needs competitively yet is the world's largest market for manufactured goods. This reliance on the U.S. market, and the trade surplus, creates a kind of vulnerability for Japan, as it is thereby subject to U.S. pressures at both macro and specific commodity levels. It would be difficult and costly for Japan to try to reduce this vulnerability. Either it must diversify its exports away from the United States, thereby forgoing many opportunities the U.S. market offers, or it must find ways to import more from the United States. The former course implies a lessened relationship. The latter requires special Japanese efforts and policies, such as decisions *not* to diversify away from U.S. sources of supply of agricultural products and other raw materials. This will require in turn export commitments on the part of the United States, including supply guarantees for foodstuffs and perhaps even coal and other energy sources. The United States should also expand its export effort, particularly toward the Japanese market, with all that entails — competent staff in Japan, market research, product redesign, sales and service infrastructure, advertising.

The overall bilateral relationship is likely to be plagued in the future, as in the past, with periods of cyclical tension. The experience of the 1970s suggests these will occur when the U.S. global balance of payments goes into serious deficit and the bilateral trade deficit with Japan becomes even more visible. Tension will be exacerbated when Japan concurrently is running a substantial surplus in the current account of its global balance of payments. It seems likely that in the long run Japan will again achieve surpluses, perhaps substantial. Much depends on the persistence of high private savings rates, private domestic investment demand, the maintenance of export competitiveness in a number of manufacturing sectors, and public policies to absorb and channel saving and to manage the exchange rate. As argued above, Japan is likely to become a capital-exporting nation in the long run; this can be achieved only through current-account surpluses. The size of the surpluses will be both a cyclical and a structural issue vis-à-vis the United States and others, especially if OPEC-nation surpluses persist. The extent to which cyclical patterns can be understood, dampened, and accepted by both countries will be one key to successful management of the bilateral economic relationship.

It is probably inevitable that, at the micro or sectoral level, trade problems in specific industries will become significant from time to time. These difficulties emanate, as already discussed, from evolving comparative advantage, attendant loss of competitiveness of certain import-competing sectors in both countries, and the time and cost required for appropriate adjustment. Where these sectors have political clout they will attempt to use it. Such protectionist pressures, always difficult to contain because of the nature of interest-group politics, will be exacerbated in times of tension in the macro bilateral relationship. Japanese agriculture and U.S. steel will continue as problem areas. Japanese exports of automobiles loom as an important new issue, although much depends on how rapidly and effectively U.S. producers shift to small-car production to meet consumer preferences as gasoline prices continue to rise. Semiconductors, symbolic of high technology for the future, have already appeared on the horizon as a potential source of dispute. Past Japanese policies of protection of infant industries from foreign competition by restrictions on imports and foreign investment are no longer appropriate. Indeed, given the liberalization steps taken by Japan throughout the 1970s, culminating in the signing of the MTN agreement in 1979, such protectionist actions would contravene Japanese policy as well as its international commitments. One future task for management of the economic relationship will be to devise rules that both recognize legitimate national interests in encouraging certain industries and assure that such support is not based on restrictions on imports and/or foreign direct investment.

Problems Each Partner Faces

Any overt ruptures in the partnership will probably emanate from the United States. Much depends on how the United States handles the ongoing problems of structural adjustment discussed earlier. Reasonable projections strongly indicate the ever-increasing salience of economic issues in world affairs. From the viewpoint of U.S. foreign policy globally and regionally in Asia, as well as bilaterally with Japan, the following trends are likely: Economic issues will become of increasing importance in U.S. foreign relations, and there will be an increasing linkage between economic and military-strategic or political domains as issues in one sphere spill over into others. More than ever, U.S. world leadership will require as a necessary, although not sufficient, condition a commitment to a market-oriented international economic order that promotes the relatively free, multilateral flow of goods, services, and capital. This is an essential component of the basis upon which the legitimacy and credibility of U.S. leadership depend.

An insidious threat to U.S. global leadership, not to mention the bilateral partnership, therefore, is the tendency toward protectionism as the politically easiest response to the adjustment problems certain industries face from import competition. A slide into protectionism by the United States by a series of ad hoc restrictive measures, rather than by any explicit shift in policy, certainly is possible. It would be disastrous for overall U.S. foreign policy. The United States successfully dealt with one potential turning point by enacting the Trade Act of 1979, which embodied the results of the successful Tokyo Round of multilateral trade negotiations. But that alone will not resolve the problems of ongoing, ad hoc protectionist pressures. Until the United States succeeds both in handling domestic problems of adjustment for industries facing severe import competition and in generating a new momentum in exports, the danger of protectionism is likely to be an ongoing issue of major dimensions in U.S. foreign economic policy.

More fundamentally, the United States needs to achieve effective management of its economy, at the levels of both public policy and private enterprise. Inflation must be brought and kept under control, ways must be found to reverse the decline in the rate of productivity growth, exports must rise not just absolutely but as a share of GNP, and energy must be conserved even as alternative sources are developed. These problems are interrelated, so their solution will require a comprehensive package of policies. At the same time, the

United States has moved into greater economic interdependence with the rest of the world. No longer can it pursue completely autonomous economic policies. To have the cooperation of its allies, including Japan, the United States must be prepared to cooperate, to take into account the policies and needs of other nations, and to consult with them in order to reach jointly agreed upon decisions.

Let us assume that the United States maintains its commitment to the system of relatively free trade. Does the United States have a desirable, or even viable, alternative to alliance with Japan as the linchpin of its Asian policy? Careful consideration suggests the answer is negative.

In the euphoria following the normalization of relations and the visit of Vice-Premier Deng Xiaoping to the United States, China may have appeared to some a real alternative. Opportunities for trade with and lending to China have become real; they should be seized with all appropriate caution. But expanding economic relations is one matter; regarding China as a major friend and ally is another.

For Japan the alternatives to alliance with the United States appear even less attractive, strategically and economically, than the Chinese alternative does to the United States. This perception has led some U.S. policymakers to support a tougher stance in negotiations on specific issues with Japan. This is a short-sighted approach. It inhibits the building of the long-run trust essential for a true partnership. It does not recognize that even in the short-run Japan does have increasing options at the margin within the alliance.

Both nations will have to work at the relationship if it is to be more sound in the future. U.S. policymakers must not continue the practice of largely ignoring Japan until difficulties develop and then mobilizing poorly informed forces for a crisis-management approach. Not only must Japan continue to reduce trade barriers, it must tell its story better—and louder—in the United States. Less well recognized is the fact that U.S. public relations efforts in Japan are even more minuscule and less effective than Japanese efforts in the United States.

Japan faces problems of economic interdependence and domestic structural adjustment similar to those faced by the United States and presents similar problems for the rest of the world. It is necessary but increasingly difficult to shift resources out of sectors that are technically efficient but economically inefficient—not just agriculture, but industries such as pulp and paper that require scarce water and land resources, labor-intensive standard-technology manufacturing, and energy-intensive industries such as petrochemicals and minerals processing. Like the United States, Japan will face increasing competition from the newly industrializing countries (the NICs), not just in its export markets but increasingly at home. The temptation for ad hoc protectionism will be as strong in Japan as in the United States.

More fundamentally, Japan psychologically is an inward-oriented society, both hesitant and arrogant in dealing with foreigners. Its self-perception is one of weakness and vulnerability, a country beset by external forces beyond its own control. This self-image is belied by the realities of Japan's economic power as a trillion-dollar economy and of the interdependence of other nations with Japan. The great task for Japan, more difficult probably than structural adjustment, is to open up as a society and economy in this increasingly interdependent world. The rest of the world will look increasingly to Japan for positive, even generous, leadership in international economic policy. To handle that role well will require a more open, self-confident Japan, a substantial widening of perspective and of definition of national interest.

For Japan the realities of its economic interdependence are crucial. The events of the 1970s have forced Japan to redefine its national security interests in more comprehensive terms. Some degree of self-sufficiency in food is regarded as essential, as Japan now imports more than half its caloric intake, a higher proportion than the United Kingdom or any other major industrial nation. High-technology goods, especially computers, are also considered of strategic importance. To continue at the forefront of the world's industrial powers in the coming decades will require great and diversified use of computers, whose hardware and software are readily available domestically.[46]

Japanese policymakers and strategists regard the possibility of interruption of foreign supplies of oil and other energy sources, minerals, foodstuffs, and other raw materials as the most serious threat to national well-being. Security of access to these commodities is thus vital. Japan has sought commodity security in various ways: diversification of sources of supply; foreign direct investment and long-term contracts with suppliers; provision of foreign aid to those with large, desired resources; a friendly and nonthreatening stance toward all nations; and maintenance of close, special ties with resource-rich nations, especially those regarded as politically stable, such as the United States, Australia, Canada, and Brazil.

Such security concerns have major implications for the United States and for the partnership. In food the trade implications are direct. As the major supplier to Japan and the world, will the United States guarantee access of supply to Japan? On what terms? Will Japan be prepared in turn to guarantee purchases, to share in enhanced stockpiling and its associated costs, and to provide other incentives to maintain or expand rather than cut back U.S. farm production? Or should Japan attempt to diversify substantially— invest in soybeans in Brazil, beef in Indochina, and fish farming elsewhere so as to hold down meat consumption, which relies on imported grains? These are important issues for producers and consumers in both nations, as well as for strategic policy. Both countries would benefit from the development of long-term agreements that guarantee Japan specified supplies at prevailing world prices.

The energy problem is more profound. It involves one of the most basic commodities, oil, and some of the most sophisticated of technologies, especially in nuclear energy but also in coal gasification. Energy issues have probably the greatest potential in the bilateral economic relationship both for cooperation and for severe conflict. The United States and Japan can cooperate in various types of R&D projects, in the development of U.S. coal mines and exports to Japan, and in the swapping of Alaskan for other supplies of oil.

In the long run, the world must rely on alternatives to oil. Technology is the key—but technologies are unproven, uncertain, or not yet known, hence risky and expensive. Development of efficient, reasonably economical new energy sources will depend on successful research and development. In November 1978 Japan and the United States signed a scientific research agreement to develop a cooperative energy research and development program, focusing initially on magnetic fusion and coal liquefaction, at a cost of $1 billion over ten years. Partnership on energy R&D will have direct benefits for both and be generally supportive of the alliance.

Global and Regional Dimensions of the Partnership

Over time the U.S.-Japan partnership has added to its direct bilateral relationship a global dimension. As a major economy, Japan has joined the United States as an important force in the determination of the rules of the game in the international economic order. Both face the same multilateral problems, and increasingly the bilateral relationship has come to be seen within the global context. Both nations have strong, similar interests in a liberal international economic system. Recent events in the bilateral relationship as well as respective global balance-of-payments positions underscore the need for an international economic system that has built-in flexibility to cope with random or occasional disruptions and disequilibria, as well as systemic changes in underlying economic circumstances. A framework for cooperation is required in which the ordinary competitive forces of the private marketplace for individuals and business can most effectively operate in achieving private and social benefits. In particular, if a system of safeguards for protecting domestic industries from substantial injury by foreign competition is devised, then it should provide protection only for a specified, relatively brief period, while requiring that domestic adjustment steps be taken. Safeguards in any form ("orderly markets," textile agreements, or whatever) should not become another mechanism for long-run protection. Indeed, how the industrial economies, through private markets and public policies, resolve structural adjustment problems from import competition over the next five to ten years will greatly shape the nature of the world economic system. Neither Japan nor the United States is very far along in developing adequate, positive policy solutions, although the Japanese may have progressed further simply because they debate so intensively current issues of structural adjustment.

In addition to the bilateral and global contexts of the U.S.-Japan economic relationship, recently perceptions of an important Asian-Pacific regional context have begun to emerge. Much of the discussion in the region on this topic, which became increasingly common beginning in 1979, was in response to the initiative of Prime Minister Ohira in establishing a task force to examine the prospects for Pacific economic cooperation. This Japanese initiative, a major new constructive step, triggered discussions in the United States, Australia, and eventually in all the Asian developing market economies.[47] One concrete suggestion, put forward initially by scholars in Japan and Australia, is that there be formed an Organization for Pacific Trade and Development, comprising private-enterprise, market-oriented Asian-Pacific economies actively engaged in international economic intercourse.[48] Consideration of possible institutional arrangements, governmental or private, has only just begun; it will take considerable time before anything concrete emerges.

In terms of the interests of both Japan and the United States regional economic cooperation is a desirable course. What the two countries do in their bilateral relationship vitally affects the other Asian-Pacific nations; the spillover and transmission effects are large, as already noted. The Pacific Basin was, and will probably continue to be, the most rapidly growing part of the world economy. The United States and Japan have mutual interests in its peaceful development. Moreover, tensions are likely to be mitigated and the bilateral relationship strengthened by the process of attempting to understand and accommodate each other's interests in a broader regional framework.

Two cautionary points should be made concerning any such regional approach. First, it should not be restrictive or in any way impede the U.S. and Japanese commitments to a global economic system. At the same time it should be recognized that in the United States "global" tends to have a predominantly Atlantic, or North-South, orientation; Americans need to be more aware of the Pacific and the manifold opportunities it presents. Few Americans are aware that U.S. trade with the Pacific since 1972 has been greater than that with the Atlantic. Much can be done within the Pacific region to enhance trade and capital flows without contravening global commitments.

Second, U.S.-Japan cooperation vis-à-vis the rest of the Asian-Pacific region must be handled very carefully at both national and business levels. It must be perceived by the Association of Southeast Asian Nations (ASEAN) and the other Pacific nations not as a "Gang of Two" trying to exploit them—not as a new East Asian Co-Prosperity Sphere with U.S. participation—but as a genuine effort to accommodate their needs and interests for the mutual benefit of all. At the business level the rules of competition and open access must prevail; U.S. and Japanese firms must not be seen as establishing collusive joint ventures or cartels to the disadvantage of the other Pacific nations, or indeed of consumers in their own countries.

It is possible to remain somewhat optimistic about the prospects for the U.S. partnership and alliance with Japan. The economic, security, and other interests of the two nations overlap significantly, and the interrelationships are critical to both; interdependence now flows both ways. In times of stress both sides tend to focus on difficulties and problems. Neither side must be blind to the opportunities the other offers. In purely economic terms, the United States is the largest private market in the world. Japan is the second largest. The Japanese market will continue to grow rather rapidly, at perhaps 5–6 percent on annual average for the next ten to fifteen years. The decade of the 1970s has highlighted the fact that the partnership is evolving and that neither nation can take the other for granted. Much hard work still needs to be done by both nations to strengthen the partnership and to prevent the tendency to drift apart, the tendency to draw down past stores of goodwill. With work, an overarching vision for the relationship, and with luck, the partnership can be of continuing immense benefit to both.

Discussion of Tables

Tables 5.1–5.4 provide summary data over time for the United States and Japan of current-account and merchandise-trade transactions on both global and bilateral bases, together with relevant ratios. The appropriate focus is upon the current account, because transactions in transportation, services, and other invisible items are important components of the international (and bilateral) transactions of both the United States and Japan.

U.S. and Japanese balance-of-payments and trade data are based essentially on the same definitional standards; the major difference is that U.S. data include reinvested income of foreign affiliates as both a current-account (investment income) and capital-account transaction. Respective estimates of bilateral merchandise trade differ modestly, as shown in Table 5.4; the main exception was in the different treatment of the 1978 Japan "emergency import" prepayment for enriched uranium. Otherwise the merchandise-trade differences are probably due mainly to the timing of trade departures and arrivals.

Conceptually, it is preferable to use current account rather than merchandise trade as a measure of the bilateral economic relationship, as bilateral invisible transactions are significant. In practice, however, there are substantial problems of definition and measurement between U.S. and Japanese estimates, as shown in Table 5.4. In addition, unlike with bilateral trade data, estimation and publication of bilateral current-account estimates are sufficiently delayed in both countries that they are of limited use for short-run policy purposes. According to U.S. data, Japan tends to run a small bilateral surplus on invisibles; the current-account balance could be estimated through its relationship with the trade balance. The simple regression relationship (million dollars, annual data 1953–1978) is

$$\text{Current Account} = 184.8 + 0.971 \text{ Trade Balance}$$
$$R^2 = 0.9847$$
$$\text{d.w.} = 0.9450.$$

Table 5.4 provides a comparison of U.S. and Japanese estimates of the main components of the bilateral current account. The U.S. estimates show a substantially large bilateral deficit on current account. Most occurs in the measurement of invisibles transactions. Japanese coverage is much more comprehensive than U.S., as reflected in the respective estimates for both receipts and payments.

Japan's data-reporting and -collection system is probably better than that of the United States. In addition, there are significant differences in definition, especially regarding shipping and other transportation. The Japanese procedure of regional transportation estimation is to attribute payments to the country in which the operating company is located, not where it registers its ships (hence U.S.-owned ships registered in Liberia or Panama are treated as American). Japanese trading companies and shipping companies provide data on freight rates by commodity and country, charterage arrangements, and the like. Hence Japanese data on Japanese receipts (U.S. payments) are likely to be more accurate than data on payments.

TABLE 5.1
United States and Japan Global Exports of Goods and Services, Current
Account Surplus, and Bilateral Current Account Balance ($US million)

	United States		Japan		U.S. – Japan
	Exports of Goods and Services (1)	Current Account Surplus (2)	Exports of Goods and Services (3)	Current Account Surplus (4)	Current Account Bilateral Balance* (5)
1953	21,215	-1,952	2,458	-185	330
1954	20,896	-266	2,651	-15	76
1955	22,328	-420	2,906	-41	264
1956	26,284	1,478	3,304	34	132
1957	29,168	3,492	3,703	-384	-209
1958	25,606	-132	3,660	511	178
1959	25,683	-2,252	4,249	339	383
1960	28,861	2,824	4,927	111	50
1961	29,936	3,821	5,166	-982	-480
1962	31,804	3,388	5,994	-48	8
1963	34,215	4,414	6,526	-780	-346
1964	38,824	6,822	8,026	-480	-211
1965	41,090	5,435	9,897	932	365
1966	44,565	3,034	11,569	1,254	710
1967	47,318	2,587	12,411	-190	280
1968	52,373	621	15,358	1,048	829
1969	57,529	406	18,940	2,119	1,270
1970	65,659	2,360	22,978	1,970	857
1971	68,790	-1,407	28,406	5,797	2,750
1972	77,197	-5,979	34,270	6,624	4,782
1973	109,853	6,885	44,757	-136	1,631
1974	149,086	1,719	66,511	-4,693	1,048
1975	155,655	18,445	68,232	-682	1,372
1976	171,274	4,338	80,485	3,680	5,286
1977	183,214	-15,221	95,606	10,918	8,149
1978	221,019	-13,467	115,122	16,534	11,676
1979	286,312	-317	126,625	-8,693	--
1977 I	44,446	-2,459	21,195	893	1,122
II	48,138	-2,101	23,406	2,183	2,098
III	45,221	-5,183	24,502	3,261	2,301
IV	46,787	-4,349	26,503	4,581	2,628
1978 I	46,643	-5,805	25,997	3,971	3,092
II	55,754	-2,858	27,910	4,579	3,291
III	54,080	-5,955	29,834	5,146	2,967
IV	63,372	722	31,381	2,931	2,116
1979 I	64,941	274	28,966	-711	--
II	67,818	-810	30,497	-1,126	--
III	74,752	1,139	32,399	-3,229	--
IV	78,800	-923	36,763	-3,577	--

Note: U.S. data since 1960 include reinvested earnings of company affiliates.
*Negative figures indicate Japan in deficit.

Sources: Columns 1, 2, 5: Various issues of U.S. Department of Commerce, Statistical Abstract of the United States and Survey of Current Business. Columns 3 and 4: Bank of Japan, Economic Statistics Annual and Balance of Payments Monthly; Office of the Prime Minister, Bureau of Statistics, Japan Statistical Yearbook.

TABLE 5.2
United States-Japan Bilateral Merchandise Trade--Amounts, Shares, and Trade Balance
($U.S. million)

	Japanese Merchandise Exports to U.S.			Japanese Merchandise Imports from U.S.			
Year	Amount (1)	% of Japan Total Exports (2)	% of U.S. Total Imports (3)	Amount (4)	% of Japan Total Imports (5)	% of U.S. Total Exports (6)	U.S.-Japan Trade Balance* (7)
1953	262	18.3	2.4	686	31.5		-425
1954	279	17.3	2.7	693	35.3	4.6	-414
1955	432	22.7	3.8	683	31.3	4.4	-251
1956	558	22.0	4.5	998	33.0	5.3	-440
1957	601	21.1	4.6	1,319	37.9	6.4	-719
1958	667	24.0	5.2	987	34.8	5.6	-320
1959	1,029	30.3	6.9	1,080	31.0	6.2	- 51
1960	1,149	27.2	7.8	1,447	34.6	7.1	-298
1961	1,055	25.2	7.3	1,837	36.1	8.9	-783
1962	1,358	28.5	8.4	1,574	32.1	7.4	-216
1963	1,498	27.6	8.8	1,844	30.8	8.0	-346
1964	1,768	27.6	9.5	2,009	29.4	7.7	-241
1965	2,414	29.3	11.3	2,080	29.0	7.7	334
1966	2,963	30.4	11.7	2,364	27.9	7.9	599
1967	2,999	28.8	11.2	2,695	27.5	8.7	304
1968	4,054	31.5	12.3	2,954	28.9	8.7	1,100
1969	4,888	31.0	13.6	3,990	33.3	9.3	1,399
1970	5,875	30.7	14.8	4,652	31.0	10.9	1,223
1971	7,259	31.2	15.9	4,055	25.7	9.3	3,204
1972	9,065	30.9	16.4	4,965	26.0	10.1	4,101
1973	9,676	25.6	14.0	8,313	25.5	11.8	1,363
1974	12,456	22.4	12.4	10,679	20.1	11.0	1,877
1975	11,425	20.0	11.5	9,563	19.2	8.9	1,862
1976	15,504	22.0	12.5	10,144	18.6	8.9	5,360
1977	18,547	23.4	12.2	10,414	16.8	8.7	8,133
1978	24,458	25.6	13.9	12,885	18.2	9.1	11,573
1979	26,243	25.9	12.4	17,579	17.7	9.7	8,664
1977 I	3,914	22.3	10.7	2,809	19.0	9.5	1,105
II	4,589	23.7	12.0	2,553	16.4	8.0	2,036
III	4,810	23.8	12.7	2,475	16.0	8.5	2,335
IV	5,232	23.5	13.3	2,724	16.8	8.7	2,503
1978 I	5,730	26.7	13.7	2,628	16.8	8.5	3,102
II	6,241	26.8	14.2	3,025	18.1	8.3	3,216
III	6,347	25.6	14.4	3,332	19.1	9.7	3,015
IV	6,239	24.0	13.5	3,907	18.7	9.8	2,332
1979 I	6,297	27.5	13.2	4,200	19.8	10.1	2,097
1979 II	6,731	27.5	13.4	4,080	17.8	9.5	2,651
1979 III	6,481	24.9	11.9	4,574	17.3	9.7	1,907
1979 IV	6,747	24.2	11.4	4,475	15.5	8.9	2,272

Notes: U.S. data on f.a.s. (free alongside ship) basis, Japanese data on f.o.b.
(free on board) basis, so that both exclude shipping, insurance, and related costs.

*Negative figures indicate Japan in deficit; discrepancies in columns (1), (4), and
(7) due to rounding.

Sources: All columns except (2) and (5): U.S. sources cited in Table 5.1; columns
(2) and (5): Japanese sources cited in Table 5.1.

TABLE 5.3
United States - Japan Bilateral Goods and Services Trade (Current Account Basis),
1970 - 1978 (U.S. $ million)

	Japanese Goods and Services Exports to U.S.			Japanese Goods and Services Imports from U.S.			U.S.-Japan Current Account Balance (7)
Year	Amount (1)	% of Japan Total Exports (2)	% of U.S. Total Imports (3)	Amount (4)	% of Japan Total Imports (5)	% of U.S. Total Exports (6)	
1970	8063	34.9	12.7	7206	34.1	11.0	857
1971	10014	35.1	14.3	7258	31.9	10.6	2756
1972	12096	35.2	14.5	8745	31.5	11.3	3351
1973	13441	29.9	13.1	13337	29.6	12.1	104
1974	18163	27.2	12.6	18856	26.4	12.9	-693
1975	16679	24.4	12.2	17614	25.5	11.1	-935
1976	21488	26.6	12.9	18051	23.4	10.5	3437
1977	25892	27.0	13.0	19122	22.5	10.4	6770
1978	32188	28.0	13.7	23523	23.9	10.6	8665

Note: The current account balance estimates here are noticeably lower than in Table 5.1;
they are from Japanese data. The differences are due primarily to definition and
coverage of invisible items, especially transportation, as well as Japan's 1978
emergency import program; see Table 5.4 and the statistical notes to these tables.

Source: Bank of Japan Balance of Payments Monthly, various issues, and Table 5.1.

TABLE 5.4
Comparison of United States and Japan Estimates of Current Account Bilateral Balance ($ million, U.S. perspective)

	1975 U.S.	1975 Japan	1976 U.S.	1976 Japan	1977 U.S.	1977 Japan	1978 U.S.	1978 Japan
Merchandise balance	-1,690	-1,045	-5,335	-5,531	-7,984	-8,984	-11,529	-10,611
U.S. imports	11,257	10,930	15,531	15,635	18,545	19,388	24,474	24,652
U.S. exports	9,567	9,885	10,196	10,104	10,561	10,727	12,945	14,041
Invisibles balance	361	1,907	98	1,999	107	1,848	-64	1,803
U.S. receipts	3,159	7,553	3,169	7,746	3,633	8,225	5,005	9,216
U.S. payments	2,798	5,646	3,070	5,747	3,740	6,377	5,069	7,413
Unilateral transfers	-43	73	-49	95	-43	43	-81	140
Current account balance	-1,372	935	-5,286	-3,437	-8,134	-6,770	-11,675	-8,668
Note: Invisible Items								
Transportation balance	194	954	24	1,173	-290	1,101	-395	1,132
U.S. receipts	923	3,399	1,029	3,758	1,105	3,861	1,164	3,879
U.S. payments	729	2,445	1,005	2,585	1,395	2,760	1,559	2,747
Investment income balance	130	298	-47	128	38	46	-17	-696
U.S. receipts	1,208	1,836	1,028	1,474	1,319	1,589	2,314	1,476
U.S. payments	1,078	1,538	1,075	1,346	1,281	1,543	2,331	2,172

Note: The substantial difference in U.S. and Japanese estimates of U.S. exports in 1978 is because the former excludes $1 billion in Japanese uranium enrichment prepayment and the latter includes it.

Source: U.S. Department of Commerce, Survey of Current Business; Bank of Japan, Balance of Payments Monthly.

Notes

1. The current account is conceptually a better measure than the (merchandise) trade account because it includes transactions in a variety of services that are important components of the ongoing economic relationships of both the United States and Japan with the world and with each other. Henceforth, references to "trade imbalances" or other trade relationships are meant in current-account terms to include both goods and services.

2. Useful discussions include Franklin B. Weinstein, ed., *U.S.-Japan Relations and the Security of East Asia* (Boulder, Colo.: Westview Press, 1978); and Daniel I. Okimoto and John K. Emmerson, "The U.S.-Japan Alliance: Overview and Outlook," in V. A. Johnson and George Packard, eds., *The Common Security Interests of Japan, the United States and NATO* (Cambridge, Mass.: Ballinger, 1981), pp. 87–129.

3. The now-standard quotation is from the speech of Secretary of State Vance to the Asia Society on June 29, 1977: "Of our allies and old friends, none is more important than Japan. Our mutual security treaty is a cornerstone of peace in East Asia."

4. For a comprehensive appraisal of the Japanese economy, see Hugh T. Patrick and Henry Rosovsky, eds., *Asia's New Giant—How the Japanese Economy Works* (Washington, D.C.: Brookings Institution, 1976).

5. For a detailed analysis, see Gary Saxonhouse and Hugh Patrick, "Japan and the United States: Bilateral Tensions and Multilateral Issues in the Economic Relationship," in D. C. Hellmann, ed., *China and Japan: A New Balance of Power* (Lexington, Mass.: D. C. Heath, 1976), pp. 95–157.

6. For data on bilateral merchandise-trade and current-account totals, balances, and shares in each other's global trade, see Tables 5.1–5.4, and the accompanying statistical note, at the end of this chapter.

7. "U.S. shipments of agricultural products to Japan are two and a half times larger than to our next most important national customer." U.S. General Accounting Office, *United States–Japan Trade: Issues and Problems*, ID-79-53 (Washington, D.C.: Government Printing Office, September 21, 1979), p. 3, commonly referred to as the *GAO Report*.

8. Data are for 1979, based on U.S. Department of Commerce, Bureau of the Census, *Highlights of U.S. Export and Import Trade, December 1979* (Washington, D.C.: Government Printing Office). The ratios of course change somewhat from year to year.

9. See, for example, the Congressional Research Service, Library of Congress Study for the Congress, *Project Interdependence: U.S. and World Energy Outlook through 1990*, Publication No. 95-31 (Washington, D.C.: Government Printing Office, June 1977). Even if more recent efforts to reduce oil imports are successful, the hard fact remains that the United States will continue to rely heavily on large amounts of oil imports for the foreseeable future.

10. The argument is as follows: Increased oil imports can be paid for only by restricting other imports or by larger export earnings; import restriction implies higher direct, informal or formal barriers (quotas, "orderly

marketing" arrangements, trigger-prices, and similar barriers) beyond relative price adjustments; however, maintenance of U.S. economic leadership requires a relatively open and free trade policy; therefore, to maintain a liberal trade policy the United States must place greater priority on exporting.

11. It should be recognized that certain assumptions about Japanese domestic economy, balance-of-payments, and exchange-rate policies as well as economic performance are implicit in this prediction. Essentially, I assume that at full use of human and capital resources Japanese saving will tend to outstrip domestic investment demand and that Japan will not be constrained by its major trading partners to appreciate the yen so much that the country would have a zero current-account position over the long run. Further, I assume that rises in imported energy prices will be offset, with time, by increases in exports. These secular forces will be somewhat reduced, and appear blurred, by continuing cyclical deficits, as in 1979–1980, if oil prices should rise dramatically from time to time.

12. An earlier crisis was brief but intense, involving the domestic politics in Japan of revising and renewing in 1960 the security treaty with the United States and culminating in the cancellation of the planned first visit of a U.S. president (Eisenhower) to Japan.

13. It is this fact that distinguishes Japan from West Germany and that, rather than racism, accounts predominantly for the U.S. focus on problems created by Japan. U.S. trade with Germany is relatively modest, and the bilateral imbalance small. See, for instance, *GAO Report*, pp. 4–14.

14. The administration tended to have a substantially more global orientation than the Congress, which had a strongly bilateral focus.

15. For a current evaluation, which concludes that such a mechanism would no longer work sufficiently because of the large size of the Japan economy, leading to adverse foreign responses, see Hugh Patrick, "What the Japanese Economy Needs Now: Moderation and Stimulus," in Hisao Kanamori, ed., *Recent Developments of Japanese Economy and Its Differences from Western Advanced Countries*, Center Paper No. 29 (Tokyo: Japan Economic Research Center, September 1976).

16. For estimates of the gap between actual and full-capacity GNP see Japan Economic Research Center, *Quarterly Forecast of Japan's Economy*, no. 41 (May 1979):42. This gap is estimated at 8.4 percent in fiscal 1977 and 8.1 percent for 1978 and is projected at 8.2 percent for 1979. An important adjustment process since 1974 has been the sharp reduction in full-capacity output growth through the decline in private enterprise investment rates.

17. The U.S. position is articulated in U.S. House of Representatives, Committee on Ways and Means, Subcommittee on Trade, *Task Force Report on United States–Japan Trade* (Washington, D.C.: Government Printing Office, January 1979), commonly referred to as the *Jones Report*. It is noteworthy that some Japanese see trade liberalization as one means of opening up, liberalizing, and "internationalizing" Japanese society.

18. Some barriers to trade are not amenable to policy action by the government of Japan, such as the Japanese language itself; others require

some change in Japanese values and attitudes, such as enactment and enforcement of antitrust legislation; for still others, such as rationalization of the distribution system and the phasing out of now uncompetitive industries such as aluminum smelting, the adjustment process will take a considerable time to work itself out.

19. See *Jones Report*, pp. 45–47. Reorganizations in late 1979 expanded the role of the Office of the Special Trade Representative and gave greater responsibility for foreign trade to the Department of Commerce.

20. A comprehensive and reasonably objective description of the many economic aspects of the bilateral relationship during 1978 is provided in U.S.-Japan Trade Council, *Yearbook of U.S.-Japan Economic Relations 1978* (Washington, D.C.: U.S.-Japan Trade Council, 1979), p. 131. A 1979 yearbook is forthcoming.

21. See Tables 5.1–5.4 for annual data and for quarterly data for 1977–1979.

22. The Japan Economic Research Center *Quarterly Forecast* for May 1979 (p. 30) estimated Japan's global current-account surplus at $7.2 billion for calendar 1979 and $6.4 billion for fiscal 1979. Interestingly, these forecasts were far below those of the previous report (no. 40, January 1979). Subsequent quarterly projections continued to revise sharply downward these estimates.

23. As shown in Tables 5.1–5.4, U.S. data indicate almost the same numbers for bilateral trade and current-account balance, while Japanese data estimate a substantially lower current-account surplus, almost $2 billion annually on average for 1975–1978. Bilateral current-account estimates for 1979 are not yet available.

24. This was reflected in the low-key way in which the Joint Economic Committee, chaired by Senator Lloyd Bentsen, received the *GAO Report* at its October 10, 1979 hearing. It should be noted that this report was prepared in response to a request by Senator Bentsen to determine if legislation for a special surcharge on imports from Japan was appropriate. By October interest in that measure had ended; the U.S. perception was that Japan had finally responded appropriately.

25. The fiscal 1979 budget (beginning April 1) had a deficit of 39.6 percent, requiring the issuance of $80 billion in government bonds, equivalent of about 6.6 percent of GNP. These amounts and ratios were far higher than in the United States or Western Europe. See *Japan Economic Journal*, February 6, 1979, p. 4.

26. At the same time the quantitative impact of "imported inflation" on U.S. prices should not be exaggerated, as trade is a small proportion of GNP. The direct effect of yen appreciation probably was very small; multiplication of appreciation (35 percent) by Japan's share in U.S. trade (about 12.5 percent) and by the U.S. share of imports in GNP (about 3 percent) provides a maximum estimate of 0.35 percent increase in U.S. prices. This figure is low, however, because it does not take into account indirect and feedback effects as import-competing U.S. producers raise prices and as inflationary increases work their way through the system. Other estimates suggest that

an increase in the average exchange rate and prices for all U.S. imports by 10 percent would raise the U.S. domestic price level by about 1.75 percent over three years. This suggests that a 35 percent yen appreciation, everything else being equal, would have increased U.S. price levels by only about 0.75 percent. For a survey of various elasticity estimates, see Peter Hooper and Barbara Lowrey, "Impact of the Dollar Depreciation on the U.S. Price Level: An Analytical Survey of Empirical Estimates," International Finance Discussion Paper No. 128 (Washington, D.C.: Board of Governors of the Federal Reserve System, January 1979).

27. *Jones Report*, p. 11, n. 10.

28. Morgan Guaranty Trust Company, *World Financial Markets*, April 1979. On April 13 the yen/dollar spot rate was 206.2; it depreciated further during the course of 1979 to about 240 (239.8 on December 28).

29. The preliminary 1979 data were announced by the Economic Planning Agency on March 7, 1980. See *U.S.-Japan Trade Council Report #13*, April 4, 1980.

30. IBM Inc., *Monthly Report for January* (January 1980), p. 28.

31. In addition, import quotas, and also exclusive sales-agency arrangements with U.S. or other suppliers, have created monopoly profits for selected importers. Not surprisingly, they strongly oppose complete import liberalization and allegedly make substantial financial contributions to friendly Diet members and other politicians.

32. Robert Brusca, "United States Export Performance," Federal Reserve Bank of New York *Quarterly Review* 3, no. 4 (Winter 1978-1979). Between 1974 and 1977 the average market share (in volume terms) in rest-of-world trade of the United States decreased from 15.1 percent to 13.5 percent, while West Germany went from 12.5 percent to 12.3 percent and Japan from 7.2 percent to 8.3 percent.

33. For good discussions see Hideo Sato, "Japanese-American Relations," *Current History* 75, no. 441 (November 1978):145–148, 180–181; as well as other articles in this special issue on Japan; Robert A. Scalapino, "The American-Japanese Alliance—Cornerstone or Trouble Zone?" in Leon Hollerman, ed., *Japan and the United States: Economic and Political Adversaries* (Boulder, Colo.: Westview Press, forthcoming); and I. M. Destler, "United States–Japanese Relations and the American Trade Initiative of 1977: Was This 'Trip' Necessary?" in U.S. House of Representatives, Subcommittee on Trade of the Committee on Ways and Means, *Background Articles on United States Trade Issues* (Washington, D.C.: Government Printing Office, September 27, 1978).

34. This is especially true of agriculture; beef is the most extreme example and one that contributes dramatically to Japan's bad image abroad. It is interesting that some 400,000 households produce beef; they represent less than 2 percent of the total number of households in Japan. Yet they, together with the other beneficiaries of import restriction, are able to keep prices of beef for the other 98 percent of Japanese consuming households at about five times U.S. levels.

35. For a detailed study see I. M. Destler, Hauchiro Fukui, and Hideo

Sato, *The Textile Wrangle* (Ithaca, N.Y.: Cornell University Press, 1979).

36. At the same time it must be recognized that the United States has lost an overwhelming market share to Japan in a number of industries, requiring considerable reallocation of labor and capital, without the issue's becoming highly politicized; examples include motorcycles, black and white televisions, cameras, and stereo equipment.

37. A case-study approach is essential. For a good analysis see I. M. Destler et al., *Managing an Alliance — The Politics of U.S.-Japanese Relations* (Washington, D.C.: Brookings Institution, 1976). For a useful discussion of the way both countries prepared for negotiation within the Tokyo Round MTN context, see Michael Blaker, ed., *The Politics of Trade — U.S. and Japanese Policymaking for the GATT Negotiations* (New York: East Asian Institute, Columbia University, 1978).

38. Also underlying the bilateral negotiations was the U.S. administration strategy of defusing potential industry and congressional opposition to the MTN legislation. This was apparently the case of U.S. negotiations with Japan regarding liberalization of import quotas on beef and especially oranges. The intensity of U.S. pressure resulted in a substantial political price in Japan. As the value of U.S. exports to Japan thus liberalized was quite modest, the payoff has to be seen in different terms: Congressional passage of the MTN legislation in July 1979. While the U.S. strategy is generally regarded as highly successful, one issue is whether such prices paid to obtain congressional support were excessive. For a good study see Gilbert R. Winham, "Robert Strauss, the MTN, and the Control of Faction," paper presented at the American Political Science Association annual meeting, August 31–September 3, 1979.

39. An editorial in the prestigious *Japan Economic Journal*, May 15, 1979, while stressing the need for Japanese action to reduce the economic strain between Japan and the rest of the world, includes the following: "Many of the charges against Japan don't make sense to the Japanese. Demands on Japan mounting in the U.S. Congress, particularly, seem not reasonable but heavy-handed pressure. U.S. strategy so far has been to bring the problems of individual industries to the diplomatic negotiating table with Japan. In so doing, the U.S. has tried little to increase exports and lower the inflation rate at home. This may be just another demonstration of egocentric behavior by a big power." A study of the attitudes of selected U.S. business and other leaders is Arthur D. Little, Inc., *The Japanese Non-Tariff Barrier Issue: American Views and the Implications for Japan-U.S. Trade Relations*, NRC-78-12 (Tokyo: National Institute for Research Advancement, May 1979.)

40. James C. Abegglen, "Narrow Self-Interest: Japan's Ultimate Vulnerability?" paper presented to Lehrman Foundation study group on U.S.-Japan relations, April 17, 1979.

41. Robert C. Angel, "Japan's Most Serious Economic Problem in the United States — The Image of an 'Unfair Japan,'" Washington, D.C. United States–Japan Trade Council, September 1978.

42. The causes of this decline are not simple and certainly not based

solely on economic tensions, which nonetheless, because of their high visibility through the Japanese mass media and their immediacy for affected persons, have had substantial impact.

43. Japanese complaints have begun to be voiced more openly. See, for instance, Saburo Okita, "Japan, China and the United States—Their Relations and Problems," *Foreign Affairs* 57, no. 4 (July 1979).

44. The effect of recession depends in substantial part on its source, duration, effect on employment, and the importance attached to employment. Thus, for instance, as U.S. economic growth slowed during 1979, import growth also slowed and the U.S. trade and current-account balances, globally and with Japan, improved. (See Tables 5.1 and 5.2.) This will probably reduce tensions and protectionist sentiment in 1980 even while recession-generated unemployment may increase pressures toward protectionism.

45. For a useful analysis, see Lawrence B. Krause and Sueo Sekiguchi, eds., *Economic Interaction in the Pacific Basin* (Washington, D.C.: Brookings Institution, 1980).

46. Okita, "Japan, China, and the United States," stresses the "absolute necessity" of Japan's policy of encouraging the "development of knowledge intensive industries and the high technology sector."

47. Lawrence B. Krause, "The Pacific Economy in an Interdependent World," and Peter Drysdale, "Australia's Economic Relations with Asia and the Pacific: Past Perspectives and Future Prospects," in Kermit O. Hanson and Thomas W. Roehl, eds., *The United States and the Pacific Economy in the 1980s* (Indianapolis: Bobbs Merrill, 1980).

48. For an appraisal in terms of U.S. national interests, see Peter A. Drysdale and Hugh Patrick, "Evaluation of a Proposed Asian-Pacific Regional Economic Organization," in *An Asian-Pacific Regional Economic Organization—An Exploratory Concept Essay* (Washington, D.C.: U.S. Senate, Committee on Foreign Relations, July 1979).

6

The U.S.-Japan Trade Conflict: An Economist's View from Japan

Ryutaro Komiya

In recent years economic as well as cultural relations between the United States and Japan have become closer and more intense. It is perhaps not surprising that as the world's two largest market economies become more closely tied, cases of economic conflict, especially in trade, arise more frequently. Some of them have been difficult to resolve and remain serious diplomatic issues between the two countries. This chapter reviews the recent history of trade conflict between the United States and Japan from an academic economist's point of view. It attempts to interpret this important problem in a macroeconomic perspective, with the hope of promoting a better understanding of the problem among the general public, government officials, and politicians, both in Japan and in the United States.

Trade Conflict and Overall Imbalance

Since the late 1960s diplomatic tensions between the United States and Japan have become acute during several "waves," due to conflicts in trading. The first major wave began to gather momentum in 1969, toward the end of the Bretton Woods regime, when Japan's balance-of-payments surplus on its current account began to increase markedly under the old parity of 360 yen to a dollar. During

An earlier draft of this chapter was first delivered at a seminar at Stanford University on September 1979. I would like to thank Dr. Glen Campbell, director of the Hoover Institution, who was my host, as well as the staffs of the institution and of the Department of Economics, Stanford University, for their helpful suggestions. The draft was revised in December 1980 in view of recent developments and comments.

this time the United States was experiencing increasing payment deficits. This wave reached its peak in 1971–1972 when Japan's surplus and the United States's deficit in their respective current accounts and the U.S.-Japanese bilateral trade imbalance all reached unprecedented highs. It subsided in 1973 when payment and trade imbalances almost disappeared as Japan, and the rest of the world, ran into rapid inflation. The tension was almost totally absent in 1974–1975, when Japan was struggling with its balance of payments and the very high inflation that followed the first oil crisis, while the United States recorded a very sizable current-account surplus.

The second major wave of heightened tension began in the summer of 1976. At that time Japan's exports to the United States, as well as to Europe, rapidly increased under conditions of stagnation and unemployment, which all the advanced industrialized countries were experiencing. The wave reached a peak in 1978, a year in which both Japan and the United States again recorded an unprecedentedly large current-account surplus and deficit, respectively. This wave of increased tension began to subside in 1979 as both countries' payment imbalances were quickly corrected. In fact, Japan's huge current-account surplus began to dwindle rapidly in the last quarter of 1978, and the account then evolved into one of rapidly increasing deficit in the beginning of 1979. At about the same time the U.S. current-account deficit almost disappeared and even moved into a small surplus in the first and third quarters of 1979.

But this time diplomatic and political tension over the trade issue persisted, although it eased considerably, particularly in 1979. Substantial imbalances remain in the U.S.-Japanese bilateral trade account. As a result of the second oil crisis—a massive worldwide rise in oil prices toward the end of 1978—Japan's balance of payments moved into a huge deficit again in the middle of 1979, and in the first half of 1980 the deficit (on an annual basis) amounted to more than $20 billion. Japan's oil-import bill swelled from the second oil crisis; the rate of growth of GNP went up from about 2.6 percent in 1978 to 5.8 percent in the first quarter of 1980. Japan had to increase its exports to pay the bill, and it did so rapidly once again. This increase in exports was particularly conspicuous in the case of a few specific items. One of these was automobile exports to the United States: In 1979 the number of Japanese passenger cars sold in the United States increased more than 30 percent over the previous year, and the Japanese automakers' share in the U.S. passenger-car market went up sharply, from 16.6 percent in 1979 to 21.8 percent in the first half of 1980. No wonder Japan's automotive exports to the United States constituted one of the most serious trade issues between the two countries. At the end of 1980 several other trade issues still remained difficult to resolve and for some of them prolonged negotiations, both formal and informal, were still going on.

The two major "waves" of tension between the countries coincided with the period in which Japan had a large payment surplus and the United States as large a deficit. Although the tension was caused by a variety of issues (e.g., the sharp increase in Japan's export of certain products, alleged cases of dumping, nontariff barriers, and the Japanese government's control of direct investment and operations of foreign banks in Japan), it appears to me that the basic economic condition in which the U.S.-Japanese trade conflict became critical was the large imbalance in the trade, or payments, between the two countries. When the balance of payments of the respective countries becomes greatly imbalanced, the trade flow between the two closely integrated economies swells in one direction and causes various kinds of friction. Should Japan's exports of certain manufactured products to the United States rapidly increase, industries in the United States producing the same or similar products will be affected and will often request restrictions on these imports from Japan. When the payment imbalance is large and the affected industries are numerous and politically powerful, the trade friction is more or less politicized and brings about increased diplomatic tension.

However, it is important here to identify the real issues to be considered and remedied by governmental policy. What should be the objectives of economic policy in the two countries?

Attention is sometimes focused on the trade-account balance — the difference between a country's merchandise exports and imports — rather than the balance of payments on its current account. Thus an imbalance in merchandise trade is thought of as something that should be corrected; a balance of trade — equal values of exports and imports — is implicitly taken as a target of economic policy. Quite often the U.S.-Japanese trade imbalance is thought of in the United States as an undesirable object that must be eliminated or at least diminished. The report of the United States–Japan Task Force of the House Subcommittee on Trade, published in January 1979 (to be referred to hereafter as the First Jones Report), states that "because the automotive trade imbalance with Japan is so extraordinary, it is hoped that the Japanese Government could give some additional special consideration to imported autos,"[1] as if the large automotive trade imbalance was something undesirable and in need of remedy.

But I contend that correction of trade imbalances is not a proper objective of economic policy and that it is not legitimate for the government of a country to request the government of another country to diminish or correct any of these imbalances. First, there is no reason to treat the balance of payments on the merchandise-trade account separately from the balance on the service account. The balance on services, which is the most important component of the current account next to the merchandise-trade account, is perennially in a state of large deficit in Japan and in large surplus in the United States. It is necessary for Japan to have a substantial surplus on its trade account to pay for the large net import of services such as shipping, insurance, patent and know-how royalties, and tourism. In addition, from an employment viewpoint, although some payments on the service account, such as patent and know-how royalties or dividends, have little employment-creating effects in the receiving countries, some others, such as tourism, are largely labor-intensive expenditures.[2]

Second, both the United States and Japan, as leading members of GATT, should believe in the virtue of free, multilateral, and non-discriminatory world trade. It is neither unnatural nor undesirable for certain bilateral trade accounts to move continuously into large deficit or surplus within the free-world trade system. What seems unreasonable is for a member of GATT to request that another member take measures to reduce the bilateral imbalance between them. This was the position the United States took repeatedly in the 1950s and the early 1960s when it had a large bilateral trade surplus vis-à-vis Japan (see Table 6.1).[3]

On the other hand, I do not deny the necessity of dealing with trade friction in specific areas. It may be necessary to interfere in order to maintain or recover orderly market conditions when a sudden flood of imports, dumping, or heavy, concentrated foreign purchases abruptly raise domestic costs. But these problems, which arise whether the relevant country's overall payments are in deficit, surplus, or balance, should be considered conceptually different from the problem of the overall imbalance. They should be dealt with according to the international rules under GATT, like those against import flooding or dumping. If a country finds these international rules unsatisfactory, it should initiate negotiations to revise the rules on a multilateral basis. If a major country takes a unilateral action—disregarding the GATT rules—such action may well be quite harmful to the multilateral trade community.

The Second Jones Report, published in September 1980, seems to largely accept the "economic" argument along the lines stated above. In part it reads:

TABLE 6.1
The Balance of Payments on Current Account and Bilateral Trade Account of Japan and the United States:
1960–1980 (unit: $U.S. billion)

	Overall Balance of Payment on Current Account		Japan's Export to United states (f.o.b.)	Japan's Import from United States (c.i.f.)	Japan's Bilateral Trade Account with United States
	Japan	U.S.			
1960	0.1	1.8	1.1	1.6	(-)0.5
1961	(-)1.0	3.1	1.1	2.1	(-)1.0
1962	(-)0.05	2.5	1.4	1.8	(-)0.4
1963	(-)0.8	3.2	1.5	2.1	(-)0.6
1964	(-)0.5	5.8	1.8	2.3	(-)0.5
1965	0.9	4.3	2.5	2.4	0.1
1966	1.3	2.3	3.0	2.7	0.4
1967	(-)0.2	2.1	3.0	3.2	(-)0.2
1968	1.0	(-)0.5	4.1	3.5	0.6
1969	2.1	(-)1.0	5.0	4.1	0.9
1970	2.0	0.4	5.9	5.6	0.4
1971	5.8	(-)3.8	7.5	5.0	2.5
1972	6.6	(-)9.8	8.8	5.9	3.0
1973	(-)0.1	0.5	9.4	9.3	0.2
1974	(-)4.7	2.1	12.8	12.7	0.1
1975	0.7	18.3	11.1	11.6	(-)0.5
1976	3.7	4.4	15.7	11.8	3.9
1977	10.9	(-)14.1	19.7	12.4	7.3
1978	16.5	(-)14.3	24.9	14.8	10.1
1979	(-)8.7	0.7	26.4	20.4	6.0
1980	(-)10.3	5.1	14.9	12.1	2.8
(Jan. - June)					

Source: IMF, International Financial Statistics; Bank of Japan, Economic Statistics Annual.

From an economic point of view, a bilateral merchandise trade deficit should not be an object of great concern, as long as a nation's world-wide current account (goods and services) is in rough balance. This economic truth, however, is a political falsity. Writing as Members of Congress, in the heat of the political process, a merchandise trade deficit of the size we have been experiencing with Japan is a serious object of concern. For millions of Americans this highly visible deficit erodes their support of open trade: it creates tensions which threaten to spill over into unrelated sectors of our bilateral relationships.[4]

This is a very strange statement indeed. If it is "an economic truth" that "a bilateral merchandise trade deficit should not be an object of concern, as long as a nation's worldwide current account is in balance," then wouldn't the most important task of members of Congress be to report this truth to their constituents, rather than to put unreasonable pressure on the governments of other countries? The above statement is very dramatic: It reveals that responsible U.S. politicians working in the center of "the heat of the political process" to resolve the U.S.-Japanese trade conflict already know very well that millions of Americans are seriously — and erroneously — concerned with something that would in fact not be "an object of great concern" if they understood the economic truth of the matter.

Macroeconomic Developments and the Balance of Payments

At the beginning of what I described as the first wave of tension between the United States and Japan, the U.S. economy was booming and in a process of accelerated inflation (1966–1969), while the Japanese economy was experiencing a mild recession (1968–1969). Toward the end of the old IMF system in 1971 the dollar was greatly overvalued and the United States's current account, as well as its capital account, was in heavy deficit. Under the adjustable-peg system with fixed exchange rates, however, the United States refused to use the legitimate procedure to revise the parity of the dollar,[5] and essentially there was no effective means readily available to correct the "fundamental disequilibrium." The old IMF system was broken down by the United States's unilateral action, but the U.S.-Japanese trade imbalance persisted until the beginning of 1973. Japan was in a fairly deep recession in 1971–1972, and the appreciation of the yen from the time of the Smithsonian Agreement did not have much of an immediate effect until 1973 because of the so-called J-curve effect.[6] The appreciation was probably too small to quickly correct the large existing imbalance. The imbalance was corrected only when it ran into a great but short-lived boom, accompanied by rapid inflation, beginning in the latter half of 1972. The lagged effect of the yen appreciation under the Smithsonian Agreement, and the effect of a further appreciation of the yen after the shift to the float rate in February 1973 (up to about 265 yen per dollar—about 36 percent above the old IMF parity level), would probably have greatly contributed to the correction of the imbalance, but the ensuing oil crisis drastically changed the underlying conditions.

The imbalance that gave rise to the second wave of trade tension was again caused by diverging business-cycle developments in the United States and Japan in 1976–1978. The U.S. economy experienced a prolonged boom, with rates of growth in real GNP of 5.7, 4.9, and 4.0 percent in 1976, 1977, and 1978, respectively. The corresponding figures for Japan are slightly higher: 6.5, 5.4, and 5.6 percent. But business conditions differed greatly in the two countries. Although the U.S. economy was experiencing a boom, as accelerating inflation and the improving employment situation over those three years indicate, the Japanese economy was in a deep depression through the end of 1978. This statement may seem strange in view of the higher rate of growth in Japan than in the United States and also in view of Japan's unemployment rate, which was very low by international standards.

But the depression following the first oil crisis was a very severe one in Japan. The rates of growth quoted above are only about half the average rates of the 1960s. Also, those rates were achieved primarily by the expansion of exports, the cause of conflict and tension with Japan's trading partners. The unemployment rate was low primarily because of the different employment practices in Japan. Japanese firms continued to keep on the payroll much of their redundant labor, which around 1975 was estimated at roughly 10–15 percent of total industrial employment. In the manufacturing sector, the sector most closely related to international trade, production went down by more than 20 percent from the peak level recorded at the time of the first oil crisis; output did not return to March 1974 levels until four years later. Because of redundant labor and excess capacity on one end, and tight monetary and fiscal policies on the other, the wholesale price index was stabilized by 1975 and the consumer price index also stabilized by 1977. Japanese corporate finances were in much worse shape than those of their counterparts in the United States or Europe in 1975–1977 and they improved only gradually thereafter.

In an advanced industrialized economy, the balance of payments on a current account tends to deteriorate when it experiences a boom and to improve in a recession or depression. This general tendency is accentuated in Japan's case for two reasons. First, large Japanese firms do not dismiss or lay off their employees except in severe financial straits, and regular (with the exception of temporary or part-time) employees normally serve in the same firm for the whole length of their careers unless they wish otherwise. This pattern of business employment is generally referred to as "lifetime" or "permanent" employment. Because of this practice, wages and salaries, excluding overtime payments and bonuses,[7] are in substance fixed costs from management's point of view, like plant and equipment. This means that the real marginal cost for additional output is very low during a deep depression, when firms have redundant labor and idle capacity.

In the postwar Japanese economy, recovery from a recession or depression has almost always been led by the expansion of exports. Cyclical booms were usually ended by tight monetary and fiscal policies, necessitated in order to curb inflation and/or reduce balance-of-payments deficits. As domestic demand became depressed and excess capacity developed, firms stepped up efforts to find outlets for their products abroad. Thus their sales effort shifted from domestic to export markets. This pattern is called the "export-drive effect," which pulls the economy out of a recession while improving the balance of payments; monetary and fiscal restraints are eased, and plant and equipment investment rebound.

Would the general tendency for a country's balance of payments on its current account to deteriorate in a boom and improve in a recession remain the same under fixed and floating exchange-rate systems? In my view there is no reason why the two systems would produce different results. If foreign exchange authorities refrain from strongly intervening in the exchange market under the float, it is likely that the country's exchange rate would depreciate in a boom and appreciate in a recession, both to a limited extent. Yet these changes will not be able to affect the current-account balance much in the short run because of the J-curve effect. But the capital flows will respond to the change in the exchange rate and will have, by and large, an equilibrating effect over the medium run. This happens because a slight change in the exchange rate will eventually induce capital flows to move into the country whose currency is expected to appreciate and out of the country whose currency is expected to depreciate. That is, capital flows will go into an economy when it is in a boom, financing its current-account deficit, and go out of the country in a recession. Hence, this general tendency and the export-drive mechanism will remain largely the same under the fixed and floating exchange-rate systems.

The second reason why a swing in the current-account balance during a business cycle tends to be especially large in Japan relates to the composition of its imports. A large proportion of Japan's imports consists of raw materials and fuel used by the manufacturing and transportation industries. Finished products, especially manufactured consumer goods, account for only a small proportion of Japan's imports.

Recently the United States and Europe approached the Japanese government concerning this matter, claiming that this composition must be due to various trade barriers imposed by Japan. However, the peculiar composition of Japan's imports is a result of (1) Japan's comparative advantage in international trade and (2) its economic-geographical location in the world economy. In my view, Japan's tariff and nontariff barriers have little to do with the very low proportion of manufactured products among its imports.

Japan, a country with little land and few natural resources, yet rich in human capital and technology, has a strong comparative advantage in manufactured products and a disadvantage in industrial raw materials and food. It therefore exchanges the former for the latter through international trade. Japan can generally produce manufactured goods more cheaply than it can import them, although there are many notable exceptions.[8] The United States, for example, still has a comparative advantage over Japan in many high-technology industries, such as those producing aircraft, computers, pharmaceutical products, chemicals, atomic energy, industrial machinery, and so on. Many Japanese industries still have much to learn from their U.S. counterparts. The large amount of patent and know-how royalties and dividends paid annually to the United States is essentially the price paid for imported industrial technology.

As the United States is rich in land, minerals, and forestry and fishery resources, it naturally has a comparative advantage in agriculture and other resource industries. The United States cannot ignore its comparative advantage in these industries, nor the substantial export of these products, whereas Japan cannot help specializing in the manufacturing industries.

Japan does not necessarily command a comparative advantage in industries using the most advanced technology. It has had a competitive edge mainly in "assembly" industries such as shipbuilding, cameras, iron and steel, automobiles, and electronics, which use fairly standardized medium-to-high-level technology. The competitiveness of such industries generally does not depend on intensive R&D, but rather on cost control, uniform product quality, steady productivity, and quality improvement.

Some critics, not satisfied with the above explanation, point out that many European countries equally poor in natural resources import many more finished products than Japan and that within Europe a great deal of horizontal trade takes place in which manufactured goods are exchanged for manufactured goods. That is true, but economic-geographical factors play an important role. Western Europe is a well-integrated market; there are many adjoining countries with more or less similar income levels, cultures, customs, and languages, and as a result a great deal of trade in finished products takes place. Japan has not yet been blessed with these kinds of neighboring countries. The geographical—and perhaps psychological—distance between Japan and Europe and between Japan and the eastern United States, is a considerable obstacle to trade in manufactured products. European or U.S. efforts to market manufactured products in the remote, isolated country of Japan have generally been limited, although there are many notable exceptions, such as IBM, Nestle, Olivetti, Volkswagen, Coca Cola, Colgate, Braun, Esso (Exxon), and Shell.[9]

The cyclical swing in output is greater for the manufacturing industry than for the economy as a whole. As I said earlier, for Japan's manufacturing industry the pre-oil-crisis peak was recovered only in March 1978, while the growth of the whole economy (real GNP), from the first quarter of 1974 to the first quarter of 1978, amounted to 23.2 percent. Thus the depression in Japan—and in many other countries after the oil crisis—was much more severe for manufacturing than for nonmanufacturing sectors. As Japan's imports consist mainly of industrial raw materials, fuel, and food, import levels remain low during a depression, when the manufacturing industry is stagnant.

Policies to Correct the Imbalance

The U.S. Side

It is a simple macroeconomic proposition that the balance on the current account of a country is equal to the difference between its total production (GNP) and its total effective demand or total expenditure (gross national expenditure). Or to put it differently, the current-account balance is equal to the difference between gross domestic investment and gross domestic savings. A country that is spending more than it is producing, that is, investing more than saving, has a deficit in the balance of payments on its current account. In order to invest more than the country has in savings, it has to borrow from abroad; its capital account must be in a state of surplus, that is, there must be a net import of capital equal to the size of the current-account deficit.

Hence, if a country with a current account in deficit should wish to diminish the deficit—to "improve" its balance of payments— there are basically two ways of doing so. The first is to reduce its total expenditure, especially in government, as well as in various categories of domestic investment. This reduction in expenditure will affect domestic production unfavorably, but if government policy succeeds in reducing total expenditures more than total production, or in reducing investment more than savings, the current-account balance will improve. Savings are necessarily reduced by a decline in income resulting from the cutback in government expenditure (investment), but normally by less than the reduction in investment; the saving-investment balance is thus improved by the expenditure-reducing policy.[10]

During the 1976–1978 boom, domestic investment in the United States was higher than domestic savings, and the balance of payments on its current account was in deficit. But Washington was unwilling to reduce government expenditure or to take measures to curb domestic investment in order to improve its balance of payments, as these actions were thought to increase unemployment. At that time a reduction in unemployment was perhaps the most urgent macroeconomic policy target for the administration.

The second course to be taken to improve the balance of payments is to increase domestic production. But as production responds to demand in a market economy, the government must accomplish an increase in the demand for the country's output without simultaneously increasing total expenditure, or more precisely, without increasing expenditure as much as the increase in demand. This is what Harry G. Johnson called the "expenditure-switching policy,"[11] and it is achieved by a depreciation in the exchange rate or by the promotion of exports and reduction of imports. Through an expenditure-switching policy, both foreign and domestic expenditure are shifted from foreign-produced goods toward domestic products; hence domestic production will rise. With domestic production increasing, expenditures will increase too, but normally by less than production, thus improving the production-expenditure or savings-investment ratio, or in other words, the current-account balance.

This course, from the U.S. point of view, may have been the most desirable to correct the U.S.-Japanese trade imbalance in 1976–1978. A few remarks should be made, however. First, although the effect of a change in the exchange rate might be substantial over the long run—provided the change is large enough—its effect is limited in the short run because of the J-curve effect. Secondly, a large appreciation of the yen means a fairly large depreciation of the dollar and a decline in its international value. Statements made by U.S. officials between 1976 and 1979 were often contradictory in this regard. Some of them urged substantial appreciation of the yen and the German mark in order to correct the trade imbalance. Others, or even the same person on a different occasion, stated that the value of the dollar must be kept stable, because a stable dollar was essential not only for the United States but also for the world economy. Obviously one cannot have both a stable dollar and large yen and mark appreciation at the same time.

Third, the effect of most commercial policy measures negotiated between the United States and Japan is likely to be very small, especially in the short run. This is partly because there has been a long-run effort to liberalize trade and eliminate disorderly market conditions between the two countries. Consequently the remaining trade barriers on Japan's side are difficult to remove for political reasons. Even if the Japanese government removed all tariffs, the immediate effect on imports would be very small. This was borne out by the fact that a very substantial appreciation of the yen did not have much effect in the short run. The effects of eliminating nontariff barriers would be similar. Liberalizing import quotas on oranges, citrus juice, high-quality beef, and other items would alter the trade ledger by at most a few hundred million dollars a year. The amount is almost insignificant when weighed against the overall trade imbalance, in 1976–1978 around $7 billion to $10 billion annually.

Fourth, the expenditure-switching policy—whether through exchange-rate depreciation or commercial policy measures—is inflationary unless accompanied by measures to reduce expenditure and production elsewhere. A very large U.S. current-account deficit in 1977–1978 mitigated inflationary pressures in the United States. A large current-account deficit means that more goods and services were supplied from abroad than were withdrawn for sales abroad. Thus if the balance of payments on the current account was to be improved, whether by expenditure-reducing or expenditure-switching policies, government expenditure, domestic investment, and/or some other component of gross national expenditure would have to be reduced in order to counteract the inflationary pressure resulting from a decline in the current-account deficit. In 1976–1978, however, the U.S. government appeared unwilling to consider such macroeconomic policies to reduce domestic expenditure.

The Japanese Side

Now let us look at the Japanese side and consider what policy measures might have been usefully taken in 1976–1978 to reduce the huge Japanese current-account surplus. There were essentially two courses, parallel to those discussed above: an expenditure-increasing policy and an expenditure-switching policy.

After the first oil crisis in 1973–1974, the household savings ratio, already very high by international standards, rose markedly. The Japanese people felt insecure and cautious because of major economic upheavals, worldwide inflation, the oil crisis, and the following depression. They saved an even larger proportion of disposable income than before to prepare for the unknown. This is in contrast to the situation in the United States, where household savings steadily declined. Japan's business sector, which used to absorb most of the savings generated by the household sector through heavy investment in plant and equipment, almost stopped doing so as the level of business investment fell sharply. A large part of household savings was absorbed by the government sector, which ran a huge deficit. In the years following the first oil crisis the government deficit exceeded 7 percent of GNP. In 1978, about 40 percent of the central government's general account was financed by issuing national bonds. This deficit was larger in absolute amount than the government deficits of the United States, West Germany, and the United Kingdom combined. But even Japan's extraordinarily large deficit was not enough to absorb all the excess savings supplied by the household sector; the remainder spilled over into the external sector, leaving a surplus on the current-account balance of payments.

In 1976–1978 it was very difficult for the Japanese government to take measures to promote domestic expenditure. Households were cautious and timid, saving heavily and being reluctant to build or buy a new house. Business investment was stagnant, partly because of excess capacity and partly because of a very uncertain business outlook. The government pursued the typical Keynesian counter-cyclical policy of deficit financing, but politicians and the Ministry of Finance, and perhaps the populace as well, were becoming reluctant to further increase deficit-financed government spending, for two reasons. First, they were all afraid of rekindling inflationary expectations; there was the potential threat, not well defined, that an accumulated public debt might somehow be monetized rapidly, giving rise to rampant inflation like that the Japanese experienced in the 1930s and during and immediately after World War II. Second, many were also concerned about the erosion of fiscal discipline, if the beneficiaries of public expenditure and the public became accustomed to increasing government deficits. Thus there were obvious limits to the expansion of government expenditure and also, in general, to the expenditure-increasing policy.

What about the expenditure-switching policy? The Japanese government appeared to be reluctant in the beginning to let the yen appreciate even moderately, and in the first half of 1976 it tried to stabilize the dollar-yen exchange rate at around 300 yen per dollar. The Bank of Japan's purchase of dollars in early 1976 evoked criticism by the U.S. government and others. It was believed that the Japanese government was trying to keep the yen undervalued in an attempt to promote Japan's exports, shifting the burden of domestic unemployment abroad. The Japanese government denied this, and from the autumn of 1976 to September 1977 it rarely intervened in the exchange market. The yen gradually appreciated about 7 percent from the beginning of 1977 through September, up to 266 yen per dollar. Then came a period of sharp, successive appreciations as the large and increasing balance-of-payments surplus became clear to the public.

Nothing could stop the rapid appreciation of the yen. Even a very extensive intervention in the exchange market by the Bank of Japan largely failed, and the yen continued to appreciate through a series of speculative waves until October 1978, when it reached a peak of 176 yen per dollar, more than 70 percent higher than at the beginning of 1976. Thereupon, with expectations reversed, the yen began to depreciate. It fluctuated between 200 and 220 yen per dollar for most of 1979 and went down to 250–260 yen in November 1979 and in April 1980.

As already mentioned, Japan's current-account balance was in deficit in the early part of 1979. The current-account surplus was very large in 1977 and 1978: $10.9 and $16.5 billion respectively. It was especially large in the first three quarters of 1978: $5.1, $4.8, and $4.6 billion respectively (see Table 6.1).

It appears that the J-curve effect was quite pronounced in this case: The largest quarterly surplus was recorded after a very substantial appreciation of the yen. Exports did not begin to decline until the second quarter of 1978 and did so only moderately (see Figure 6.1). Imports began to increase only around the middle of 1978 (see Figure 6.2). The price index of exports in terms of the dollar rose

FIGURE 6.1
Changes in Japan's Export Prices, Volume of Exports, and Exchange Rate (seasonally adjusted, January 1977 = 100)

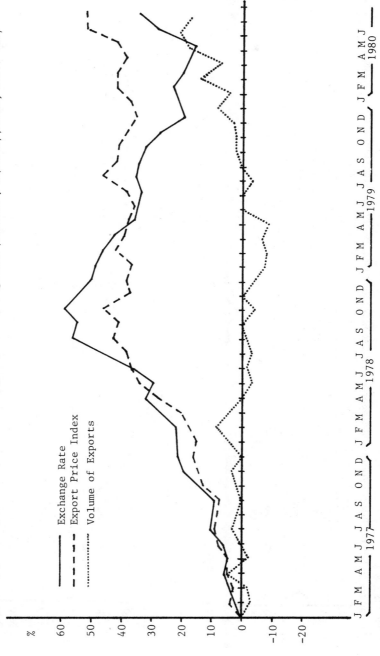

Note: Export price is given in terms of U.S. dollar; exchange rate is U.S. dollar per unit of yen.

FIGURE 6.2
Changes in Japan's Prices, Volume of Imports, and Exchange Rate (seasonally adjusted, January 1977 = 100)

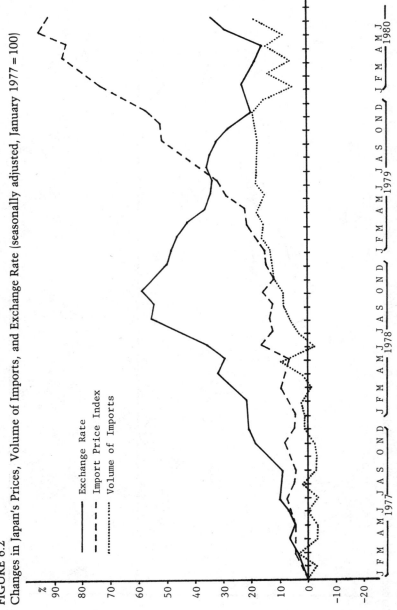

Exchange Rate ——
Import Price Index – – –
Volume of Imports ·······

Note: Import price is in terms of U.S. dollar.

sharply, while that of imports rose much less, improving Japan's terms of trade more than 20 percent during the year ending in September 1978. From the second quarter of 1978 to the first quarter of 1979, the export dollar price index was continuously less than 35 percent, but the rise in the import dollar price index was only 4.4 and 6.2 percent higher, respectively, in the second and third quarters of 1978. The latter index began to rise in the middle of 1978, but it was only 18.3 percent higher in the second quarter of 1979 than in the last quarter of 1976, even after a sharp increase in oil prices (see Figures 6.1, 6.2, and 6.3).

As a result of these quantity and price developments following the sharp appreciation of the yen, the peak in export value (in terms of the dollar) was recorded in November 1978, more than a year after the yen started to appreciate sharply (see Figure 6.4). This is a typical J-curve phenomenon: The current-account surplus continued to increase rather than decline for some time after the sharp appreciation of the yen began and remained very high until the third quarter of 1978.

The drastic decline in Japan's current-account surplus in the last quarter of 1978 may be accounted for by the following factors: (1) Domestic private demand in Japan rallied in the last quarter of 1978, for almost the first time since the first oil crisis; (2) the substantial appreciation in the yen in 1977–1978 began to exert its full force, following the J-curve effect; (3) the U.S. economy slid into a mild recession after a long boom, and with the appreciation of the yen, the expansion of Japan's exports to the United States came to an end; and (4) the rise in oil prices increased Japan's import bill.

Nontariff Barriers

In the United States, as well as in Europe, there appears to be a widespread notion that Japan is a closed market surrounded by high tariff and nontariff barriers. In my opinion, this is not the case. Why this notion has become so prevalent is an interesting question. In fact, the Japanese economy is at present — although it was not in the past — about as open as any advanced industrialized economy in Western Europe and North America, excluding perhaps such natural barriers as distance, language, culture, and social customs.

Although international comparisons of the average level of tariffs are difficult, there is general agreement that Japan's average tariff on manufactured products is now lower than that of the United States or Europe; this is a result of the successful conclusion of the Tokyo Round negotiations under GATT. A few Japanese tariff rates are still

FIGURE 6.3
Changes in Japan's Terms of Trade (seasonally adjusted, January 1977 = 100)

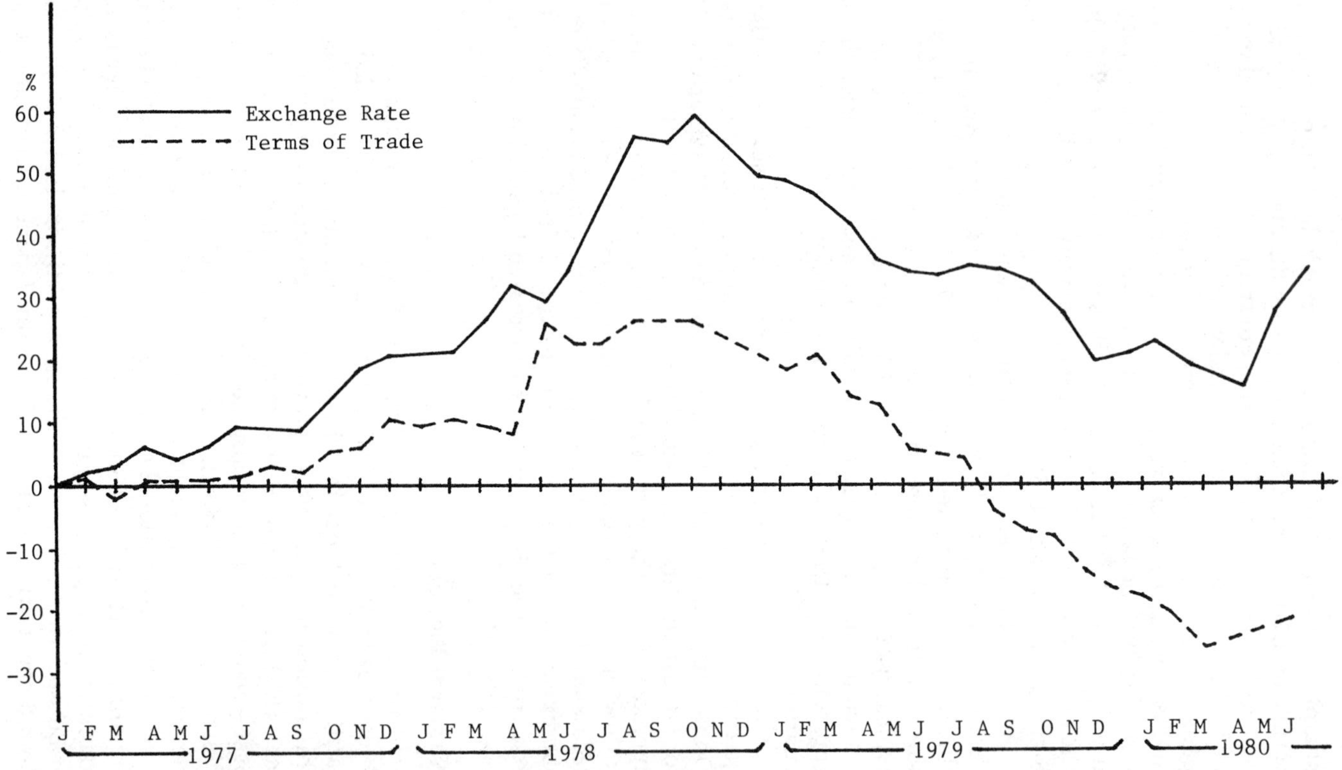

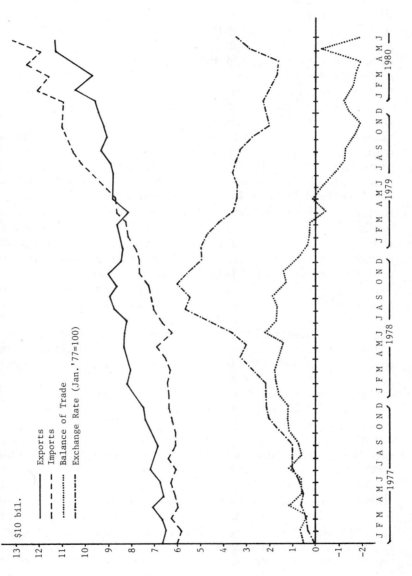

FIGURE 6.4
Value of Japan's Exports and Imports and the Balance of Trade (seasonally adjusted)

as high as 25 to 30 percent, but such rates, and even higher ones, are also found in the U.S. tariff schedule.

Nontariff trade barriers are hard to define and even harder to identify. Nontariff trade barriers may be defined as artificial barriers set up by the government. Barriers such as geographical distance, language, and social customs are *not*, conceptually, nontariff barriers. When comparing nontariff barriers internationally, Japan's do not appear conspicuously higher than those of the United States or Western European countries.

Certain governmental regulations or procedures may be considered undesirable nontariff barriers from the view of exporting countries but may not be regarded in the same way by the importing country if they are socially necessary regulations applicable to imports and domestically produced goods alike. In my opinion the question of whether something is a nontariff barrier or not should be considered solely from an economic and social point of view, not from a legal one. Whether a certain regulation is legally acceptable under existing international agreements is irrelevant, because nontariff barriers are a problem of trade policy, and in any discussion of economic policy problems, the purpose is to examine whether or not existing government policy needs to be changed. Thus a trade barrier, although legally acceptable under existing international agreements, may constitute a serious nontariff barrier. When judging from an economic and social point of view one must rely on vague and changing criteria that inevitably involve value judgments. Whether a certain regulation constitutes a nontariff barrier, therefore, may well differ from country to country or even from person to person.

One of the reasons I have come to believe that Japan is as open as the United States or Western European countries regarding nontariff barriers stems from the First Jones Report. This report, which grew out of Congressman James Jones's trip to Japan in 1978 to investigate Japan's trade barriers in view of its huge payments surplus in 1977–1978, was able to identify only a few barriers, in spite of its unusually critical and severe tone, as seen in its assertion that "there is still a wide range of trade and structural barriers in Japan which restricts import, interferes with the currency alignment process, and perpetuates the U.S.-Japan trade imbalance."[12] Moreover, the First Jones Report contains a number of erroneous assertions regarding Japan's trade barriers. An example is the statement concerning the many informal "import cartels which restrict, usually with government aid or acquiescence, the volume or price of imports, thus ensuring the continued survival and profitability of the domestic industry." But the only concrete example given in the report, that of an import cartel on phenol, is based on incomplete information from a U.S. source.[13] The Japanese business world is highly and sometimes even fiercely competitive, and unless some formal arrangements are made under governmental approval or guidance it is difficult to restrict competition. Needless to say, those companies involved in illegal cartels may well be, and actually are, prosecuted by the Japanese antitrust authorities (the Fair Trade Commission).

The Second Jones Report seems to be in general agreement with my view that the Japanese economy is at present as open as any industrialized economy in Western Europe or North America. It concedes that "Japan is today a reasonably open market for many products, other than agricultural and other high technology items" and supports the view that "this [U.S.-Japan] trade imbalance has resulted more from the disparity between the effort made by Japanese exporters to develop U.S. markets for their goods and the efforts made by U.S. companies to develop markets for their goods than from any remaining Japanese nontariff barriers."[14] As the subject is often the source of misunderstanding, let us assess here the nontariff barriers in Japan and the United States.

Quantitative Import Restrictions. Quantitative restrictions (QR) on imports classified as "residual" under GATT involve twenty-seven items for Japan and seven for the United States. This may give the impression that Japan has many more residual import restrictions than the United States, but for the most part this disparity is due to a peculiar historical reason. Twenty-two of Japan's twenty-seven residual QRs are placed on agricultural products, compared with one (sugar) of the seven residual QRs in the United States. When GATT was originally concluded, the U.S. administration chose to endorse it as an administrative agreement, as it was thought rather difficult for the United States to ratify GATT as an international treaty. Because of this an anomaly has persisted. Most member countries ratified GATT as an international treaty, and each country's legislature is clearly bound by GATT, whereas the U.S. Congress does not consider itself legally bound by the original GATT treaty and sometimes behaves as if it can ignore the treaty. When entering into the original GATT treaty, the United States requested and obtained a waiver from GATT for a QR on agricultural product imports, as domestic prices were supported by federal government programs. Thus, even today the U.S. QRs on butter, cheese, milk, cream, cotton, and peanuts are not considered residual QRs. There are also import restrictions at the state level, such as those on citrus fruits for quarantine reasons. As far as nonagricultural products are concerned, Japan, with five items (including coal, hides, and leather) has fewer residual QRs than the United States (six items).

Self-Restraint. A trade barrier closely related to the QR is export "self-restraint." When exports of a certain group of goods to the United States sharply increase, the government, instead of restricting imports through a quota system, sometimes chooses to ask the exporting countries (e.g., Japan, Korea, Taiwan, Hong Kong) to reduce exports. These export self-restraints have often been negotiated under the threat of higher tariffs, import quotas, or dumping charges. This is because export self-restraint is often more convenient than a revision of tariffs or an introduction of quotas. In recent years there have been self-restraints on Japanese exports to the United States covering a wide range of products, including textiles, iron, steel, and television sets. Ironically, Japan recently negotiated with Korea for export self-restraint on some of Korea's textiles exports to Japan.

Trigger-Price Mechanism. Another serious nontariff trade barrier in the United States is its arbitrary—from the Japanese point of view—application of antidumping measures. For example, when a Japanese steel product is sold below a certain prescribed minimum price, it is automatically considered a potential case of dumping and an investigation is triggered. This is an example of the "trigger price mechanism," an artificial trade barrier set up to restrict imports. It puzzles me why this kind of arrangement, which in substance amounts to a price cartel, is not considered illegal under U.S. antitrust law.

Safety and Environmental Regulations. The First Jones Report complains of the strict regulations on automobiles for safety and environmental purposes enforced by the Japanese government and the cumbersome procedures with which the regulations are implemented. Similar complaints arise from time to time in regard to regulations on medicine, food additives, and the method or chemicals used in processing foods, such as the fungicide used in preserving citrus fruits.

Unfortunately, the report fails to mention the equally strict regulations and cumbersome procedures enforced on automobiles, medicines, and food additives in the United States. When a Japanese automaker decides to market a new model in the United States, it has to send, by air, *forty* new-model cars to Ann Arbor, Michigan, for testing by U.S. environmental authorities. It is true that when only a few thousand of each foreign-car model are sold in Japan, environmental and safety testing adds considerably to the cost. But there is no reason why regulations should be relaxed when the number of cars or the amount of medicine imported annually is minimal.

U.S. and European automakers and their governments have complained that Japanese emission standards were too strict and could not be met by foreign producers. The Japanese government thereupon agreed to postpone its enforcement of these standards for some time. This is an unusual concession from the standpoint of environmental policy, especially as industrial and transportation activity in Japan emits a great deal of pollution in a very narrow piece of land. It is only natural that automobile emission standards should be more strict in Japan than in countries endowed with a larger land area. It seems unreasonable to label Japanese emission standards as a nontariff barrier, simply or primarily because U.S. and European automakers cannot meet the standards.

Sometimes U.S. businessmen and others complain that in regard to safety, hygienic, and other regulations, Japanese authorities do not accept test results obtained in the United States or other countries and take their time in approving testing in Japan. However, the same is true for almost any country, including the United States. Some drugs and food additives approved by Japanese authorities and widely sold and used in Japan are not approved by U.S. authorities. Japanese and European pharmaceutical companies generally agree that, among major countries, the food and drug authorities in the United States are generally the most stringent in approving a new drug. The question of whether government safety standards constitute a nontariff barrier, or how to remove or change it, would be best left to a neutral, bilateral, or multilateral body composed of impartial experts.

Restrictions on Foreign Banks. The First Jones Report asserts that foreign banks in Japan face restrictions not imposed on domestic banks, and "since banks can and do encourage trade between countries" these restrictions have possibly "contributed to the trade gap between Japan and the United States." But some of the charges of discriminatory treatment against foreign banks are apparently based on misunderstanding. Admittedly, banking is one area in Japan in which the Japanese government (and the Bank of Japan) too often directly intervenes, and I would welcome some relaxation of government regulations.

Yet it is far-fetched to argue that restrictions on foreign banks contribute to the trade gap between Japan and the United States. Although Japanese banks are subject to a wide range of regulations and "administrative guidance," they are highly competitive, and U.S. exporters and importers, and U.S.-owned firms operating in Japan, can and do get from Japanese banks any banking service available to their Japanese competitors on equal terms. It is unlikely that Japanese banks would eagerly provide services conducive to exports and not to imports.[15]

Procurement Policies of Public Corporations. One of the most difficult issues between the United States and Japan, which began in the "second wave" period, is concerned with the procurement policies of Japan's governmental corporations, such as Japan National Railroad (JNR) and Nippon Telegraph and Telephone Corporation (NTT). The negotiation over the latter's procurement policy has been perhaps the most difficult and troublesome in recent U.S.-Japanese economic relations, second only to the painful textile negotiation in 1969–1972.

The issue is a complicated one. The United States takes the position that NTT should buy more U.S. telecommunication equipment by adopting an open system of bidding under GATT's Government Procurement Code and that Japan should make its telecommunication market more open and accessible to foreign manufacturers and telecommunication service companies. The telecommunication market is rapidly developing worldwide — one of the "industries of the future" — and is one in which many high-technology industries are related.

Japan's, or NTT's, position is that certain types of telecommunication equipment requiring a very high degree of reliability must be developed through joint R&D effort by NTT and its manufacturers and cannot therefore be purchased on an open-bidding basis; telecommunication companies or agencies in the United States and in almost all European countries do not adopt an open-bidding system for certain high-technology equipment. NTT emphasizes that because of the very high level of reliability required and the need for prompt service in cases of emergency and because joint research work extends over many years, it prefers domestic manufacturers to foreign ones for the supply of vital equipment.

I cannot judge which of these two positions is more reasonable. I note, however, that the U.S. position is unilateral: The telecommunication field and railroads are run as private enterprises in the United States and are not subject to the Government Procurement Code; foreign governments cannot criticize the procurement policies of private telecommunication or railroad companies even if they are publicly regulated. The Second Jones Report points out that because bilateral trade in telephone terminal and switching equipment is in large surplus in Japan's favor, NTT should buy more from U.S. manufacturers. This is not a convincing argument. The fact that Pan American (or any other U.S. airlines, as well as Japan Airlines) buys aircraft only from U.S. manufacturers does not mean that it (or others) should buy from Japan as well. In other words, the pattern of procurement may be a reflection of underlying comparative advantage.

On the other hand, my impression of JNR and NTT is that their procurement policies, especially the latter's, have been so closed that many domestic manufacturers have also been complaining. If NTT makes its procurement more open, the chief beneficiaries could well be major Japanese manufacturers that are not members of the NTT "family" and hence have not yet been able to sell much to NTT. Because a publicly owned corporation is not subject to profit incentives, persuading it to adopt a policy, procurement or otherwise, that departs from past practices is not going to be easy.[16]

A solution to the NTT problem may be to change it into a private enterprise. This "solves" the problem in that its procurement would not be covered by GATT's Government Procurement Code, and foreign governments could not then complain about procurement policies. Also, it would be subject to profit incentives, making it more cost-conscious and perhaps more eager to buy from the cheapest sources (although such incentives are generally weak for natural monopolies like telecommunications or public utilities).

Automobiles. As already mentioned, the automotive trade imbalance between Japan and the United States (and also between Japan and Europe), already conspicuous at the time of the First Jones Report, has become even more so. When Japanese automotive exports first began to increase, the United States and Europe complained about Japan's antipollution standards, inspection procedures, and high domestic excise taxes on larger passenger cars. But it has gradually become obvious that Japanese cars are widely judged to be of better quality than similarly priced U.S. and European cars. Although it is true that the Japanese government protected the automobile industry heavily in its earlier years, it is now clear that Japan has a comparative advantage in automobiles. Japanese automobiles are competitive in overseas markets even after paying transocean shipping costs and tariffs. If U.S. and European automakers cannot compete successfully with Japanese automakers in their home markets, they cannot expect to do so in the Japanese market after paying shipping costs.

One can understand why an importing country would want to restrict imports when confronted with a sudden increase, as such an

increase leads to a rise in unemployment and to failures in home industries. Because the automobile and related industries employ a
large number of workers, companies and labor unions have a great
deal of political influence in most countries. It is therefore not surprising that protectionist movements in the United States and
Europe have arisen requesting measures to restrict automobile imports from Japan. In Europe, a few major countries have already
taken measures to restrict automobile imports from Japan, perhaps
illegally under the terms of GATT.

In the United States, Japanese automobile imports have come to
be restricted by an "orderly marketing agreement," with the grudg-
ing consent of the Japanese government and automakers. Such an
agreement offers no permanent solution to the problem. It would be
awkward for the U.S. government to continue this kind of restriction indefinitely, as it would be tantamount to admitting that the
United States's foremost industry cannot compete with foreign
manufacturers even in its domestic market and has to depend on
protectionism for its survival.

Soliciting direct investment by Japanese automakers in the
United States does not seem to me a workable solution, either.
Private companies cannot be forced to undertake direct investment;
they do so only when cost conditions are favorable. At present it is
generally still cheaper and more dependable to produce in Japan; the
wages of U.S. autoworkers are high by international standards, and
their work incentives and morale are too low for Japanese automakers to want to manufacture automobiles in the United States.

The only viable, long-run solution to the problem seems to me for
U.S. automakers to improve their products, raise productivity by investing in new plant equipment, and take better quality-control
measures and for autoworkers to become more productive relative
to their wages. Over the long run the appreciation of the yen and the
rise in Japanese real wages will help to shift relative competitiveness in the United States's favor. This shift may eventually promote
Japanese direct investment in the United States.

Although it is desirable to remove and reduce trade barriers in
order to enjoy the benefits of freer international trade, it should be
understood that existing tariff and nontariff barriers are the result of
many years of institutional developments promoted by, and
political power games played among, a country's various interest
groups. There are almost always groups in a country that are unfavorably affected by the removal of trade barriers. Therefore, the
reduction of barriers should not be considered a measure that can be
used readily to correct the payment imbalance in the short run. It

should also be noted that the increase in Japan's imports that would result from such reduction is likely to be very small, even if the Japanese government agreed to take drastic measures to reduce trade barriers in regard to any of the items discussed by the United States and Japan in 1977–1978. In short, the removal or reduction of trade barriers should be considered a long-run policy objective, not an effective short-run measure to correct a payment imbalance.

The reduction in trade barriers is usually accompanied by political, social, and administrative difficulties. The government must assist in the adjustment of those who are adversely affected and occasionally compensate them for losses. This is often a painful political process. Nations have known for a long time that if they wish to gain from freer trade they must share in the burdens of political adjustments by *reciprocally* reducing tariff and nontariff barriers under a bilateral trade agreement. The policy of requesting unilateral concessions under pressure or threat, like that pursued by the United States toward Japan in 1969–1972 and 1977–1978, may appear successful to some extent in the short run, but the resentment it creates can be substantial and the policy will essentially be unworkable in the long run.

Agricultural Protection

Everyone knows that the Japanese government heavily protects agriculture and that as a result the prices of many agricultural products are much higher in Japan than in other countries. At the same time, however, Japan depends heavily on food imports. The degree of dependence can be measured in several different ways, but on a caloric basis Japan is said to import slightly more than 50 percent of its food. A very large part of this comes from the United States. No other large industrialized country (with the possible exception of the United Kingdom) relies so heavily on imported food. Primarily because of this already high degree of dependence, Japan's protection of its agricultural sector is unlikely to change substantially in the near future.

Japanese voters generally seem to support a policy of producing a considerable portion of their food supply in Japan, even at substantially higher costs. This was particularly evident after the worldwide food shortage and commodity booms in 1972–1973 and the first oil crisis in 1973–1974. These events revealed just how vulnerable the Japanese economy is to external disruptions in the supply and price of imported food, raw materials, and fuel.

An important event that profoundly shook the composure of

many Japanese was the embargo placed by the U.S. government on soybean exports in the summer of 1973. Soybeans are a very important source of protein in the Japanese diet; soy sauce (*shōyu*), bean paste (*miso*), fermented soybeans (*nattō*), and bean curd (*tōfu*) are made from soybeans. Until the 1920s Japan was nearly self-sufficient in soybean production, but during the 1930s Japan became increasingly dependent on imports from China. After World War II Japan again became nearly self-sufficient in soybean production because of the shortage of foreign exchange, but imports from the United States gradually increased. Under U.S. pressure and as a result of repeated negotiations, Japan agreed to liberalize restrictions on the import of soybeans, and thereafter the domestic supply diminished rapidly to only a small percentage of total consumption. At the time of the 1973 embargo, about 90 percent of Japan's total demand for soybeans was met by imports from the United States.

Prices of feed for cattle, including soybeans, soared in 1972–1973 as a result of a poor catch of Peruvian anchovies. In June 1973 the U.S. government placed an embargo on soybean exports. Even shipments to Japan of soybeans that had been previously contracted for were prohibited. The embargo did not last long, but soybeans were in acute shortage in Japan until early 1974. The Japanese government tried to diversify its sources of supply and to expand domestic production, but with little consequence over the short run. Japanese consumers had a hard time obtaining *tōfu* and *shōyu* for some time.

This event may not have been as shocking to the Japanese as the oil crisis that broke out a few months later, but it revealed the high degree of vulnerability of the Japanese economy because of its heavy dependence on foreign food supplies. What made it particularly shocking was the fact that the U.S. government, which had been urging Japan to liberalize its agricultural import policies, decided to clamp an embargo at a critical time on one of Japan's most important, and heavily depended on, food imports.

Since the worldwide food shortage of 1972–1973, and especially after the oil crisis, Japanese public opinion appears to have shifted toward support of self-sufficiency. The rural populace, as well as the majority of the urban populace, now feels that Japan should not increase its degree of dependence on imported food any further but should maintain a reasonable level of domestic production by protecting agriculture. This policy is deemed necessary to maintain a minimum supply of food during times of emergency. Precisely what emergency contingencies would be covered by this policy has never been made clear; nor is it clear why the Japanese prefer food self-sufficiency through protection over some other alternatives, like stockpiling major foodstuffs or diversifying supply sources. Perhaps the majority would like the government to pursue not just one but some combination of each of these alternatives. At any rate, agricultural protection for emergency preparedness has taken on the status of a national consensus as a result of the external economic vicissitudes of the 1970s. It has become, in short, an integral part of Japan's national security policy.[17]

In Japan, rural voters, who favor an agricultural protectionist policy, can exert much stronger influence on agricultural policy than urban consumers, who might prefer a more liberal one. Japan's urban voters are not strongly against a protectionist agricultural policy—this may be in part because of the older generation's remembrance of days of hunger during and immediately after the war and its fear of possible emergency shortfalls. Also, in Japan today agriculture is attended to by relatively poor farmers. There is little resentment by urban consumers of those who benefit from agricultural production. The overwhelming majority of Japanese were poor farmers one or two generations ago, and most urban residents still have ties to their rural roots; parents or close relatives still live in the countryside, and visits usually are made twice a year during the New Year holiday and during the August Festival. Japanese rural society has been transformed by rapid industrialization and the great exodus of people from rural to urban areas. Many urban residents do not want to see further changes in their homeland brought about by the lifting of agricultural protection.

Conclusions

As a result of continued prosperity, relative peace, technological progress (especially in transportation and communication), and strenuous efforts to lower the number of tariffs and nontariff barriers to trade, advanced industrialized economies today are much more closely tied to each other than in the past. The major market economies of the world have never been as closely integrated as they are now. Under present conditions, divergent business-cycle developments can give rise to large swings in the balance of payments on current accounts, whether exchange rates are fixed or floating.

As shown in Figure 6.5, swings in the current-account balance have been much larger, relative to GNP, in European countries than in the United States or Japan, as European countries are more closely integrated with one another. As national economies become

FIGURE 6.5

Swings in the Balance of Payments on Current Account of Major OECD
Countries (percentage of GNP/GDP)

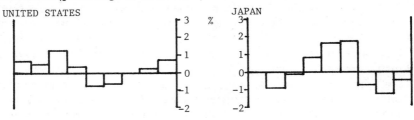

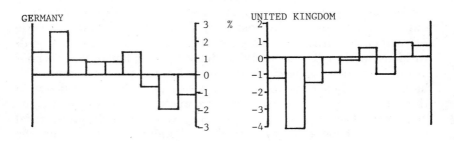

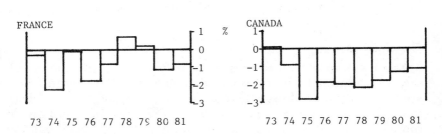

73 74 75 76 77 78 79 80 81   73 74 75 76 77 78 79 80 81

Source: OECD, Economic Outlook, December 1980, p. 65. Figures for
1980 and 1981 are forecasts made by the OECD secretaries.

more closely integrated, governments and people must be prepared
for larger swings in the current-account balance than heretofore experienced.

From the point of view of both individual countries and the world
economy as a whole, it is desirable for the current-account balance
of a country experiencing a boom to move into deficit and for that of

a country in a recession to move into surplus. In this way inflationary pressure in a booming economy is mitigated, while excess
capacity and underutilized labor in an economy in recession are
usefully mobilized to satisfy demands elsewhere. The situation in
which one country or a group of countries experiences a boom while
others are in a recession, and in which the current-account balances
of the former swing into deficit while those of the latter swing into
surplus, is preferable to one in which the business cycles of all major
economies are synchronized giving rise to a worldwide boom (as in
1972) or recession (in 1974–1975). As long as each country pursues
an independent fiscal and monetary policy under the floating
exchange-rate system and follows its own course of cyclical developments, its government and its people should be prepared to accept
swings in the current-account balance that arise from diverging
business-cycle developments vis-à-vis its trading partners.

Under the floating exchange-rate system an important rule that
should be observed by individual countries is that their governments and/or central banks should refrain from intervening in the
exchange market, except to "smooth out" short-run problems or to
cope with unexpected emergencies. "Smoothing out" here means intervention to reduce short-run fluctuations in the exchange rate so
that purchases and sales net out approximately to zero over the
short run. If a government intervenes in other ways, especially in
order to stabilize the exchange rate in a recession, it will leave itself
open to the criticism that it is pursuing a "beggar-thy-neighbor"
policy of exporting unemployment. Fluctuations in exchange rates
are likely to remain within reasonable limits, provided major countries do not run into accelerating inflation; such fluctuations will
not adversely affect international trade and investment to any great
extent, as evident in developments since 1973.

It is unreasonable and even irrational for a GATT member country to request that its trading partner alter the size of the bilateral
trade balance. This runs counter to the multilateral principle of
GATT. It would be reasonable to request that the surplus country
move more vigorously to lower its tariff and nontariff trade barriers,
if the surplus or deficit refers to an overall balance on the current account rather than a bilateral trade balance and to secular rather than
cyclical surpluses.[18]

A country's balance of payments on its current account is equal to
the gap between the total expenditure of its households, firms, and
government and total domestic production; it cannot be remedied
unless expenditures are reduced or output increased. Over the short
run, the effect on the current-account balance of currency deprecia-

tion or appreciation, a change in the tariff rates, or a removal or lowering of nontariff barriers is likely to be quite small because of the J-curve effect, and because of various secondary effects in the reverse direction.

I do not mean to ignore the necessity of dealing with friction in trade, which will arise from time to time in specific sectors. Cooperating to resolve sectoral problems on a bilateral and multilateral basis, and to lower tariff and nontariff barriers, is essential for the promotion of multilateral trade. Coping with sudden increases in imports to avoid or mitigate a rapid increase in unemployment and/or disorderly market conditions is also obviously important. However, sectoral trade-policy issues ought to be distinguished conceptually from macroeconomic problems of an overall trade or payments imbalance.

Notes

1. U.S. House of Representatives, Committee on Ways and Means, Subcommittee on Trade, *Task Force Report on United States–Japan Trade* (Washington, D.C.: Government Printing Office, 1979), p. 28.

2. This is not to be taken as asserting that from an economy policy point of view the balance of payments on the current account should be brought into balance. Even over the long run a country may well have fairly large deficits or surpluses on the long-term capital account. But this is not the place to discuss targets for economic policy in the area of balance of payments.

3. It should be pointed out here that generally it is not easy to "correct" a bilateral imbalance within the GATT framework. When a country with a bilateral trade deficit with another country asks the latter to grant trade concessions to increase the former's exports, the latter's concessions are made available automatically to other member countries under the nondiscrimination (MFN) principle of GATT. Therefore, the former must choose an area in which other GATT members' competitiveness is weak. Moreover, although the former's exports in which concessions are granted may increase to some extent, unless the domestic macroeconomic situation remains unchanged the export of other products may well decline and the size of the overall or bilateral deficit is likely to remain largely unchanged, as will be further explained.

4. U.S. House of Representatives, Committee on Ways and Means, Subcommittee on Trade, *United States–Japan Trade Report* (Washington, D.C.: Government Printing Office, 1980).

5. See R. Komiya, "Recent U.S. Foreign Economic Policy from a Japanese Point of View," in *Towards a New World Trade Policy: Maidenhead Papers,* ed. C. Fred Bergsten (Lexington, Mass.: D. C. Heath, 1975), pp. 359–363.

6. The J-curve effect is a phenomenon in which a country's balance of payments, following a depreciation (appreciation) of its currency, deteriorates (improves) for some time (several months to half a year) before it begins to improve (deteriorate), thus giving rise to a J-shaped curve in the movement of the balance over time.

7. A bonus is a lump-sum payment given to each permanent employee once or twice a year. The amount depends on the company's profit and the monthly salary of the employee. It normally amounts to two or four months' salary and is frequently up to five to seven months'. If the company is not making a profit the bonus will be very small, or possibly nothing.

8. The *United States-Japan Trade Report* (1980) states: "A comparison of our leading exports to Japan versus our imports from her is devastating. The data seems to indicate that (aircraft excluded) we are a developing nation supplying a more advanced nation—we are Japan's plantation: haulers of wood and growers of crops, in exchange for her high technology, value-added products . . . we believe this relationship is not acceptable, and can be corrected, through changes in trade and domestic policy."

9. A number of foreigners have stated that the Japanese distribution (wholesale and retail) system is so complicated that it is difficult for foreigners to understand and deal with it and that it constitutes one of the most serious nontariff barriers. But a country's distribution system has become what it is through a long history of developments and cannot be said to constitute a nontariff barrier unless the government interferes in such a way as to restrict distribution of imports or foreign firms' access to it. My impression is that whether or not it is more complicated than a system in another country, the Japanese distribution system is highly competitive, efficient, and rapidly changing. Also, when a foreigner says that it is difficult to understand, how does he explain the great success in marketing by the companies cited above?

10. The reader who is not familiar with these macroeconomic propositions is referred to the classic article by Harry G. Johnson, "Towards a General Theory of the Balance of Payments," in H. G. Johnson, ed., *International Trade and Economic Growth* (London: Allen and Unwin, 1958), pp. 153–168.

11. Ibid., p. 162.

12. *Task Force Report on United States–Japan Trade* (1979), p. 4.

13. Ibid., pp. 25–26.

14. *United States-Japan Trade Report* (1980), pp. 12–13. Yet there still remain misconceptions in this Report, based upon hasty and casual observations. For example, it states that "Japanese buyer preference for goods produced in Japan . . . is based largely on multi-generation buyer-supplier relations" and that "groups that would be competitive in the United States have been united in a web of marriages and family ties that would confound a C. Wright Mills" (p. 35). This is far from reality. It is true that buyers prefer stable and reliable supply sources in Japan, as in any other country, but competition among vendors in postwar Japan has been very severe, perhaps more severe than in most other industrialized economies. If not, why is such a

great emphasis placed on marketing by Japanese firms, and why are they so successful in marketing abroad? Postwar Japan is an egalitarian society, and marriage and family ties play a minimal role in business. Not only do the large trading companies compete, but many smaller ones also compete in the importing business. Imported luxuries today are conspicuously advertised in newspapers and magazines, and anyone who visits Japanese plants in heavy industry will undoubtedly find imported machine tools and equipment in use.

15. The Task Force now seems to be aware of this point. See *United States–Japan Trade Report* (1980), p. 30.

16. For public corporations profit motives may be weaker than nonprofit motives, such as keeping close ties to suppliers so it can "sell" members of its top and middle management to the latter as future executives.

17. Thus there are considerable similarities in the motives of Japan's agricultural policy in maintaining a certain degree of self-sufficiency in its food supply and the U.S. energy policy aimed at becoming more self-sufficient in its energy supply.

18. It may be noted, however, that a country having a secular surplus on its overall current account may be performing a valuable service to the world economy by providing urgently needed long-term capital.

7
The Economics of National Defense

Daniel I. Okimoto

Of all the discontinuities brought about by the end of World War II, none is more dramatic than Japan's nearly complete military about-face. The "bully" of prewar Asia, whose international orientation had been determined by strategic power calculations, laid down its arms following defeat in 1945. Under the tutelage of the U.S. occupation, Japan embarked upon a new international course, characterized by a disavowal of military violence as an instrument of national policy. So thoroughgoing was this transformation that the concept of military security, the crux of Japanese foreign policy from 1868 to 1945, all but disappeared from the early postwar vocabulary. Resources and energy, once directed toward the creation of a colonial empire, were rechanneled toward the goal of economic growth and prosperity. This reorientation fit perfectly into the United States's vision for a new postwar order, based on the principles of free trade knitting together democratic states in a network of alliances and held together by a preponderance of U.S. power.

A telling indicator of Japan's military *volte-face* is its record in public finance. Military outlays in the prewar period, from 1868 to 1945, averaged more than 10 percent of national income per year, reaching as high as 17 percent on the eve of Pearl Harbor. They constituted the largest single item in the national budget.[1] In the postwar period, by contrast, the Japanese government has kept military spending generally below 1 percent of GNP. Defense expenditures have exceeded 1 percent of GNP in only six out of the nearly thirty years the Self-Defense Forces (SDF) have been in existence—and

An earlier version of this chapter was given at the Council on Foreign Relations–Japan Center for International Exchange conference in 1981. The author wishes to thank the Hoover Institution for a National Fellowship during which this chapter was begun and the Northeast Asia–United States Forum, Stanford University, for support that permitted its completion. Thanks are also due to Daniel J. Levy and Alan Herbert for assistance in the simulation.

only during the early years. The figure hit a high of 1.75 percent in 1954, sinking gradually to 1.14 percent in 1959 and falling below 1 percent in 1960, where it has since stayed. The figure is by far the lowest of any major industrial state, as seen in the comparison in Table 7.1.

Japan's defense outlay is so low, in fact, that it has given rise to the charge that Japan is receiving a "free ride." Calls to step up the level of defense spending have begun to be heard from an ever-widening circle of U.S. leaders. Since the mid-1970s, the frequency and volume of calls for "steady and significant" increases in Japanese defense expenditures have picked up noticeably. Members of the Carter administration, for example, had wanted Tokyo to double its military expenditures, from less than 1 percent to roughly 2 percent of GNP, over an eight-to-ten-year period.[2] Although the Reagan administration has refrained from spelling out specific target figures, it has by no means abandoned the notion that there should be "steady and significant" increases. Indeed, if anything, the expectation may be stronger than ever, now that the Reagan administration is committed to steep increases in the United States's own defense budget. The $134 billion allocated in 1981 is projected to expand to nearly $300 billion by fiscal 1985; if these figures are in fact reached—a prospect by no means certain—the U.S. military budget will be pushed to nearly 8 percent of GNP—all at a time when other expenditures are being ruthlessly cut back.[3] Such sharp increases, coming at a time of fiscal belt-tightening, may place U.S. allies under growing pressure to contribute more to the common defense.

Japan's reluctance to allocate more resources for its own defense—not to mention that of the Western alliance—is especially irritating to U.S. leaders because the United States's once-dominant economy appears to be sliding down a slippery slope of declining productivity and world market share and Japanese industries seem to be climbing relentlessly upward—at the United States's expense. The "flood" of Japanese automobile imports, claiming more than 20 percent of the U.S. domestic market, is symptomatic of these trends. "We can't understand how Japan can say . . . that its hands are tied on defense spending," exclaimed one U.S. congressman, "when its growth rate is nearly double ours, its savings rate several times higher, and its inflation and unemployment rates substantially lower."[4] Echoing these sentiments, one executive of a U.S. semiconductor firm remarked, "The Japanese should not be allowed to get away with spending less than one percent of GNP on defense when we must allocate five or six times that amount—in part to guarantee the defense of Japan itself."[5] The presumption is that, if

TABLE 7.1
Defense Spending as Percentage of GNP (1979)

United States	5.2
United Kingdom	4.9
France	3.9
West Germany	3.3
Italy	2.4
Japan	0.9

Source: The Military Balance, 1980–1981 (London: International Institute for Strategic Studies, 1980), p. 96.

Japan had to divert more of its capital and labor from commercial to military applications, its economy would not be as dynamic. While this view may not be either correct or typical, it is far from uncommon.

The military burden is believed to hamper the U.S. economy in several ways: (1) by narrowing the band of fiscal flexibility; (2) by diverting finite resources from more productive channels; and (3) by contributing to a huge, cumulative deficit that complicates the government's management of monetary policy and price stabilization. The resentment against Japan's "free ride" is grounded, therefore, in the perceived economic costs of having to assume a disproportionate share of the burdens of collective defense. Implicit are the presumptions that (1) Japan's economy is fully capable of shouldering a heavier burden; (2) larger Japanese outlays will relieve the United States of some of its current and projected defense responsibilities; and (3) a greater Japanese defense capability will upgrade the overall structure of Western deterrence. Here again, as this view is based on counterfactual logic, the argument is hard to substantiate or to refute. Nevertheless, the circle of those who subscribe to this view, or some modified version of it, is by no means insignificant.

The Japanese rebuttal is economic in nature. Pushing through steep increases in defense expenditures, they say, runs counter to the logic of budgetary incrementalism and is likely to arouse stiff opposition from the Ministry of Finance, which is determined to cut back the extraordinarily high rate of deficit spending, currently standing at around 30 percent of the general accounts budget. If the ministry fails to put public finances back on a sound footing, the argument goes, the government will be saddled with a serious problem of fiscal discipline somewhere down the road.

Tokyo officials have also sought to cast the 1 percent "ceiling" in a more positive light. They point out that, although the percentage of defense spending has remained constant, Japan's military expenditures, adjusted for inflation, rose around 7 percent per year between 1967 and 1982, thanks to steep gains in productivity. This means that in real terms, Japanese defense expenditures from 1965 to 1980 rose faster than those of the United States or most NATO nations, albeit starting from a much lower baseline. In dollar figures, the 1980 budget of more than $10 billion placed Japan *eighth* in the world. The figure would be even higher if different accounting procedures were followed. Using NATO accounting categories, which include the costs of helping to finance Japanese employees on U.S. base facilities, Japan's defense budget would be calculated at around 1.2 percent of GNP rather than the widely cited and criticized figure of 0.9 percent.

Observe that the defense dialogue—including U.S. criticisms and Japanese rejoinders—pivots on fiscal, economic, and statistical arguments, not on issues of military strategy, threat perceptions, or specific military missions that need to be carried out. This preoccupation with the economics of collective defense is a curious and striking feature of the U.S.-Japanese defense dialogue. How and why is it that military questions have come to be cast so centrally in economic terms of reference? In what sense, if any, is the "free ride" hypothesis accurate and relevant? Why has Japan been so reluctant to devote more resources to military defense? Would higher military expenditures lower Japanese growth rates? These are but a few of the questions that this chapter will attempt to analyze.

Low Defense Expenditures: The Historical Background

The U.S. Occupation and Creation of the SDF

To understand how and why Japan came to spend so little on defense requires going back in history. The vision of postwar Asia conceived by U.S. policymakers in 1944 called for: (1) the complete dismantling of Japan's wartime machine; (2) the democratization of its political system as a guarantee against the revival of militarism; and (3) Japan's reemergence as a peace-oriented economy. The intent of the United States was clear: to prevent Japan from ever again menacing peace and stability in Asia.

This vision of a demilitarized Japan guided U.S. occupation policy for several years following Japan's surrender. It was apotheosized in Article 9, the famous "no war" clause, of Japan's postwar "peace" Constitution, drafted by U.S. occupation officials in 1946 and ratified by the Japanese Diet in 1947. Article 9 reads:

> Aspiring sincerely to an international peace based on justice and order the Japanese people forever renounce war as a sovereign right of the nation and the threat of force as a means of settling international disputes.
>
> In order to accomplish the aim of the preceding paragraph, land, sea, and air forces, as well as other war potential, will never be maintained. The right of belligerency of the State will not be recognized.

The utopian sentiments embodied in Article 9 meant that Japan would have to entrust its security to the "good faith and justice of the peace-loving people of the world."[6] Some officials believed this could be accomplished through common guarantees among the region's four powers—the United States, USSR, China, and Great Britain.

The deterioration of the world's security environment, however, soon dashed such visions. A series of world crises set the stage for Japan's eventual rearmament—at the urging of the United States: the sequence of events in Europe leading to the proclamation of the Truman Doctrine, the communist triumph in China, the signing of the Sino-Soviet Friendship Treaty, and the outbreak of the Korean War. Early hopes for an unarmed and neutralized Japan gave way to a Cold War strategy of establishing Japan as the cornerstone of an anticommunist arch extending from the Aleutians down through the Philippines and into Southeast Asia.

Even before the outbreak of the Korean War, a number of U.S. policymakers, including George Kennan, had come to believe that leaving Japan disarmed, defenseless, and utterly vulnerable to possible Soviet blandishments would be to court potential disaster.[7] In a world dominated by Soviet-U.S. confrontation, Kennan proposed that a defense network be established in Asia, "which would assure the security of that country [Japan] from Communist penetration and domination as well as from military attack by the Soviet Union and would permit Japan's economic potential to become once again an important force in the affairs of the area, conducive to peace and stability."[8]

Reflecting Kennan's concern about Japan's security and the protection of U.S. interests in Asia, the U.S. National Security Council (NSC) called for the creation of a 150,000-strong police force in Japan. Initially, General Douglas MacArthur resisted the NSC proposal, but in July 1950, following the invasion of South Korea, he promptly requested that Prime Minister Yoshida Shigeru create a National Police Reserve (Kokka Keisatsu Yobitai) of 75,000 men, the embryo of what was later to become the Self-Defense Forces (Jieitai). Looking ahead to the day when the occupation would end, U.S. and Japanese leaders also formulated plans for a U.S.-Japan security alliance, which would retain U.S. forces on Japanese bases for an indefinite period. John Foster Dulles pressed Prime Minister Yoshida to organize a defense force of 325,000 to 350,000 men. Although Yoshida agreed, in principle, that Japan needed a defense capability and although he was anxious to bring the occupation to an end, he rejected the idea that so large a defense force needed to be created, citing a number of reasons:

1. *Political infeasibility.* The strength of pacifist sentiment and the power of opposition parties to mobilize resistance made rearmament at the 350,000-man level politically impossible.
2. *Constitutional constraints.* Questions concerning the constitutionality of defense forces also ruled out Dulles's proposal.
3. *Civil-military relations.* Memories of military rule made Yoshida uneasy about recreating a military force of such size so soon after the end of the war.
4. *Low external threat of aggression.* Yoshida assigned low probability to military invasion of Japan; China, he felt, lacked the air and amphibious capabilities, and the Soviet Union had been too badly hurt by the war.
5. *Regional reactions.* Asian countries might react negatively to Japan's sudden and large-scale rearmament; it would slow down the process of winning reacceptance in the international comity of nations.
6. *Involvement in Korean War.* If Japan rearmed quickly and on the scale desired by U.S. leaders, Yoshida was afraid Japan might be asked to participate in the Korean War.
7. *Protection under U.S. military superiority.* A defense alliance with the United States, then unquestionably the dominant military power in the world, would guarantee Japan's security and obviate the need for massive rearmament.
8. *Economic strain.* The overriding consideration was economic. Japan's fragile economy, trying to recover from wartime devastation, simply could not sustain the costs of maintaining so large a defense force; as economic recovery had to be the country's first priority and the best hedge

against communist insurrection, Yoshida argued that rushing ahead on the military front would undermine the United States's long-term interests in Japan and Asia.[9]

The arguments were sufficiently compelling to forestall U.S. pressures. The National Police Reserve stayed at 75,000 for the rest of the occupation period and was increased to 110,000 in October 1952; the Self-Defense Forces were not formally created until 1954.

The U.S.-Japan Security Treaty, signed in September 1951, diminished the urgency of Japan's rapid rearmament, because the U.S. military umbrella was extended over Japan and the region. However, it is worth noting that the text of the original treaty made reference to the "expectation . . . that Japan will itself increasingly assume responsibility for its own defense against direct and indirect aggression."[10] Yoshida himself acknowledged that the U.S. security guarantee "cannot be continued indefinitely. That is why we must undertake to build up a self-defense power of our own gradually according as circumstances and resources permit. . . ."[11]

In the revised treaty, signed in January 1960, this reference to Japan's eventual assumption of responsibility for its own defense was deleted. It is hard to say why. One could conjecture that, as the point had already been made in the text of the original treaty, reiteration would only have belabored the obvious. Perhaps the political delicacy of passing the revised security treaty through Japan's Diet—in the face of emotional opposition and the danger of mass protests in the streets—may have made Japanese and U.S. leaders cautious. Whatever the explanation, too much should not be made of the omission. It is doubtful that U.S. leaders in 1960 had abandoned hopes of persuading Japan to assume more responsibility for its own defense. The United States could live with the status quo as long as the U.S. military commanded a preponderance of power, but there was no guarantee that that situation would last.

Economics, Defense, and National Interests

The negotiations between Dulles and Yoshida thus reveal that, from the very beginning, the question of rearmament had become inextricably entangled with economic considerations. Until the 1960s Japan's economy had not gained sufficient strength to sustain the magnitude of expenditures that Dulles's proposal would have required—at least not without incurring heavy costs in other areas. U.S. officials, perfectly aware of the trade-offs, recognized that economic reconstruction had to be given priority. It held the key to the realization of several U.S. objectives: (1) Japan's democratization and long-term stability; (2) preemption of the communist threat in Japan; (3) Japan's prosperity and acceptance in the world; (4) ripple-effect benefits of Japanese growth for the rest of Asia; and (5) consolidation of a world order based on free trade.[12]

With the onset of the Cold War, U.S. leaders stepped up efforts at Japan's economic reconstruction. These efforts took the form of changes in occupation policies from punitive reparations and deconcentration to the facilitation of full recovery. Dulles came to believe that, in order to give Japan a fair chance at recovery, Southeast Asian countries had to scale down their wartime reparations demands; he argued that excessive reparations could boomerang if Japan was forced to default on payments.[13]

There was a more immediate and tangible reason why U.S. officials were eager to see Japan's economy back on its feet again: namely, to ensure that the United States would not be stuck with a huge foreign aid bill to keep Japan solvent.[14] From 1945 to 1948, the U.S. government had provided Japan with more than $750 million in direct assistance; estimates place the total by the end of the occupation in 1952 somewhere around $2 billion.[15] No wonder sentiment in the U.S. Congress favored an early peace settlement and support for Japan's reintegration into the world economy. With the rehabilitation of Europe to worry about, legislative leaders did not want the federal budget to continue carrying the weight of Japan's economic backwardness.

At the same time, Japan's economic resurgence would require that certain adjustments be made. Prior to the war, Japan's colonial empire had supplied a large portion of its raw materials and overseas markets. New sources and trade partners had to be found. Obviously the United States would have to play a major role in filling that need.[16] As leader of the capitalist world, the United States stood to gain a great deal from the relationship, not only in terms of bilateral trade, but also from the perspective of building a viable capitalist structure in Asia. But to gain these benefits, it had to accept policies and practices in Japan that were not fully tolerated in Europe: namely, strict foreign exchange and direct investment controls. As a consequence, U.S. firms were denied an opportunity to invest heavily in Japan — in contrast to U.S. penetration of Europe. Behind protective barriers, Japanese companies extended control over their own markets and, using economies of scale, launched successful export drives, aimed particularly at the U.S. market.

For France and Britain, colonial powers in prewar Asia, the specter of an economically resurgent Japan, purchasing raw materials from and selling finished products to Southeast Asia seemed threatening to their continuing commercial interests in the region. Japan appeared to possess all the assets necessary to dominate trade in Asia: proximity, a skilled labor force, a history of prewar industrial development, large trading companies, low wages, and so on. France and Britain were worried that they might be "crowded out," but neither nation could prevent Japan from establishing a dominant position in the region. The only country that might have, the United States, saw only positive consequences emerging from Japan's growing interdependence with Southeast Asia. It even hoped that Japan might be a catalyst for the region's economic "take-off."

For a variety of reasons, therefore, not the least of which involved U.S. perception of its national interests, the United States seemed almost as anxious as Japan itself to see Japan's economy restored to good health. One immediate way of facilitating this process was to help Japan cope with its balance-of-payments problem, a chronic headache for a country lacking in natural resources — a deficiency that was especially acute in the aftermath of the war, when its capital stock had been badly depleted. As Japanese leaders claimed the country could not balance its international payments through normal channels of trade, U.S. officials in 1953 agreed to use the U.S. program of military assistance (under the Mutual Security Act of 1951) to strengthen Japan's economy and relieve its current-account deficits through military procurement orders that would supply much-needed foreign exchange. Military procurements and other spillover spending connected with the Korean War had already stimulated Japan's economy, helping it to recover from the devastation of war. The Mutual Defense Assistance Agreement, signed by the United States and Japan in 1954, alludes explicitly to the relationship between economics and defense: "In the planning of a defense assistance program for Japan, *economic stability will be an essential element for consideration in the development of its defense capacities, and . . . Japan can contribute only to the extent permitted by its general economic conditions and capacities.*"[17]

Because U.S. leaders understood the importance of economic priorities, not only for Japanese but also for U.S. interests, the early impasse over the scope and pace of Japan's rearmament could be amicably resolved. Instead of 350,000 troops and 2 or 3 percent of GNP, Japan recruited 110,000 troops in 1952 and allocated slightly more than 1 percent of GNP until 1960. Subsequent events helped to alleviate pressures on Japan to move more rapidly toward an autonomous defense capability: (1) general equilibrium in Northeast Asia's balance of power; (2) no eruption of war following the Korean conflagration; (3) the Sino-Soviet split; (4) massive demonstrations against the passage of the 1960 security treaty; and (5) U.S. military dominance in the region.

In summary, one can say that the primacy of economic recovery and growth, and the United States's extension of a military umbrella over the region, gave Japan the opportunity, almost unheard-of among major nation states, to mobilize its considerable skills and energies single-mindedly in pursuit of economic development without the heavy drain of military expenditures. Favorable developments in the region, and the continuing credibility of power of the U.S. military umbrella, combined to keep the defense equation from crowding to the forefront of U.S.-Japan relations until the mid-1970s — long after Japan had not merely recovered but had become the noncommunist world's second largest economy.

The Significance of Low Defense Expenditures

For more than a quarter of a century, the U.S.-Japan defense alliance functioned fairly smoothly within the framework of the U.S. military umbrella and Japan's minimalist military posture. Both sides accepted the incremental nature of increases in Japan's capabilities. What have been the political and international consequences of Japan's de-emphasis on defense? How has it affected U.S. and Japanese interests? Answers to these questions can be sought at several different levels: systemic, regional, bilateral, and domestic.

Systemic and Regional Stability

E. H. Carr has argued that the causes of World War II can be traced to the failure of the interwar hierarchy of power — which he saw as rigid and inequitable — to accommodate the interests of such rapidly rising states as Germany and Japan.[18] Faced with a growing discrepancy between the extant order and the realities of their military power and regional ambitions, the Axis "outsiders" rose up to challenge the status quo. The key to the stabilization of the postwar world — not to mention regional peace in Asia and Europe — lay in the reorientation of Japan and Germany as commercial countries with vital stakes in a peaceful new world order. Viewed in this light, the military "de-fanging" of Japan and Germany, and their transformation into merchant states, would remove a major source of systemic instability. Extant states would not feel threatened by their economic resurgence, because the two former Axis powers would keep economic gains decoupled from military power. Their spectacular economic ascent could be accommodated without giving rise to structural strains that would cause another violent realignment of power through world war. The other notable benefit would come in the enhancement of political stability within both countries, a development that, in turn, would contribute to the equilibrium of the postwar order.

From a broader perspective, Japan's military *volte-face* neutralized the one indigenous power capable of disrupting the region. Countries that had been overrun by Japanese troops during the war were relieved of anxieties about military domination. Together with China's unification, Japan's peaceful reorientation stabilized what had been, until then, a dangerously volatile area.

It goes without saying that U.S. military might provided the necessary underpinning for the postwar transformation of Germany and Japan. Even today, the credibility of the U.S. umbrella holds the key to the continuing stability of the world order, not to mention the viability of Japan's low military posture. For years, going back to the mid-1960s, crystal-ball gazers have predicted that Japan would try to reattain the military grandeur it once knew, citing a variety of reasons: e.g., historical tradition,[19] nationalism,[20] a Gaullist desire for security independence,[21] protection of overseas economic interests,[22] and a compulsion to bring its politico-military influence more in line with its economic power.[23] What these predictions failed to take adequately into account—and perhaps the underlying reason why they have not so far materialized—is the continuing credibility of U.S. power as the backstop for Japan's strictly commercial orientation. The loss of that credibility is more apt to hasten Japan's remilitarization than any factor cited above.

Remilitarization could occur in one of two ways: either through the abrogation of the U.S.-Japan Mutual Security Treaty (MST) and the acquisition of an independent military capability; or through heavier rearmament within the framework of the bilateral alliance—perhaps in response to "soft spots" in the Western alliance. Whether Japan can continue as a lightly armed economic superpower—few, if any, nations historically have managed to do so—depends largely on the stability of the bipolar international system and on the capacity of the United States to maintain the military balance.

Consolidation of the U.S.-Japan Alliance

Japan's metamorphosis from militaristic to merchant state took place within the structure of the U.S.-Japan alliance, one of the truly seminal developments in postwar Asia. The benefits of that alliance for both countries have been incalculable:

- A stable, coherent, and predictable foreign policy orientation
- An effective structure of deterrence

- A greater sense of security than either side had known in prewar Asia
- Opportunities for cooperation in the management of the world economy
- A dynamic Japanese economy
- Economic complementarity and the stimulus of vigorous competition
- Japan's role as a catalyst for regional development under capitalist auspices
- Japan's considerable symbolic and functional value as a showcase of democracy

Until the late 1970s, Japan's low military posture removed what might otherwise have been a serious irritant, given the political sensitivity of the defense question in Japan. It provided the bilateral relationship much-needed time to heal old wounds and to forge new and lasting ties of economic interdependence. As a result, the alliance has blossomed into the kind of relationship that only the most far-sighted policymakers ever envisioned: enduring, founded on a bedrock of common interests, and held together by an elaborate structure of interlocking ties.

The Domestic Dimension: Japanese Politics

Military de-emphasis has also had positive effects on Japanese politics. Among the outcomes to which it has directly or indirectly contributed are:

- removal of the uniformed services as dominant actors in policymaking
- elimination of the danger of a military takeover during times of national crisis
- clear acceptance of the principle of civilian control
- single-minded pursuit of economic interests and objectives
- facilitation of national consensus (due in part to the concentration on economic objectives)
- spillover benefits from rapid and sustained growth for the stabilization of domestic politics
- avoidance of political polarization, which might have resulted if military rearmament had been given higher visibility and priority
- containment of military controversies within the sphere of "nonissues," thereby sidestepping potential problems for the Liberal Democratic party (LDP) in managing the Diet and staying in power

- time for popular support to congeal around the U.S.-Japan defense alliance
- greater sensitivity to the nuances of public opinion than would otherwise have been possible

The insulation of postwar politics from the volatility of rearmament issues, in effect, gave the political system time and optimal circumstances under which to sink firm roots. Features of that system gradually emerged as semipermanent fixtures: the power of the bureaucracies; the influence of business interests; the primacy of commercial concerns; the relative weakness of labor unions; the dominance of the conservative, pro-business, pro-U.S. LDP; and unparalleled overall stability. The consolidation of this system has furthered U.S. national interests, at the same time advancing Japan's.

On the other hand, the military low posture has not been cost-free. To cite one example, the elementary level of public discourse concerning issues of military security — standing in stark contrast to the highly sophisticated level of economic analysis — is both a reflection and a by-product of the low visibility given questions of national defense. Moreover, the duration of Japan's military weakness and political isolationism — long beyond the period of healing — has led to resentment and a sense of crisis on the part of Americans. A somewhat quicker acceptance by Japan of military responsibilities and of a more positive political and economic role might have diminished the resentments that accumulated, especially as it became clear that the United States no longer possessed the unquestioned superiority it once enjoyed over the Soviet Union.

On balance, however, when viewed from the perspective of domestic politics, the benefits have clearly outweighed the costs. Until the middle-to-late 1970s, political circumstances in Japan were not ripe for an acceleration of rearmament. Any attempt to force Japan to move at a significantly faster pace would probably have backfired. Opposition parties would have banded together to attack the LDP; the LDP itself might have succumbed to bickering and internal division; public opinion would surely have become polarized; the whole political climate might have been thrown into turmoil — with orderliness restored perhaps only by the sacrifice of democratic processes. Given the fragility of democracy, and its failure to survive during the prewar era, democratization might have been much harder to maintain had there not been an interlude of military decompression. The long-term benefits for democracy were every bit as valuable as the opportunities created for high-speed economic growth. In laying the groundwork for the bilateral alliance, Japanese and U.S. leaders can be given credit for having had their long-term priorities straight: Economic recovery and growth and the consolidation of the democratic party had to be given early priority over military rearmament.

Political Predictability and Fiscal Expectations

Foreign observers often express bewilderment that the Japanese government should feel that its hands are tied by the "1 percent ceiling" on defense expenditures.[24] But the tumultuous protests against the passage of the revised U.S.-Japan Security Treaty in 1960 revealed how suddenly and massively political opposition could be set off by the mishandling of military issues. Owing to such sensitivity, the conservative ruling party has been more vulnerable to attack over security imbroglios than over any other issue.

One way of bringing down political temperatures was to adhere to limits on defense spending. In the early 1960s, the ceiling stood at slightly more than 1 percent of GNP, or around 10 percent of the general accounts budget. By 1967, the figures had fallen below 1 percent, reaching a low of 0.8 percent in 1970, and staying below 1 percent through the 1970s (see Figure 7.1). The military's share of the annual budget also fell steadily, dipping below 6 percent in 1977. Yet because of the rapid expansion of economic output, the absolute yen amounts kept climbing. The decade of the 1960s saw, in short, the consolidation of a de facto "1 percent GNP" system.

The practice of allocating no more than 1 percent had the effect of depriving opposition parties of an easy target for partisan attack. Expectations were stabilized, uncertainties and anxieties reduced, and fiscal processes routinized. The politics of national defense became highly predictable. As predictability is often the key to avoidance of conflict, military matters gravitated to the periphery of controversy as time passed. Except for occasional incidents—like the revelation of military contingency plans involving the USSR as Japan's hypothetical enemy (the so-called Three Arrows contingency plan)—public protests triggered by the mishandling of military issues subsided. By 1970, the year the revised security treaty came up for review, the political climate had calmed to such an extent that the treaty could be extended without provoking massive demonstrations in the streets.

Fixing a tacit ceiling also gave the LDP fiscal flexibility to fend off criticisms in another area of vulnerability: namely, inadequate welfare and social overhead investments. By holding down military outlays, the LDP government was able to divert ever-larger sums to social security and the promotion of science and education. In 1960, as seen in Figures 7.2 and 7.3 (A, B), the three items—defense, social

FIGURE 7.1
Defense Spending as Percentage of GNP

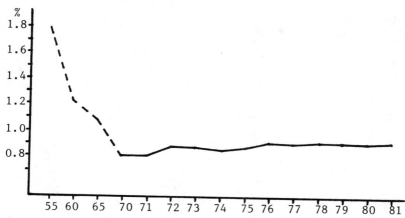

Source: Japan Defense Agency, Defense of Japan, 1981, pp. 291-292.

FIGURE 7.2
Defense Spending Relative to General Account Budget

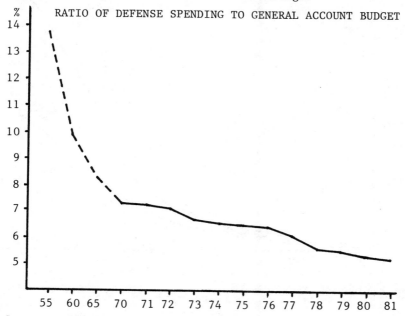

Source: Japan Defense Agency, Defense of Japan, 1981, pp. 291-292.

FIGURE 7.3A
Defense Spending Relative to Other Expenditures (in million yen)

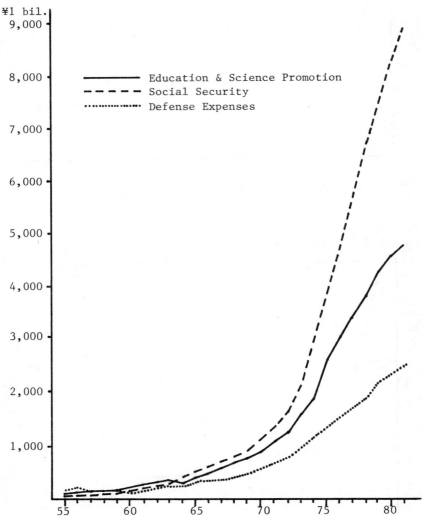

Source: Japan Defense Agency, <u>Defense of Japan, 1981</u>,
pp. 291-292.

FIGURE 7.3B
Defense and Other Expenditures as a Percentage of the General Account
Budget

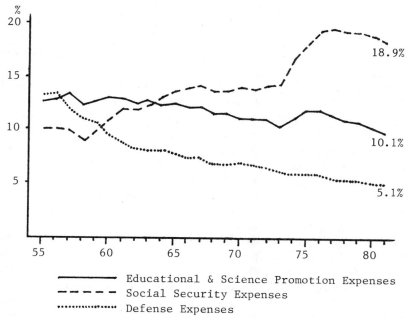

Source: Japan Defense Agency, Defense of Japan, 1981,
pp. 291-292.

security, and education and science — were quite close in terms of
annual expenditures: 10 percent, 11.4 percent, and 13.6 percent of
the general accounts budget respectively. However, social security
and education and science rose steeply after that, leaving defense expenditures lagging far behind. In 1982, the government spent twice
as much for science and more than three times as much for social
security as it did for national defense. Spending on social security as
well as science and education rose monotonically during the early
1970s, when the LDP found itself losing voter support and opposition parties stepped up their attacks on the social costs of rapid
growth — particularly environmental pollution and lagging welfare
benefits. Large welfare increases were approved in an attempt to arrest the LDP's relentless decline. By bringing welfare spending up to
the standards of other industrial states, the LDP hoped to neutralize

the appeal of socialist and communist parties. Although establishing causality is always difficult, the rapid expansion of welfare benefits appears to have helped the LDP halt the erosion of its popular base of support.[25] The conservative party has managed to hold onto its majority in both houses of the Diet (although the margins are far from large).

It is, of course, possible to argue that: (1) the shift to welfarism was inevitable, given the low level of spending prior to 1971 and Japan's aging population; or conversely (2) the rate of increase was too fast for Japan's fiscal health. What Japanese bureaucrats and political leaders failed to foresee when big increases were approved in 1971 was the onset of the oil crisis and the enormous impact it would have on the economy. As Figure 7.3 (A, B) shows, social security outlays continued to rise even after Japan's economy sputtered through the mid-1970s. It happened to coincide with a period of heavy deficit spending, necessitated by an excess of savings over investment demand and the consequent need for Keynesian measures to stimulate aggregate growth.

Perhaps one can criticize the government for raising social security payments too precipitously at precisely the time when the budget could least afford it. The so-called ratchet effects of higher welfare spending have made reductions to a lower plateau virtually impossible. In addition to the strain on public finances, the action may have limited the government's leeway with respect to national defense. However, Japan's welfare levels needed to be brought up to the levels of other industrial states; had the LDP failed to do so, that pro-U.S. conservative party might well have lost its majority in the Diet to the progressive parties,[26] and the likelihood is that a coalition government made up of these parties would have been disposed to raise welfare expenditures at an even faster rate.

The 1 percent of GNP yardstick, it should be pointed out, was never an official government guideline. It emerged, de facto, out of the pulling and hauling of the budgetary processes.[27] Over the years the ratio of military allocations became more or less fixed, with expectations hardening around the 1 percent figure. In 1975, a private study council, called the Committee to Consider National Defense (Boei o Kangeru-kai), in making recommendations to the prime minister, explained the rationale behind the 1 percent ceiling:

1.   . . . if Japan were to maintain defense power sufficient to meet any situation, costs would be astronomical. It would be inappropriate to authorize a defense budget solely on the basis of military requirements.

2. In Japan today, the maximum defense budget that the nation will tolerate seems to be within a limit of 1 percent of the gross national product. Anything over this 1 percent limit runs into great difficulty in obtaining public approval, even when the overall economy is on an upswing, and particularly at time of decline.

3. There is no practical or theoretical basis behind this 1 percent figure, but it has allowed Japan to achieve a certain level of defense power without adversely affecting the national economy, and has somehow become the magic number in public determination of whether the defense budget is moderate or excessive.[28]

As suggested in this report, economic and political considerations, not military or strategic objectives, have determined the level of defense spending. Although military appropriations in all countries emerge from a complicated process of weighing trade-offs, the Japanese case is unusual in the degree to which military considerations have been subordinated to fiscal and economic imperatives.

If the benefits of a low military posture are stressed, its costs must also be pointed out. Military de-emphasis gained time for political stabilization, but it has also led to a growing discrepancy between Japan's security posture and the changing realities of the external environment. Japanese leaders, fearful of sparking a political crisis, followed a cautious, status-quo posture for nearly two decades — during which time the Soviet Union achieved nuclear parity with the United States and dramatically expanded its air and naval deployments in the Pacific. By the mid-1970s, the situation had generated serious friction between the United States and Japan. U.S. leaders began pressing Japan to bring its security capabilities into closer and more realistic alignment with the growing requirements of protecting the interests of the Western alliance.

Defense Spending and Economic Implications

We have considered the systemic, bilateral, and political consequences of Japan's low defense budget. What about its economic effects? If the "free ride" argument is valid, Japan's rapid economic growth was possible because of the lightness of its defense burden. If Japan had been forced to assume the full costs of national defense — instead of shifting it onto the shoulders of the U.S. taxpayer — the pace of its economic growth would have been slowed significantly. The implication is that the U.S. taxpayer has borne a double burden: the direct expenses associated with extending the U.S. military umbrella over Japan and the indirect cost of seeing the Japanese bounce back from defeat to claim an ever-larger share of the U.S. market in steel, automobiles, consumer electronics, and so on. Is the "free ride" hypothesis valid? Would Japan's growth rate have been appreciably slowed by higher defense expenditures?

The Early Decades, 1945–1965

Answers to these and other questions differ according to the time frame and the counterfactual assumptions made. Heavy defense expenditures clearly would have been a net drag on Japan's economy during at least the first two decades of the postwar period. Capital was in short supply, and in view of the buoyancy of business investment demand, scarce capital would probably have had to be diverted from more productive commercial channels. To sustain a much larger defense force, the government would have had to come up with money from somewhere, whether through higher taxes, deficit financing, or reallocation of public expenditures. Each would have exacted opportunity costs. Higher taxes would probably have reduced the record rates of savings, the sine qua non of Japan's heavy business investments and system of indirect financing.[29] Deficit spending would have placed public finances in a precarious position at a time when the government was trying to solidify its financial institutions and monetary policies on the basis of a balanced budget. The third option, reordering budgetary allocations, would have curtailed government services in other areas, limiting subsidies and preferential loans that could be extended to high-priority industries. Because Japan's machinery for high growth was finely tuned, any tampering of these sorts would probably have thrown it out of kilter.

Of course, the extent to which economic growth would have been set back is hard to calculate. That would have depended on a number of circumstances: e.g., the size of the defense "bite," the composition of expenditure items (personnel, weapons production, support for base facilities, etc.), the source of funding (taxes, deficits, or fiscal juggling). It would have made a major difference whether the government allocated 2, 3, or 4 percent of GNP, whether those funds were spent in ways that yielded civilian spin-off benefits, and whether the money came at the expense of investments or consumption. One cannot reach blanket conclusions without considering the wide range of variables, any combination of which would have altered economic outcomes.

One Estimate. Two well-known economists, Hugh Patrick and Henry Rosovsky, have offered a quantitative estimate of the effects of higher defense spending, based on the following set of admittedly extreme assumptions:

1. Defense expenditures would be set at 6 or 7 percent of GNP (presumably because Japan would not have the U.S. umbrella on which to depend for its own security).
2. Military outlays would come at the expense of capital investments rather than consumption.
3. No spillover benefits would exist for the civilian economy (no technological spinoffs, no demand stimulus, no multiplier effects).
4. The average capital-output ratio would be constant.[30]

Clearly, such assumptions are unrealistic. Yet, they can be useful if one wants to measure maximal rather than probable impact. By assessing maximal impact, one can come to grips with the "free ride" criticism that Japan's growth was possible because of the low level of defense spending.

Even with an overestimation of military appropriations, Patrick and Rosovsky discovered that Japan's annual growth rate would have fallen by around 2 percent per year. Although relatively minor for any given year, the reduction would have registered a significant cumulative impact over a twenty- or twenty-five-year period. From 1952 to 1974, the cumulative costs of defense would have reduced the overall size of the economy by a factor of around 30 percent — a major opportunity cost but by no means crippling for what would still have been the fastest-growing economy in the industrial world. The authors concluded, therefore, that low defense expenditures did not account for much of the variance in Japan's remarkable postwar growth. Even under the worst-case scenario — an autonomous defense capability, costing 6 or 7 percent of GNP without returns to the civilian economy — Japan's postwar juggernaut would still have moved ahead at impressive speed.

What the Patrick-Rosovsky estimate does *not* tell us, however, is how higher spending would have affected such key areas as political alignments, social stability, industrial structure, and public finances. If capital had come out of investments, it would presumably have caused serious long-term problems for public finances. Japan's industry might have been structured differently. Less capital would have been available for social overhead investments. And whether the government would have had the fiscal leeway to ensure political stability through the extension of subsidies to the countryside or the redistribution of wealth to slow-growing regions is questionable. As a consequence, one might surmise that the political "fallout" effects could have led to the dislodging of the conservative regime. A radical change in spending priorities, in short, would have been likely to alter not only the pace and pattern of postwar growth but also the constellation of political forces that emerged from, and sustained, Japan's high-growth system.

One weakness of economic simulations, therefore, is their inability to factor political consequences into the computer's simultaneous equations. Continuity is usually assumed, even though shifts in political alignments are capable of throwing off all economic calculations. On the other hand, simulations are useful in demonstrating that, under certain assumptions and controlled conditions, the economy would have yielded a certain level of production and growth. Like laboratory experiments, simulations isolate an independent variable and measure how it alters the outcome of a dependent variable, controlling for intervening factors. In interpreting the Patrick-Rosovsky results, we need to keep in mind their assumption that certain conditions—such as conservative, pro-business rule and political stability—would have stayed constant. Their finding that low military spending constituted only one factor, and at that not a primary or decisive one, in Japan's rapid economic growth is enlightening in trying to come to terms with the "free ride equals rapid growth" hypothesis, but it must be understood within the limitations of its assumptions.[31]

Higher Defense Spending in the 1980s: A Simulation. If the Patrick-Rosovsky estimate places the reduction at 2 percent per year, given military appropriations from 1952 to 1974 of 6 or 7 percent of GNP, what would be the impact of spending at a more realistic level of, say, 2 percent of GNP, spread over a four-year period? Now that Japan's economy has become the second largest in the noncommunist world, behind only the United States, is it not more capable of absorbing the higher costs of defense without setbacks to its growth rates?

The question is empirically testable through the use of simulated models of growth, provided simplifying assumptions are made. First, we shall set the 1983 level of defense spending at 2 percent of GNP, an increase from 0.9 percent (the figure in 1980), with steady increments each year until 1983. The 2 percent figure could be set lower or higher, depending on what related assumptions are built into the model. The decision to peg the level at 2 percent is based on the belief that the U.S.-Japan Security Treaty will remain in effect over the foreseeable future, obviating the need for a more massive buildup. Members of the Carter administration, as pointed out earlier, had hoped to persuade Japanese leaders to lift expenditures to 2 percent over an eight-to-ten-year period.

The 2 percent figure is undoubtedly unrealistic under prevailing political circumstances. If the Japanese were to step up military expenditures suddenly, the doubling of appropriations over a three-to-five-year period would be stretching the limits of feasibility. Even at the current level of less than 1 percent, Japan's defense budget in absolute amounts places it eighth among all nations of the world; 2 percent would catapult Japan to fourth place, behind the United States, USSR, and China but ahead of NATO nations.

Our second assumption is more extreme: namely, that spending increases would come out of private and public investments rather than out of consumption. No government, certainly not Japan's, would choose to draw only upon investments, the lifeblood of productivity gains. Also factored into the model is the assumption that larger defense appropriations would not crowd out other important budget items. The government would not cut back spending for welfare, education, or other vital services. However, if Tokyo really had to finance larger defense outlays, the likelihood is that it would try to do so within the limits of natural increases in the overall budget by allowing defense expenditures to increase while holding down or cutting back on less important categories. Japan's budget contains items — like public works — in which a substantial amount of "padding" can be trimmed. Fiscal belt-tightening is one way of sidestepping deficit spending or higher taxes.

There are, of course, limits to the amount that can be squeezed out of the budget. Raising defense appropriations while holding down other expenditures like welfare may be more difficult in Japan than it is in the United States. If defense expenditures are increased, the progressive parties may insist that social security benefits also be raised. This represents a form of internal "linkage politics." Unless the political climate changes — as a consequence, say, of a national crisis — the government would have to look for categories other than welfare to do its belt-tightening.

If the government chooses not to reorder spending priorities, it could come up with money to finance higher defense expenditures through higher taxes or heavier deficit spending. There may be leeway in Japan for raising taxes, considering that the overall tax rate is among the lowest in the industrial world: 21 percent of GNP, compared to roughly 28 percent for the United States, and more than 50 percent for Sweden. (Whether or not higher taxes are politically acceptable is, of course, an altogether separate question.) This comparatively light burden, attributable in part to low defense and welfare expenditures, has had the beneficial effect of helping to sustain Japan's high savings rate, because a large proportion of disposable income — ranging from 20 to 24 percent — has gone into savings.[32] To the extent that a low tax rate is politically popular, it has also benefited the conservative regime. But taxes seem bound to go up in the future, if only because Japan's aging population, soon to become one of the oldest in the world, is going to require larger welfare outlays.

The option of heavier deficit financing has been ruled out because of the large debt the government is already servicing.[33] In 1980, the Japanese government incurred a deficit of nearly $70 billion, more than that of the United States, Britain, or France. Although the government is determined to scale down its yearly deficits in order not to lose control over prices and public finances, the macroeconomic situation suggests that there may be room for higher defense expenditures if public works and other deficit-financed programs are cut back. Defense spending might be an alternative to regional construction projects as a means of stimulating aggregate demand. By procuring equipment and investing in new plant capacity, military-related demand might be able to absorb excess savings, spur growth, help neutralize the compulsion to export, and raise demand for manufactured imports. A number of Japanese business leaders have expressed interest in, and support for, higher defense expenditures for precisely these reasons. But this scenario usually assumes that Japan's savings rate will stay high, or that capital will not flow out through offshore banking activities or through the mechanism of international arbitrage. If savings slump, or capital moves abroad, the net effect of a doubling of defense spending could well be to unleash inflationary pressures.

Our last assumption is that the composition of the defense budget will basically reflect past priorities with some modifications to take account of changing military needs. Personnel and provisions would continue to constitute the largest item on the budget, but with more money available and no major personnel expansion assumed, the percentage would drop from more than 50 to less than 45. The share of weapons procurement would rise from less than 20 percent to more than 25 percent as money is invested to upgrade Japan's air defense, antisubmarine warfare capabilities, ammunition reserves, and command-and-control and communications systems. Research and development would also be expanded, with a doubling of investment from 1 to 2 percent of the defense budget. If Japan is serious about strengthening its defense capability, it would have to bring the state of its military technology up to the level of other powers'; currently it lags far behind the United States and is curiously backward relative to the advanced state of its commercial technology.

Simulation Results. Having made our assumptions explicit, let us look now at the results of the simulation. Two forecasts had to be run in order to measure the full impact of higher defense spending. The first run is a standard forecast, based on no major changes in defense spending; I shall refer to it as the *control case* or *standard forecast*. The second run is adjusted for higher military expenditures along the lines of the assumptions already explained; I shall call it the *experimental case* or *adjusted forecast*. A comparison of the results bring to light some intriguing differences.

Because of the sudden ratcheting-upwards of defense spending, economic growth rates plunge in the second year of our forecasts from an expected 4.6 percent growth rate (standard or control case) to a net negative rate of −3.1 percent (adjusted or experimental case) (see Figure 7.4). Clearly, the suddenness of higher military appropriations sends growth rates tumbling, at least for the first few years. However, by the end of the third year, the economy rallies to make a strong comeback: Growth rates leap from −3.1 percent to a remarkable 10.5 percent, which is explainable in part as a statistical regression toward the mean, while the control case or standard forecast grows by only a modest 2.8 percent over the third year. The nominal and inflation-adjusted size of the economy is still larger in the economy that has not boosted defense spending (the standard or control case) but not by a great deal: 265 versus 256 trillion yen (nominal) and 127 versus 126 trillion yen (adjusted to 1970 prices) (see Figures 7.5 and 7.6). Hence, looking only at the first three years, we see that the overall expansion of the economy slows down as a consequence of higher defense spending.

Surprisingly, however, the adjusted economy, buoyed perhaps by the stimulus of greater military-related demand, not only makes up the lost ground but actually overtakes the standard or control case economy by the end of the fourth year. The GNP growth rate is 9.3 percent compared to 6.2 percent. The nominal size of the economy, by 1983, is roughly 300 trillion yen, compared to 290 trillion yen in the control case. In real terms, taking inflation into account, the gap is less striking but still significant: 138 trillion yen as opposed to 135 trillion. The pattern is thus clear: After sustaining early setbacks in growth rates owing to a sizable redirection of funds, the Japanese economy bounces back with remarkable resiliency to register, by the end of the fourth year, a larger economy overall and a higher growth rate. This result suggests that the Japanese economy is clearly capable of absorbing significantly higher military expenditures without adverse reductions in its aggregate size or growth rates over the long run. Old anxieties about negative aftereffects, stemming back to the Dulles-Yoshida days, no longer seem war-

FIGURE 7.4
Percentage Change from Previous Year Gross National Product

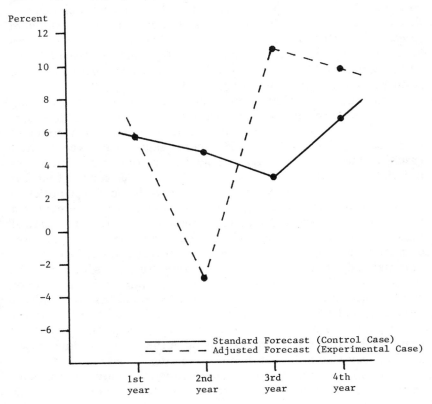

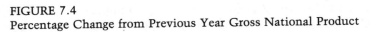

ranted, not at least on purely economic grounds. Indeed, if trends for
the final two years of our simulation are indicative, the empirical
evidence would seem to support the contention of those in favor of
higher military expenditures — that they would spur higher rates of
growth. During the recession of the mid-1970s, there was some discussion in business circles — none of it very serious — about trying to
reflate the economy through military spending.

Contrary to common belief in some business circles in the United
States, therefore, the competitiveness of Japan's economy might not
be undermined by higher defense expenditures. Indeed, the commercial strength of certain sectors, such as microelectronics, telecommunications, computers, and aircraft, would probably be
enhanced by larger procurements and government sponsorship of

FIGURE 7.5
Impact on Gross National Product—Nominal

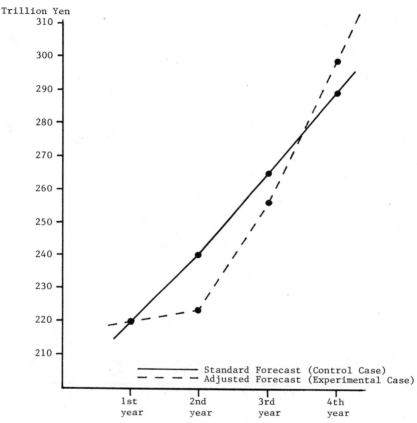

Trillion Yen

Standard Forecast (Control Case)
Adjusted Forecast (Experimental Case)

1st year 2nd year 3rd year 4th year

research and development. Of course, economic efficiency could be hurt if, because of higher defense expenditures, capital and labor flowed into industries, such as shipbuilding, aluminum, or petro-chemicals, where comparative advantage is shifting away from Japan.[34] However, as pointed out earlier, Japan is not suffering from a shortage of capital; and so long as the savings rate does not suddenly plummet, the question of capital availability should not pose a particularly serious problem. The era of heaviest industrial investment in the basic manufacturing industries is past, and with the liberalization of capital movements, Japanese companies are taking advantage of the opportunity to issue bonds and sell stock overseas. OPEC countries, hoping to diversify oil-dollar holdings, have also begun investing in Japanese securities. One suspects, therefore, that

FIGURE 7.6
Impact on Gross National Product—Real (1970 prices)

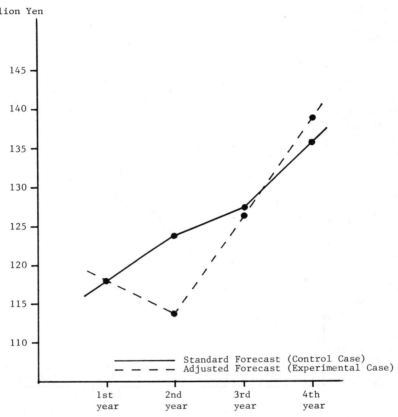

the high-growth industries—and primarily the high-technology sector—would not be hurt by higher military expenditures, particularly
in view of the demand-side boost that might be felt.

There are indications that the business community in Japan supports heavier defense appropriations for precisely such reasons. An
interview with eighteen top executives in defense-related industries
revealed that none of them accepts the validity of the government's
argument about delaying spending increases in order to restore
public finances or to keep rises in military expenditures roughly in
line with welfare increases.[35] What business leaders want is for the
government to give national defense higher priority. Not only do
they feel that Japan's economy is capable of sustaining a higher
level; a number also believe it is the only way of averting friction

with the United States and maintaining a harmonious trade relationship. Many business leaders want the ban on arms exports lifted so that economies of scale in domestic production can be achieved and commercial ties with certain nations solidified.[36] Hence, elements of the business community see Japan's economic interests enhanced by the expansion of defense capabilities. Although skepticism and opposition remain strong, support for higher defense spending—at a steady but limited pace—seems to be gathering momentum.

The Costs. What about the costs of higher spending levels? Leaving aside political fallout effects, one might perhaps expect a higher rate of inflation. The simulation exercise suggests indeed that the consumer price index would rise. Over the first two years, the rise would be steep, leveling off and dropping over the next two (see Figures 7.7 and 7.8). The consumer price index in the experimental case is significantly higher during the first two years than in the control case, but it falls back into rough alignment during the third and fourth years, somewhere around 6 or 7 percent annually. Of course, the government could dampen inflationary pressures by adjusting spending priorities, but as that option is consciously eschewed in our growth model, the consumer price index may be more susceptible to control (under more realistic circumstances) than is reflected in our simulation results.

What about industrial production? How would manufacturing output be affected? Mining and manufacturing production fall off during the second and third years and rebound strongly in the fourth year; by the end of the fourth year, in fact, the level of industrial output in the adjusted forecast clearly exceeds that of the standard forecast (see Figures 7.9 and 7.10). Here again is evidence that higher defense spending would be likely to stimulate aggregate demand over time, even though the initial years might witness a temporary falling-off in production.

Personal income follows a similar pattern, dropping off during the first two years and then rising steeply over the third and fourth years—to the point where, by the end of the fourth year, the level exceeds that of the standard, nonadjusted forecast (see Figures 7.11 and 7.12). This result may indicate that the savings rate could dip sharply over the first two years, due to the squeeze on personal and disposable income, but then rally during the next two years as personal and disposable income rebounds.

Trade is also momentarily "knocked off stride" with exports rising dramatically and imports falling precipitously over the second and third years and then reversing trends in the fourth, when exports

FIGURE 7.7
Percentage Change from Previous Year Consumer Price Index (1975 = 100)

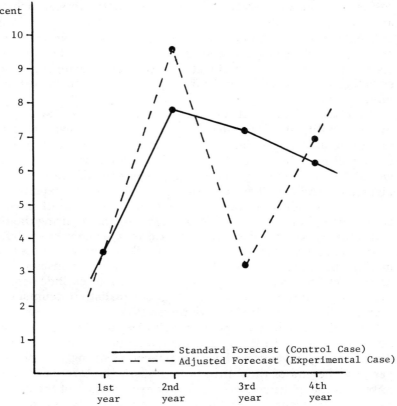

drop and imports rise (see figures 7.13 and 7.14). The pattern can be
understood in terms of the falling-off in aggregate growth rates during the second and third years; lower domestic demand usually
means a slackening of import demand. To pull out of its economic
tailspin, Japan would be likely to step up its drive to export, assuming foreign markets remain open and an imbalance of trade is acceptable to deficit countries—a major and uncertain assumption.
When domestic demand picks up again, as it does during the third
and fourth years, imports expand and exports contract. If this pattern of trade reflects what Japan might try to do (i.e., step up exports) as a means of coping with an initial falling-off in domestic
growth, it points up what could turn into a serious trade irritant. We
might question whether the politics of trade would allow Japan the

FIGURE 7.8
Percentage Change from Previous Year Wholesale Price Index (1975 = 100)

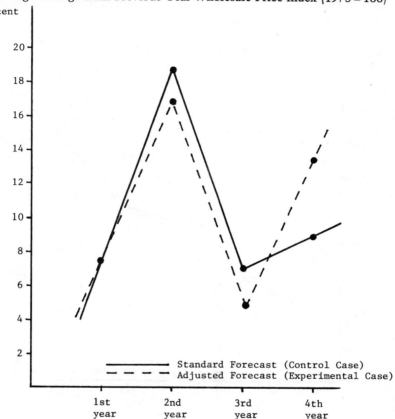

luxury of attempting to export its way out of domestic recession. Trade friction over automobiles, steel, and consumer electronics indicates that the world climate may be more protectionist than is reflected in the elasticities assumed by the simulation. Higher defense expenditures would therefore have to be handled in ways that minimized pressures on the structure of trade, particularly with the United States.

As the model assumes that capital would come out of investment, not consumption, investment rates plunge during the second and third years but rebound strongly the fourth year, exceeding levels that would have been reached without abrupt increases in defense spending (see Figures 7.15 and 7.16). *For inflation, production, personal income, and trade, therefore, the picture is quite consistent:*

FIGURE 7.9
Impact on Mining and Manufacturing

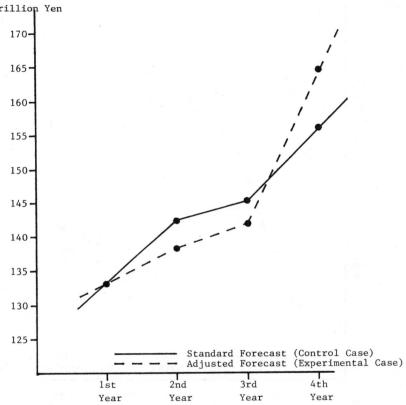

Trillion Yen

Standard Forecast (Control Case)
Adjusted Forecast (Experimental Case)

1st Year   2nd Year   3rd Year   4th Year

abrupt deviation from the normal path (of 1 percent defense spending) leading to short-term setbacks, followed by long-term adjustments and even gains.

Implications and Evaluation

Before exploring the implications of this exercise, we must again emphasize that no simulation can capture the complexity of forces at work in the real world. Certainly our own simulation is flawed by the simplifications and rigid assumptions that have been built into it. Its insensitivity, especially, to political variables ought to make us wary of interpreting the results too literally.

Having acknowledged its weaknesses, let us assess what tentative

FIGURE 7.10
Percentage Change from Previous Year Mining and Manufacturing

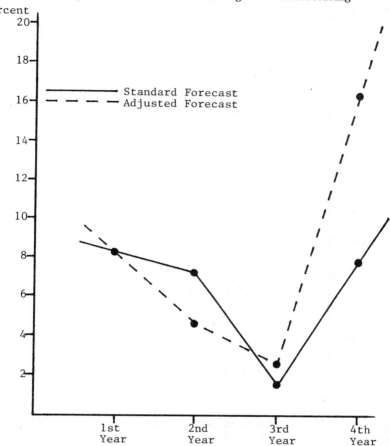

conclusions and relevant implications emerge. The simulation suggests, first of all, that economic growth in Japan is *not* dependent on keeping defense expenditures below 1 percent of GNP. The widespread notion—associated with the "free ride" argument—that growth rates would slacken if Japan were forced to shoulder a heavier defense burden is simplistic at best and inaccurate at worst. There was, of course, a period of capital scarcity—until around the middle-to-late 1960s—when a heavy defense burden probably would have reduced growth rates. But Japan's economy is clearly capable today of sustaining substantially larger defense outlays without suffering serious setbacks in either the rate of growth or the size of the

FIGURE 7.11
Impact on Personal Income

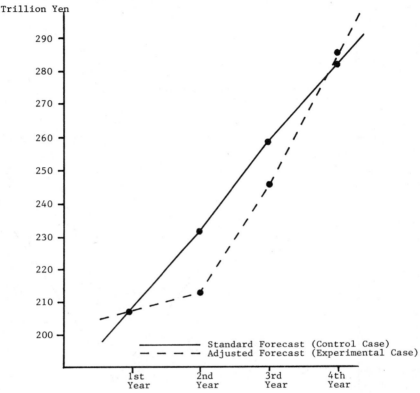

Trillion Yen

economy. If the expansion is steady and spread over a number of years, the short-term problems should require fewer and less traumatic adjustments than our simulation suggests. Short-term reductions in growth, industrial production, and disposable income; surges in inflation; and oscillations in the international balance of trade — all short-range problems in the simulation — could be avoided through skillful management. If capital can be extracted from consumption (and not just investments) and from a reallocation of spending priorities, there is no a priori reason to anticipate major disruption of the economy.

If simple-minded versions of the "free ride" hypothesis are incorrect, so too are commonly heard arguments in Japan that higher military appropriations are fiscally out of the question. This is a view that the Ministry of Finance has propounded in resisting U.S.

FIGURE 7.12
Impact on Disposable Income

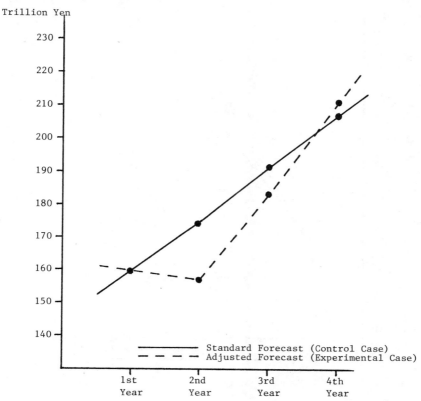

Trillion Yen

230 —

220 —

210 —

200 —

190 —

180 —

170 —

160 —

150 —

140 —

————— Standard Forecast (Control Case)
— — — — Adjusted Forecast (Experimental Case)

1st Year   2nd Year   3rd Year   4th Year

pressures. The Japanese government usually cites five reasons why fiscal reconstruction must take priority over higher defense spending: (1) inflation; (2) the "crowding out" of private investments; (3) the precarious position in which public finances would be placed; (4) fiscal and monetary rigidification; and (5) the unwitting creation of a big and inefficient government. Because of these dangers, the Ministry of Finance has set a target of deficit retrenchment of 2 trillion yen each year, starting in 1980.

From a strictly economic point of view, such concerns appear misplaced. There may be compelling reasons not to allocate more money for defense, but they cannot be convincingly based on the rationale of fiscal reconstruction. One eminent economist, Professor Uchida Tadao of Tokyo University, has analyzed the fallacies in these five points.[37] If inflation is correlated with deficits, he asked,

FIGURE 7.13
Percentage Change from Previous Year Exports

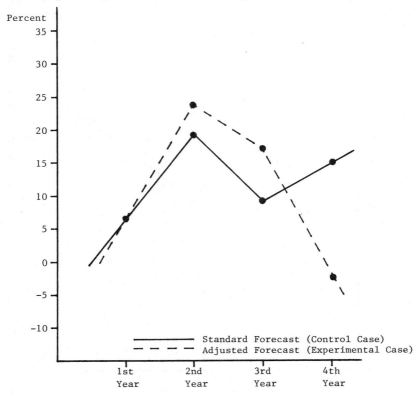

how is it that inflation rates were so low in the second half of the 1970s? Fears of a crowding-out of business investments owing to competition over capital are also unfounded, he said; the outlook is for new plant investments to exceed the growth rate of the economy. Professor Uchida also argued that Japan's overall fiscal and monetary condition, taking into account public savings at all levels of government, is much healthier than Cassandras in the Ministry of Finance would have us believe. This had led him to dismiss fears about the rigidification of fiscal and monetary policies; his own prediction, in fact, is that, even without strenuous belt-tightening, the ratio of national debt to government revenue will decline around the mid-1980s. As for the specter of a big and inefficient government, econometric calculations indicate that such fears are exaggerated. Budgetary outlays should expand at around the

FIGURE 7.14
Percentage Change from Previous Year Imports

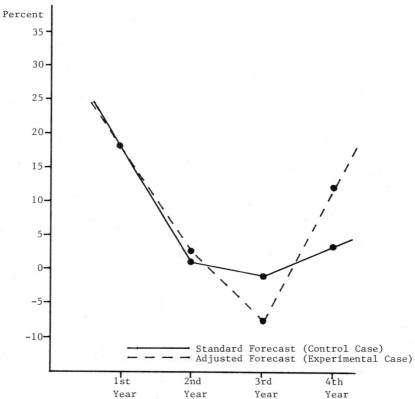

same rate as GNP growth. With an elasticity of tax revenues to GNP somewhere around 1.2 or 1.3, the government "take" is not likely to get out of hand.[38]

If Professor Uchida is correct—and the results of our simulation seem to corroborate his arguments—then the main obstacle to higher defense expenditures is not economic. It is political. Doubling defense expenditures is economically feasible, but the overriding question is this: At what political cost? Even if increases are gradual, not jerky and steep as in our simulation, would the opposition parties be willing to go along? Would the LDP's popularity be damaged and its Diet majority jeopardized? Would public opinion be polarized? Can a national consensus be mobilized?

Comprehensive Security. Many Japanese, even some of those who

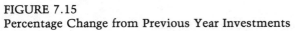

FIGURE 7.15
Percentage Change from Previous Year Investments

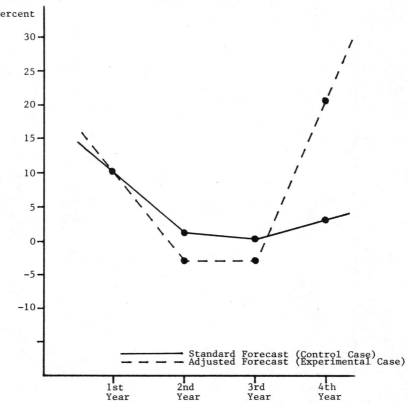

dismiss the "fiscal reconstruction" argument, believe Japan should concentrate on increasing its foreign aid rather than its military capabilities. Economic assistance falls into a broad definition of security, which is referred to as "comprehensive security" (*sogo anzen hosho*), a term covering economic as well as political and military contingencies. The idea of pursuing an international division of labor where security responsibilities are concerned, "specializing" in areas where a country's comparative advantage lies, is one that enjoys fairly widespread support in Japan. Professor Uchida is among its proponents. Although he is in favor of higher defense expenditures within limits—at around 1.5 percent of GNP—he believes more resources should be channeled into non-military contributions to international security. In a broad category

FIGURE 7.16
Impact on Investment

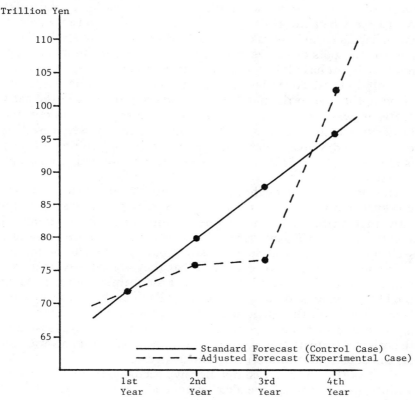

Trillion Yen

Standard Forecast (Control Case)
Adjusted Forecast (Experimental Case)

called "international cooperation" (*kokusai kyoryoku*), which encompasses everything from defense expenditures to economic assistance and research and development—all of which presumably promote the collective good—Japan currently spends about 4 percent of GNP, compared to around 8 percent for the United States. Professor Uchida would like to see that gap narrowed over the next decade, principally through massive increases in economic assistance and research and development.[39] Believing in the essential "substitutability" (*daigasei*) of economic and military means of international security, he has pointed out that Japan is in a logical position to contribute to economic security.

Stepped-up efforts at international cooperation would seem to make sense. An emphasis on the economic dimensions of security would be more palatable politically, as Japan's own national security is defined so overwhelmingly in economic terms of reference, and Japan is in a position to contribute to the stabilization of the world's economic order, not to mention its own national security.[40] At a time when the United States is cutting back on foreign aid, Japan seems capable of taking up at least some of the slack. There are trouble spots of strategic importance where aid can make a difference. Japan has already broken with past patterns of channeling aid only to those countries in which it has a commercial stake and of tying that aid to the purchase of Japanese products. In the early 1980s it was extending help to such countries as Turkey and Pakistan, which are central to the world balance of power, as well as to Oman and Kenya, where there was interest in building military facilities, and to Egypt and Korea, which are politically and strategically pivotal.

The idea that there ought to be an international division of labor, however, is not immune to criticism. Some U.S. leaders, particularly in Congress and the business community, have expressed skepticism about Japan's "specialized" concentration on economic security. There is a widespread feeling that aid by itself, no matter how constructive, is not enough. What they want from Japan is a willingness to shoulder a larger share of the military burden. When the U.S. redeploys forces away from the Pacific, these leaders want Japan to help fill the vacuum created. At the very least, they want Japan to assume more responsibility for its own defense, as stated in the original security treaty, even if they understand that a variety of factors constrain military involvement overseas.

Nor has the notion of comprehensive security escaped criticism within Japan. Although the idea has generated a great deal of discussion, which has had the positive effect of heightening public awareness of the links between economic and politico-military security, it has failed so far to galvanize a national consensus. The concept has been the target of attack from opposite flanks of the political spectrum. Those opposed to Japan's assumption of a larger military role believe the pursuit of an expanded world role under the guise of comprehensive security would pull Japan into the vortex of big-power politics. As a resource-poor island nation, utterly dependent on the international environment, Japan is not suited, they believe, to play the game of power politics.

At the opposite end of the spectrum, the idea of comprehensive security is dismissed by those who argue that it does not go far enough.[41] Like it or not, the realities of the decline of the United States as world hegemon make a more active role for Japan imperative. As a consensus seems to have emerged within the U.S.

government (going back to the Carter administration) about the importance of Japan's playing an expanded role in the world, Japan can expect to come under continued pressures to upgrade its defense capabilities. For harmonious bilateral relations, not to mention the shoring-up of the deterrent in Asia, Japan may have to press forward on *both* military and economic fronts, bringing its overall contribution to world security more in line with its economic power.

Cynics see the stress on comprehensive security as little more than sleight of hand to divert attention from Japan's minimalist military stance. By including even research and development expenditures in the accounting, the overall Japanese contribution is artificially inflated. Instead of 0.9 percent of GNP, the figure is set misleadingly high at 4 percent. Although breakthroughs in know-how ultimately benefit everyone, and in that sense contribute to the collective good, it would be stretching the usual definition of international security to place R&D in the same category as official development aid. If technology is transferred as part of a program of economic assistance, helping Third and Fourth World countries industrialize, or if the research effort advances basic scientific knowledge, then perhaps the categorization may carry some credence. But Japan has not been known, so far, either for the generosity of its program in technology transfer or for its work in basic scientific research.

Whatever the ultimate mix of security expenditures, a consensus seems slowly to be emerging that the country's low posture on politico-military matters is no longer viable. The combination of factors that had made Japan's ostrich-like stance possible—particularly the military and political dominance of the United States—has changed in ways that no longer permit potentially powerful allies like Japan the luxury of pursuing a one-dimensional diplomacy: namely, that of maximizing its economic interests.

The situation today is obviously different from that in the 1940s and 1950s, when U.S. and Japanese interests converged so neatly in terms of giving priority to economic reconstruction. Regardless of what Ministry of Finance officials say, fiscal reconstruction is not as serious a stumbling block today as postwar recovery had been until the 1960s. Nor are all the beneficial consequences of low armaments alluded to earlier—economic growth, regional stability, recovery from the trauma of war, a new diplomatic reorientation, establishment of a democratic political system, continuity of conservative rule, and so on—necessarily going to be lost if Japan strengthens its defense capabilities. Japan has had time to consolidate those gains.

If there is still a roadblock, it lies in the potential complications that might result from a maladroit handling of the *politics* of national defense. Without underestimating the seriousness of the potential backlash, however, we can surmise that the Japanese government is more capable of handling domestic opposition today than it was in the 1950s or 1960s. Japanese leaders are being reminded that governments everywhere, including even the United States, incur political costs when they take finite resources away from social needs to bolster national defense. Granted, political sensitivities may be more troublesome in Japan than in most other countries, but there are limits to the mileage that can be made out of that. Indeed, from the U.S. perspective, the basic problem is not simply one of equitable economic burden sharing; it is equally one of sharing the *political* burdens of common defense. Increases in economic aid would be welcomed, particularly if funneled toward strategically pivotal countries in need of assistance. But to satisfy U.S. expectations, Japan will probably also have to demonstrate evidence of steady and significant increases in defense spending. The old rationale used to resist outside pressures no longer appears to carry convincing force.

In asking the Japanese to upgrade their defense capabilities, U.S. officials argue that trends in the world balance are such that the Western alliance badly needs Japan's potential power to shore up its defenses. By dragging its feet today, Japan runs the long-term risk that a future crisis will precipitate a crash program of military rearmament—with possibly adverse side effects for political stability. Better for all concerned to gear up gradually than to be caught off-guard and then have to embark on a crash program.

Defense Technology. During the latter years of the Carter administration, certain leaders in the U.S. Department of Defense proposed to Japan's Defense Agency that more resources be earmarked for defense-related technology.[42] Compared to Japan's highly sophisticated technology in areas like commercial microelectronics, the state of its defense-related technology is conspicuously backward. That this should be the case is hardly surprising in view of the fact that only around 1 percent of a very limited defense budget is earmarked for research and development. As the level of commercial technology is so advanced, however, it should be possible to upgrade the state of defense technology expeditiously with only marginal increments of investments.

Department of Defense leaders believe Japan's defense technology could be improved dramatically simply by doubling, over a period of several years, the amount of money in the defense budget devoted to science and technology and by expanding links with civilian industry. The Pentagon, for its part, would be willing to share U.S. military technology with Japan as part of an ongoing program of bilateral cooperation and exchange. Such a program, it is hoped, would achieve several objectives: (1) correct a glaring deficiency in Japan's defense establishment; (2) dovetail with, and facilitate, Japan's goal of improving the quality of its military hardware; (3) upgrade the overall deterrent in Asia thereby; (4) broaden technological cooperation between the United States and Japan; (5) lay the groundwork for possible weapons standardization among Japanese, U.S., and NATO forces; (6) expand civilian industry's stake in military production; and (7) thereby strengthen the hands of domestic actors in favor of an expanded security role. It would offer, in short, an alternative means of speeding up rearmament without having to bludgeon the Japanese over the controversial 1 percent ceiling. It would also extricate the bilateral dialogue from the morass of budgetary statistics — decidedly a positive step in terms of domestic deliberations.

For many years the Defense Agency has emphasized the importance of qualitative improvements in Japan's force posture. The uniformed services have often complained that the weapons systems currently deployed are at least a generation obsolete. In light of the high costs of personnel and the difficulties of competing with industry for manpower, the emphasis on qualitative improvement seems the logical route for military expansion to follow. It makes political sense also, because the replacement of obsolete weapons systems is less visible than a large-scale expansion of personnel. And it could be accomplished by tapping into the already advanced technology available in private industry — steel, automobiles, machinery, computers, telecommunications, semiconductors, and so on. Once Japan develops an infrastructure for defense production — with U.S. encouragement and assistance — it can manufacture the equipment needed to strengthen its defense: for example, an early warning radar system, antisubmarine warfare capabilities, and aircraft.

Japan is the only country close to technological parity with the United States in the vital area of microelectronics, on which U.S. defense strategy has relied to offset Soviet numerical superiority in manpower and in conventional and nuclear weapons. If, through bilateral cooperation in research and development, Japan's technological assets are harnessed, the capacity of the U.S.-Japanese alliance to lengthen its technological lead could be given a powerful thrust forward. Japanese know-how in such areas as fiber optics, lasers, and very-large-scale integrated circuits is already so advanced that the U.S. military could benefit from access to the patents. Working in cooperation on such state-of-the-art technology as very high-speed integrated circuits (VHSIC), the United States and Japan could push back the frontiers of knowledge at a pace and in ways that the Soviet Union would be hard-pressed to duplicate.

As rosy as this prospect seems, however, its implementation raises several practical questions. Can the two countries, and private firms within them, cooperate when commercial competition between them is so fierce?[43] How will such cooperation, and Japan's move into defense-related technology, affect the competitiveness of the microelectronics industries? In what ways will trade in the high-technology sector be affected? Can the always-complicated problem of technology transfer be handled, not only bilaterally but multilaterally as well? Judging from past experience, one would expect to encounter bottlenecks at each of these junctures. Some U.S. firms may not want to see their Japanese competitors move into defense-technology production. Japanese firms have not been noted for their spirit of cooperation in transferring sensitive know-how to the United States. Whether, and to what extent, a strategy of bilateral cooperation in defense technology can work — and if so, with what consequences — remains quite uncertain.

On the other hand, the defense-technology proposal is not necessarily dependent on an extensive two-way exchange of technology. If its primary purpose is the upgrading of Japan's capabilities in defense-related technology, as an essential first step toward the development of a sturdier defense network, then the objective can be achieved even without the establishment of elaborate mechanisms for technological exchange. Quite apart from its immediate impact on Japan's production of military equipment, the stress on defense technology may lead the country down the path of least resistance where rearmament is concerned. Private industry will benefit from military procurements, research and development support, and purchase of testing and assembly equipment. For industries that illustrate the principles of learning-curve theory, like the semiconductor industry, the demand-side boost provided by military contracts could help to encourage risk-taking, cushion the costs of possible failure, free up resources for other uses, enlarge market share, and reduce production costs.[44]

Of course, there could be zero-sum trade-offs, particularly in those areas in which military needs tie up resources that might otherwise be devoted to commercially more lucrative products; but as the percentage of military-related production would remain comparatively small, such concerns would not appear to loom very large.[45] Indeed, perhaps in anticipation of greater military outlays, many of the large electronics firms in Japan have already established defense production divisions to consider ways of exploiting procurement opportunities. Support for larger defense budgets could broaden in the business community, particularly among those firms that have a growing stake in defense-related production.

Even if Japan proceeds slowly in developing defense technology, it has already reached a state wherein its industrial technology has far-reaching military implications. Because the boundaries between civilian and military technology are not always distinguishable, Japan will have to consider how to handle such matters as the protection of highly sensitive technology from foreign intelligence. Leaving the responsibility solely in the hands of private industry may not be adequate insurance, as Soviet and Chinese intelligence activities in Japan are said to be intensive, yielding an ongoing harvest of technological information through electronic and other forms of surveillance.[46]

What technology to transfer, to which countries, and under what conditions pose complicated questions for Japan, as the dual-purpose nature of modern technology means that security considerations must always be weighed against commercial calculations. The U.S.-Japan relationship will also witness the spread of economic competition from the old-line industries—steel, automobiles, and so on—to the high-technology and service sectors—semiconductors, computers, telecommunications, and the like. The rapid growth of worldwide demand should mean that there is ample room for both U.S. and Japanese industries to flourish. But competition could heat up, because industries on both sides are aware of the need to expand and hold market share in order to survive. Moreover, if friction in one arena, such as automobiles, exacerbates tensions in high technology, the overall level of conflict may be substantially harder to handle than that experienced in past trade confrontations.

So much is at stake in, for example, the semiconductor competition. It is not just profit in a rapidly growing industry; what is affected is competitive advantage in a dramatically advancing technology, one that is absolutely seminal across a proliferating range of end-product applications. More important, microelectronics provides the technological basis for the West's capacity to maintain the strategic and conventional balance. Simply by virtue of reaching the frontiers of technology, Japan finds itself in a position in which its diplomatic prestige, and perhaps its leverage, are enhanced. Even though such leverage may not have been consciously sought, the possession of state-of-the-art technology itself makes Japan a more important actor than it has been on the international scene.

Japan has come to what may be regarded as a historic crossroad, not by conscious design, but as a by-product of its pursuit of purely economic goals. The irony is that by systematically eschewing military power, and focusing instead on economic enhancement, Japan has managed to construct an industrial and technological infrastructure that now makes it awkward for the country to continue assuming a posture of politico-military innocence. Even though the successes of its past policies render any radical departure improbable, its advanced economy gives it a range of options, including that of stronger arms and independence. Where it goes from here will hinge, importantly, on how well its alliance with the United States functions in the 1980s and 1990s.

The Policymaking Apparatus: Resistance to Change

We have noted the past utility of establishing fiscal ceilings to impose predictability on the potentially volatile politics of national defense. If fiscal ceilings proved useful in the past, however, their constructiveness today is being increasingly outweighed by certain dysfunctional consequences. Of these, perhaps the most serious is the deflection of attention from salient questions that need to be addressed: the nature of external threats, delineation of priority missions, identification of the hardware necessary to accomplish those missions, and so on. Instead of focusing on changes in the external environment, deliberations continue to be bogged down by Japan's peculiar preoccupation with fiscal ceilings.

Budgetary politics is currently structured in ways that render major increases in defense spending improbable, at least in the near future. The collective weight of those institutions and groups actively in favor of higher defense expenditures is comparatively weak. The Japan Defense Agency (JDA) wields considerably less clout than most other government ministries. It must provide detailed technical justification for each item listed on its proposed budget. The Ministry of Finance, strict keeper of the national purse, subjects JDA requests to the closest scrutiny, ruthlessly paring away expenditures that fail to meet standards.

The promotion of several ex-MOF officials to top positions in the JDA hierarchy might lead one to expect greater JDA "pull" within the budgetary system. However, that has not turned out to be the case. Quite the contrary, as former MOF officials depend on the

MOF for postretirement job placement (referred to as *amakudari*),[47] they may feel inhibited about pressing for larger allocations. Nor, apart from a small handful, are JDA budgetary requests significantly strengthened by the backing of powerful politicians. Electoral incentives are not structured in ways that activate large numbers to rally around the flag of national defense. As suggested earlier, certain businesses and industrial associations may feel most clearly that their own self-interest lies in lobbying for greater defense capabilities. But as the MOF guards its prerogatives against encroachment by outside groups, these interest and government groups have failed so far to secure significantly larger appropriations—even with the backing of heavy pressure from the United States. So long as defense decisions are confined to the budgetary arena, Japan's capacity to adjust flexibly to shifts in the external environment may be impaired.

Short of an unexpected crisis, which might suddenly change perceptions and restructure the whole policymaking apparatus, it seems unlikely that there will be any major shift in defense orientation in the near future. To the extent that there are increases, they will be incremental in nature and subject to the discipline of aggregate spending limits. Breaking the 1 percent barrier on the way to the 2 percent target once envisioned by the Carter administration seems to lie outside the realm of political probability. Approval of even incremental increases—larger than those granted to other budgetary items—might require the continued application of pressure by the United States. But such pressure, if required over a sustained period, could cast the United States in the role of scapegoat, a role that is not entirely unknown in U.S. economic dealings with Japan.

Japan Rearmed: Some Questions

Whether, and to what extent, the United States wants to incur the costs of applying pressure on Japan will depend on a number of factors. For reasons that have been discussed already, the U.S. government is anxious to see "steady and significant increases" in Japanese defense spending. Curiously, what may constitute the most compelling reason for Japan's buildup is seldom mentioned in official statements, although it may implicitly underlie the United States's public posture: namely, the need to keep U.S. and Japanese policies in closer alignment through a leveling-off of some of the structural asymmetries. Differences in the U.S. position as a global military power and the Japanese as a minimalist military state have given rise to inevitable differences in perceptions, capabilities, commitments, and policy objectives. One sees evidence, for example, of a fundamental divergence in such areas as U.S. and Japanese perceptions of the seriousness of the Soviet threat, appropriateness of countermeasures, and willingness to take action. Because alliance cooperation is perhaps needed as urgently now as ever before, eliminating some of the *structural* causes of friction becomes important. Although not all structural differences can be removed, some leveling-off might be useful in narrowing what could otherwise be a worrisome gap. Even if most of the presumed benefits of Japanese rearmament turn out to be false—e.g., if the burdens of the United States's defense responsibilities are not lightened—the spillover effects might still be valuable if the distance between the United States and Japan is narrowed.

Looking back at U.S.-Japan relations since the mid-1970s, we can clearly see one fundamental problem: that fissures, caused in large measure by structural asymmetries, could very well deepen in ways that would undermine alliance solidarity. If there is a convincing reason why the notion of an international division of labor by itself—to the exclusion of a steady and significant upgrading of military capabilities—may not be a viable solution in the long run, it is perhaps the argument that Japan's specialization in only the economic dimensions of security does nothing to narrow the enormous structural gap between the United States and Japan. Although in some degree a division of labor makes sense and is to be welcomed, the concept of comparative advantage ought not to be carried too far in areas to which it may not be strictly applicable, such as the balance of power. Japan's most constructive contribution could very well lie in the realm of economic or comprehensive security, but an economic role would not necessarily obviate the need for a concomitant upgrading of its military capabilities.

On the other hand, Japan's reemergence as a military force, if taken too far or too fast, could cause problems and lead to negative fallout effects. There is little evidence that, in pushing for heavier Japanese rearmament, U.S. policymakers are aware of the full range of potential ramifications. In thinking about Japan's military course, a number of hard questions need to be, but are not being, asked:

Japan's Domestic Situation

Is there a trade-off between increases in armaments and political stability? If so, at what point would the political costs outweigh the benefits of improved military capabilities?

In particular, how will the LDP majority, opposition forces, public opinion, and the policymaking institutions and processes be affected?

In what way, if at all, will the defense question affect decisions in other issue areas, such as welfare, and how will the political system as a whole be affected?

Will a greater emphasis on defense, including the possible assumption of regional responsibilities, require or cause changes, such as constitutional revision or a new security treaty?

In what ways will military-civilian relations change?

How will nationalism and perceptions of national interests be affected?

What industries, fiscal priorities, research and development strategies, and industrial policies will be affected?

U.S.-Japan Relations

Is U.S. pressure needed in Japan to strengthen the hands of those in favor of stronger defense? If so, is outside pressure likely to generate resentment against the United States?

What will be the impact of developments in the military sphere on the bilateral economic relationship? How will the trade balance, technology transfers, direct investments, and issue-area linkage be affected?

Are there differences in threat perceptions?

What specific military missions need to be carried out, against what threats, and for what contingencies?

Is the United States apt to lose influence with Japan as defense capabilities are expanded?

What are the implications and possible long-term consequences of Japan's acquisition of a greater military capability? Independence and greater neutralism?

Will the U.S. defense burden be lightened, and the collective deterrent in Asia improved, by Japan's heavier rearmament?

Japan's International Orientation

Are Japan's analytic capabilities in politico-military matters adequate to underpin a more active world role?

Is its system of policymaking, based on consensus formation, well suited to such a role?

Will Japan's ability to pursue its economic interests be impaired?

How will the alignment of domestic interest groups and policymaking institutions be affected?

How will the regional and global balance of power be altered?

How will Japan's relations with Korea, China, the Soviet Union, and ASEAN change, if at all?

Will Japan forge closer ties with NATO in a triangular relationship,

including the United States? Or will more distance be placed between these allies?

Once momentum for military armament is gathered, will it be hard
to stop?

Will Japan's international prestige and voice be enhanced?

Will Japan be pulled into the vortex of power politics and become
involved in the protection of its economic interests overseas?

Will it enter the world arms market as an aggressive exporter?

Systemic Implications

Will alliance solidarity (particularly, the U.S.-Japan alliance) be
enhanced through the elimination of structural asymmetries?

Will policy coordination with the United States be made easier?

Will Japan's military expansion speed the transformation of the
world system into a multipolar balance?

In what ways will it alter the Soviet-U.S. and Sino-Soviet rivalries?

Will Japan's militarization help arrest the decline of U.S. power and
freeze the status quo?

Will it raise the aggregate level of armaments in Asia?

Are there opportunity costs in Japan's abandonment of a purely commercial orientation, such as the sacrifice of a potentially useful
role as neutral mediator in international or regional disputes?

Does the world system need a more heavily rearmed and active
Japan — as the interwar period might have benefited from a less
isolationist United States? Or is a more lightly armed Japan more
stabilizing?

Japan stands at a critical juncture in its postwar history. The question of military rearmament goes well beyond matters of fiscal
feasibility and touches upon possible changes across a whole range
of areas: "fine-tuning" adjustments in Japan's political system,
diplomatic reorientation, alliance adaptations, and long-term re-
alignments in the international system. If Japan rearms heavily, the
direct repercussions and indirect ripple effects will be felt throughout the world. Given the significance of the transformation, moving
deliberations within Japan — as well as between Japan and the
United States — beyond the blind alley of budgetary politics becomes
essential. The litany of "free ride" criticisms in the United States
and of fiscal rebuttals in Japan has unfortunately diverted attention
for too long from the more central concerns regarding the multi-
faceted consequences of Japan's possible metamorphosis from merchant to military security state.

Notes

1. William W. Lockwood, *The Economic Development of Japan* (Princeton, N.J.: Princeton University Press, 1968), pp. 76, 142–143.

2. The Carter administration may never have gone on public record about the 2 percent target; nor is it clear that the message was ever clearly communicated to the Tokyo government. But this was the thinking of some high-ranking officials in the Department of Defense in the early phases of the administration. Interview with a high-ranking official in the Department of Defense, August 11, 1981.

3. Lester C. Thurow, "Unsolicited Advice on Japanese-American Economic Relations (1)," *Japan Economic Journal*, May 5, 1981, p. 19.

4. Discussion with a U.S. congressman, January 15, 1981.

5. At a conference sponsored by the U.S.-Japan Relations Project, Northeast Asia–United States Forum, Stanford University, "U.S.-Japan Competition in Semiconductors," Rickey's Hyatt House, Palo Alto, Calif., May 1, 1981.

6. Supreme Commander for Allied Powers, *Political Reorientation of Japan, September 1945 to September 1948*, Vol. 1 (Washington, D.C.: Government Printing Office, 1949), p. 102.

7. George F. Kennan, *Memoirs 1925–1950* (Boston: Little, Brown, 1967), p. 376.

8. Ibid, p. 381.

9. This list of factors is distilled from John W. Dower, *Empire and Aftermath: Yoshida Shigeru and the Japanese Experience, 1878–1954* (Cambridge, Mass.: Harvard University Press, 1979), pp. 369–400.

10. The text of the original security treaty is contained in Martin E. Weinstein, *Japan's Postwar Defense Policy: 1947–1968* (New York and London: Columbia University Press, 1971), pp. 137–138.

11. Quoted in Dower, *Empire and Aftermath*, p. 437.

12. Frederick S. Dunn, *Peacemaking and the Settlement with Japan* (Princeton, N.J.: Princeton University Press, 1963), pp. 6–7.

13. Ibid, p. 123.

14. Ibid.

15. Ibid.

16. Ibid.

17. Document reproduced in Japan Center for International Exchange, *A Handbook on Japanese Foreign Policy and Security* (Tokyo: Japan Center for International Exchange, March 1978), p. 38 (emphasis added).

18. E. H. Carr, *The Twenty-Years Crisis, 1919–1939* (London: Macmillan and Co., 1940).

19. Kishida Junnosuke, interviewer, *Nijusseki e no Sekai: Kissinger-shi to no Taiwa* [Toward the twenty-first century: Dialogue with Kissinger] (Tokyo: Asahi Evening News, 1978), p. 83.

20. Isaac Shapiro, "The Risen Sun: Japanese Gaullism?" *Foreign Policy*, Winter 1980–1981, pp. 62–81.

21. Kataoka Tetsuya, "Nippon Daini Kyowakoku no Koso," [The concept

of a Second Republic], *Shokun*, October 1979.

22. Donald C. Hellman, *Japan and East Asia: The New International Order* (New York: Praeger Publishers, 1972).

23. Herman Kahn, *The Emerging Japanese Superstate* (Englewood Cliffs, N.J.: Prentice-Hall, 1970), pp. 160–171.

24. Questions (and tacit criticisms) constantly come up in discussions the author has had with businessmen, academics, journalists, and policymakers in the United States.

25. Murakami Yasusuke, "Shin-chukan Taishu Seiji no Jidai" [The age of new middle mass politics], *Chuo Koron*, December 1980.

26. Martin Feldstein has discussed the rapid rise of social security benefits in the United States during the 1970s. See "Slowing the Growth of Social Security," *Wall Street Journal*, September 24, 1981, p. 24.

27. For an analysis of the budgetary processes, see Aaron Wildavsky, *The Politics of the Budgetary Process* (Boston: Little, Brown, 1964); John C. Campbell, *Contemporary Japanese Budget Politics* (Berkeley and Los Angeles: University of California Press, 1977).

28. Excerpted in Japan Center for International Exchange, *A Handbook on Japanese Foreign Policy and Security* (Tokyo: March 1981), p. 41.

29. See Suzuki Yoshio, *Nihon no Tsuka to Bukka* [Money and prices in Japan] (Tokyo: Toyo Keizai Shimposha, 1966); and *Gendai Nihon Kinyuron* [Monetary theory in modern Japan] (Tokyo: Toyo Keizai Shimposha, 1974), which has been translated into English under the title *Money and Banking in Contemporary Japan*, trans. John G. Greenwood (New Haven, Conn.: Yale University Press, 1980).

30. Hugh Patrick and Henry Rosovsky, "Japan's Economic Performance," in H. Patrick and H. Rosovsky, eds., *Asia's New Giant* (Washington, D.C.: Brookings Institution, 1976), p. 45, footnote.

31. See Edward F. Denison and William K. Chung, *How Japan's Economy Grew So Fast* (Washington, D.C.: Brookings Institution, 1976).

32. Joseph Pechman and Keimei Kaizuka, "Taxation," in Patrick and Rosovsky, *Asia's New Giant*, pp. 317–382.

33. Noguchi Yukio, "Zaisei Saiken e no Kihon Shiten" [Basic perspectives on fiscal reconstruction], *Ekonomisuto*, October 21, 1980, pp. 22–34.

34. Shinno Kojiro, "Sangyo Chosei no Kijun to Seisaku Shudan no Sentaku" [Criteria and policy measures for adjusting industrial structure], *Toyo Keizai*, October 18, 1981, pp. 36–42.

35. *Japan Economic Journal*, September 8, 1981, p. 15.

36. Daniel I. Okimoto, "Arms Transfers: The Japanese Calculus," in John Barton and Ryukichi Imai, eds., *Arms Control II* (Cambridge, Mass.: Oelgeschlager, Gunn & Hain, 1981), pp. 273–317.

37. Uchida Tadao, "Heiwa Kezai Taikoku: Nippon no Kihon Koso" [Peaceful economic power: Japan's basic thinking], *Kinkei Shirizu*, January 16, 1981, pp. 18–31.

38. Ibid., pp. 27–28.

39. Ibid, p. 26.

40. Gaimusho, *Waga Gaiko no Kinkyo* [Japan's diplomatic bluebook] (Tokyo: Gaimusho, 1980), pp. 524–572.

41. For an analysis of economic aid from a North-South perspective, see Nishikawa Jun, "Kokusai Kyoryoku to keizai Enjo" [International cooperation and economic aid], in Taigai Keizai Seisaku Kenkyu Guruupu, *Taigai Keizai Seisaku no Kihon* [Foundations of foreign economic policies] (Tokyo: Okurasho Insatsukyoku, 1980), pp. 273–299.

42. William J. Perry, under secretary of defense for research and engineering, was one of the prime advocates of this proposal. On Japan's defense technology, see Aoki Tsutomu, *Nihon no Boei Gijutsu* [Japan's defense technology] (Tokyo: Kyoikusha, 1979), pp. 69–149.

43. Daniel I. Okimoto, "The Role of the State in the Growth of the Semiconductor Industry: A Comparative Analysis of the United States and Japan," paper prepared for the project on U.S.-Japan Competition in the Semiconductor Industry, Northeast Asia–United States Forum, Stanford University, July 1981.

44. Ibid.

45. Nagamatsu Keiichi, *Nihon no Boei Sangyo* [Japan's defense industry] (Tokyo: Kyoikusha, 1979), pp. 16–17, 19.

46. Interview with a high-ranking official in the Central Intelligence Agency (January 14, 1981), who identified Japan as perhaps the prime staging area for Soviet intelligence-gathering in the area of sensitive commercial technology.

47. Ino Kenji and Hokuto Man, *Amakudari Kanryo,* [Postretirement placement of higher civil servants] (Tokyo: Hisshin Hodo, 1972).

Conclusions

Daniel I. Okimoto

Each of the seven chapters in this book has analyzed a different dimension of Japan's ongoing adjustment to changes in the international environment. There are inevitably differences of view among the seven authors with respect to preferred policy solutions, but there is consensus concerning the underlying nature of the problems and the general directions in which it would be desirable to see Japan move. Let me summarize first the commonalities in diagnosis:

The international economic system is undergoing a major transformation in response to such developments as the deterioration of the Bretton Woods system.

Sharp hikes in oil prices, uncertainties surrounding oil supplies, and other factors have contributed to, and complicated, such global or bilateral problems as stagnation, unemployment, and balance-of-payment disequilibria.

Under such circumstances, international economic frictions are apt to flare into serious conflicts as capitalist nations, operating within systems of open elections, try to balance domestic political and economic imperatives against international expectations and responsibilities.

The cushion formerly provided by rapid growth no longer provides as much insulation as it used to; forces in the external environment relentlessly intrude on the domestic economy and polity, necessitating adjustments at home and in foreign policy.

Bilateral imbalances in merchandise-trade and current accounts have become focal points of friction, even though, from an economic point of view, the multilateral balance is what counts.

Owing to the nature and composition of its trade, Japan is always going to run bilateral surpluses with some countries while incurring deficits with others.

Trade tensions have become particularly acute between Japan and the United States since the late 1970s, and although the tensions are a sign of the health and ever-growing importance of the bilateral relationship, they pose worrisome potential problems for trade in particular and the overall management of the U.S.-Japanese alliance in general.

Conditions of slow growth, high unemployment, inflation, sagging productivity, and an erosion of comparative advantage in certain manufacturing sectors tend to intensify protectionist pressures among industrialized states.

Faced with import competition for domestic market share, many industrial states have resorted to protectionism short of formal quotas or tariffs; we might even call this an era of voluntary export restraints (VERs), of orderly marketing agreements (OMAs), and reciprocity in bilateral relations.

The politicization of these problems means that there are no simple or guaranteed solutions. Nevertheless, the seven authors seem to agree on some of the factors that might go into a solution:

Japan cannot continue to follow the same domestic and international course that yielded such handsome returns during the 1950s and 1960s; it must assume more of the responsibilities of world leadership.

The precise nature of that leadership role is still unclear and subject to discussion; but if U.S. expectations have any effect, it will encompass some form of contribution not only to economic stability but to the maintenance of international security as well (whether it be in the form of greater economic assistance or an upgraded defense capability, or both).

Although Japan cannot be expected to balance trade and current-account ledgers with all countries, it must be sensitive to the political repercussions of allowing its surpluses to balloon.

Much ado is made about Japan's microlevel barriers — e.g., import quotas on agricultural products and leather, customs and inspection red tape, and the like — and although reforms here will not eliminate the aggregate imbalance (affecting trade flows only marginally), they could remove an external source of friction.

> At the macrolevel there may be limits to the degree of policy co-ordination that is either possible or desirable; nonetheless, some degree of "fine-tuning" can sometimes be helpful.
>
> Multilateral coordination would be beneficial, if it can be worked out, in the area of international energy security.
>
> Trends toward the liberalization of Japan's financial system should not be resisted, as the free movement of capital can serve to offset the merchandise-trade imbalance, move capital where it is needed, and relieve some of the pressures on the dollar as the international reserve currency.
>
> Various mechanisms for conflict avoidance and resolution — such as the creation of a trade ombudsman's office — ought to be established.

Although there are encouraging signs that Japan is reassessing its position in these areas, the problems are so deep-rooted and complex that we must guard against excessive optimism. In addition to the familiar problems associated with competition in the old-line manufacturing industries, Japan is apt to encounter a new array of conflicts emerging out of competition in the high-technology and service sectors. Looking ahead, we can anticipate such potential sources of friction as:

> Unavoidable political and security entanglements stemming from economic exchanges in high-technology goods
>
> Possible linkage, therefore, of economic and politico-military issues
>
> Conflicts over the differential role of the state in economic management, particularly the perception that the actions of one state bestow an unfair advantage over others
>
> The dangers of returning to a protectionist cycle of actions and reactions within the narrow framework of bilateralism through the use of "reciprocity" as a Trojan horse
>
> Failure to work out some common understanding of equitable burden sharing
>
> Failure to work out a coordinated framework of objectives and procedures in the area of energy security
>
> Domestic political costs of making structural adjustments to shifts in international comparative advantage
>
> Differential capacity of various governments to manage their economies in ways that obviate protectionist pressures
>
> Competition over the procurement of limited raw materials
>
> Conflicts and fissiparous pressures within the Western alliance

The possibility of greater instability in the world, with Soviet-U.S. confrontation, nuclear proliferation, and so on

Complicated questions concerning the transfer of sensitive gray-area technology, political and economic links of interdependence with adversary nations, and the like

Conflicts in the service sector exacerbated by differences in culture, social and political systems, and economic organization

Competition in certain sectors from newly industrializing nations like Korea, Singapore, and Taiwan

Japanese and U.S. competition for market share and influence in the rapidly growing Pacific Basin region

Regional tensions and instability in Asia

The problems are formidable. They will continue to test Japan's capacity to adapt. What is worrisome is that the concatenation of economic, political, and military problems threatens to occur at a time when domestic political circumstances for conflict management are far from optimal. Japan is probably in a better position to cope than most political systems; but in the face of such new and more complicated problems, past performance may not be the best predictor of future adaptation. The waning years of the twentieth century thus find Japan in the throes of transition, moving cautiously and pragmatically in response to changes in the external environment. Japan's ultimate direction may not yet be clear; but we can be certain that, whatever its course, Japan's economy will have a significant bearing on the shape of the international system.

Abbreviations

AOC	Arabian Oil Company
ASEAN	Association of Southeast Asian Nations
BA	banker's acceptance
BOJ	Bank of Japan
CCOP	Committee for the Coordination of Joint Prospecting for Mineral Resources in Asian Offshore Areas
CD	certificate of deposit
CIA	Central Intelligence Agency
c.i.f.	cost, insurance, and freight
DISC	Domestic International Sales Corporation
EEC	European Economic Community
EMS	European Monetary System
f.o.b.	free on board
GATT	General Agreement on Tariffs and Trade
GNP	gross national product
IBJ	Industrial Bank of Japan
IEA	International Energy Agency

IMF	International Monetary Fund
Japex	Japan Petroleum Exploration Company
JDA	Japan Defense Agency
JNOC	Japan National Oil Company
JNR	Japan National Railroad
JPDC	Japan Petroleum Development Corporation
LDC	less developed country
LDP	Liberal Democratic party
LNG	liquefied natural gas
LPG	liquefied petroleum gas
MITI	Ministry of International Trade and Industry
MOF	Ministry of Finance
MST	Mutual Security Treaty
MTN	Multilateral Tariff Negotiations
NATO	North Atlantic Treaty Organization
NCD	negotiable certificate of deposit
NEP	New Economic Policy
NGL	natural gas liquids
NIC	newly industrializing country
NSC	National Security Council
NTT	Nippon Telegraph and Telephone Corporation

OECD	Organisation of Economic Co-operation and Development
OMA	orderly marketing agreement
OPEC	Organization of Petroleum Exporting Countries
PRC	People's Republic of China
QR	quantitative restriction
R&D	research and development
SDF	Self-Defense Forces
SDR	special drawing right
STA	Science and Technology Agency
UNCTAD	United Nations Conference on Trade and Development
VER	voluntary export restraint
VHSIC	very high-speed integrated circuit

About the Contributors

Herbert I. Goodman: President, Gulf Oil Trading Company, with extensive experience working with Japanese on energy matters; formerly with the Department of State.

Eric W. Hayden: Vice-president, Economics and Strategic Planning, Bank of America, Asia Division.

Hideo Kanemitsu: Professor, Department of Economics, Sophia University, Tokyo; Visiting Fulbright Fellow, Northeast Asia–United States Forum on International Policy, Stanford University.

Ryutaro Komiya: Professor, Faculty of Economics, University of Tokyo.

Daniel I. Okimoto: Assistant Professor, Department of Political Science, Stanford University.

Hugh T. Patrick: Professor, Department of Economics, Yale University.

Gary R. Saxonhouse: Professor, Department of Economics, University of Michigan.

Index